THE PHOENIX AND THE UNICORN

Peter Hinssen

THE WHY, WHAT AND HOW OF CORPORATE INNOVATION

nexxworks

ACKNOWLEDGEMENTS

I would like to sincerely thank everyone who had a hand in making this book a reality. Thank you, Laurence Van Elegem, for being my superb co-pilot in this, and for hopefully many more projects to come. Thank you, Kim Indeherberg, for the excellent project co-ordination of this adventure. Thank you, Ilse De Bondt, for your support in the background. And a huge thank you to Cathy Boesmans, for your amazing strength and resilience, without whom this project would not have taken off. Thank you, Emile Piters, for giving me the idea of the Hourglass model – since then, I have been very glad to spread it to the world! And a big thanks to all the amazing input and collaboration from Edward Atkinson-Clark, Marc Lerouge, Vera Ponnet, Steven Theunis, Chantal Van de Ginste, Ivy Vanderheyden, Griet Hemeryck, Pascal Coppens, Steven Van Belleghem, Heather E. McGowan, Costas Markides, Carlota Perez, Nancy Rademaker and anyone who made this baby come alive.

My special thanks goes to the amazing nexxworks team, a wonderful family of 'crazy ones', my favorite group of round pegs in square holes. Thank you!

DEDICATION

This book is to the amazing networks of people that have inspired me over the years, from all around the world.

To the networks of companies that I've been privileged to talk to and learn from for all these years.

To the networks of friends that I've been able to make, all deeply curious, all crazy enough to think they can change the world.

Together, we can.

Table of contents

Foreword – Why I needed to write this book **8**
Introduction – The Phoenix and the Unicorn **12**

1 Innovation is the New Normal 16
The French Revolution and The State 18
The Industrial Revolution and The Firm 19
The Technological Revolution and the Empowered Individual 23
The New Normals 24
The Era of Crossroads 29
Your turn 35

2 The Hourglass model – A practical guide to the Day After Tomorrow 36
The origins of the Day After Tomorrow 37
The Hourglass Model 43
Your turn 53

3 Types of innovation – The What 54
I. Product Innovation 57
II. Market Innovation 69
III. Service Innovation 82
IV. Model Innovation 90
V. An industry case: acing innovation in the automotive sector 100
Conclusion 106
Your turn 119

4 The anatomy of a Phoenix – The How of innovation   **120**
   Vorsprung   121
   I. Customer Disruption: Extreme Customer Centricity
   in the age of 'Me'   123
   How Phoenixes can create an 'offer you can't refuse'
   for their customers – BY STEVEN VAN BELLEGHEM   130
   II. Platform Disruption: Operating in the age of platforms   139
   III. Cultural Disruption: The culture of transformation   160
   IV. Organizational Disruption: Remastering the system   179
   V. Structural Disruption: A Never Normal Design
   – BY LAURENCE VAN ELEGEM   200
   Your turn   210

5 The Proof of the Pudding   **212**
   So, tell me. Can it be done?   213
   The Phoenix from Bentonville   217

Before we part: 10 questions to spark your inner Phoenix   **229**
Endnotes   **234**
About Peter Hinssen   **236**
Other books by Peter Hinssen   **237**

FOREWORD

Why I needed to write this book

> There will come a time when you believe everything is finished; that will be the beginning.
>
> — LOUIS DEARBORN L'AMOUR, LONELY ON THE MOUNTAIN

After a very brief stint as an employee at Alcatel, a former French telecommunications giant, I started my career by moving fast and "building" things: when the Internet surfaced, I built websites, and then I built a company that built websites (well, intranets, actually). After which I founded a startup that tried to dabble in online video streaming, about 4 years before Youtube joined the world (suffice to say that it was a disaster; much too soon). Addicted to starting things from nothing, I then moved on to set up a SaaS company that became one of the pioneering cloud providers in Europe. I loved every minute of my life as an entrepreneur. It was hard, but I loved it.

But then I changed. From about 2010, I became much more interested in helping others with the experiences I had had as a struggling entrepreneur: startups, as well as large corporates. I wanted to show them how the world was changing, how this impacted (customer) behavior and how the rock stars of the business world – the Ubers, the Apples, the Haiers, the Alibabas, the Amazons but also the smaller (or, at least, lesser known or unpolished) diamonds like PerfectDay, iCarbonX or Revolut – organized themselves for innovation. I have travelled the world and the seven seas with my keynotes and my books, often upsetting the sweet dreams – about balance, margins and linearity – of decision makers (sorry about that, by the way, if I crushed yours). I moved on from building things to observing, and projecting what these observations could mean for the future of business, education and society as a whole.

That's what I'm still trying to do today: inspire others with the most beautiful success stories out there. And I still love every minute of it.

And then, a few months ago, after a keynote, I was enjoying a drink at a hotel bar with a customer, himself a friend. We talked for a long time and then a short silence ensued. He swirled the ice cubes in his glass and then he said: "Peter, I love your books, I love your vision and philosophy, your thermodynamics theory, the Day After Tomorrow and all that stuff, but why don't you ever write something that's… I don't know… more down to earth, more practical. Like a manual." I laughed and asked: "What do you want to know?" And he answered: "Well, you've travelled so much and you've seen so many companies, so you're probably one of the best out there to tell us about the why, the what, and the how of corporate innovation. Sometimes people don't need vision, sometimes they just need practical examples." I think I responded with a joke, and the conversation moved on, but his request somehow stuck.

And this book is the result of that.

I have to admit that what follows is somewhat out of my comfort zone: a lot more pragmatic than my readers will be used to: a lot more cases, of success and failure as well as small exercises at the end of each chapter. In fact, in some ways, I had to reinvent myself as a Phoenix; shifting from being an observer, and a thinker into a more pragmatic type of teacher (for lack of a better word). Don't worry, the other, observant part of me is still there. In fact, I'm already carrying around the idea of my next book, which is going to be a lot more societal, philosophical even. But I loved every minute of writing this book, thinking about the customer who challenged me to challenge myself.

I hope that 'The Phoenix and the Unicorn' will challenge you too. I hope that you'll learn a lot from the beautiful, and disastrous company cases that follow. I hope this book will both bring you down to earth, and inspire you to aim for the moon, or even further: "to infinity and beyond".

That's why I dedicate this book to all corporates around the world: these long-lasting and complex systems that get so little love and attention while the 'sexy' startups steal all of their spotlight. May it spark the fire inside them needed to reinvent themselves, like a Phoenix. May it give them the inspiration and perspective they need to turn their 'business as usual' upside down. May it help them see that endings and beginnings are merely synonyms of the word 'potential'.

Corporates, this one's for you!

INTRODUCTION

The Phoenix and the Unicorn

> I think death is the most wonderful invention of life. It purges the system of these old models that are obsolete.
>
> — STEVE JOBS

Unicorns have many aspects. Well, two actually. One shows a mythical horse-like creature with a great big spiraling horn on its head and, oh yes, magical powers. The other is almost as mythical and certainly quite as magical: the billion-dollar startups from Silicon Valley or Shenzhen that grow so quickly that they seem to defy gravity, or any other law of physics and economics.

It's the latter type of Unicorns that I refer to in the title, of course. They have captured our imagination in the last few years: with scores of young graduates wanting to join them, droves of aspiring entrepreneurs dreaming of becoming one, and stockpiles of middle-aged employees wondering how unfair it is that they never had a chance to join that movement.

We all want to be a Unicorn so bad. The truth is, however, that most of you reading this book will never become, found, or work for one.

Personally, I'm exhausted by the heaps of Unicorn stories that reared their pointy heads in the press for the last couple of years. Worse, I have often been thoroughly underwhelmed when I visited these companies during the many innovation tours run by my company nexxworks. Of course, you can't but help admire these entrepreneurs who are willing to take risks and try out entirely new business models. Some of these amazing stories can profoundly inspire us. But this interest also seems to have created an explosion of the Unicorn phenomenon, fueled by the billions of dollars of venture capital. And, sadly, this has somehow deflated the magical status of these mythical creatures.

Most of you reading this book work for traditional companies in traditional businesses. Most of you have to cope with company structures and mechanisms that force you to abide to ALL the laws of physics and economics. There's very little magic dust there, am I right?

Don't worry, I'm not in 'Unicorn Denial'. But I have recently become obsessed with another type of mythical animal. One that, in my opinion, is far more interesting than the fabled Unicorn. Let me introduce you to the Phoenix. According to Greek mythology, this long-lived bird has the ability to cyclically regenerate itself: it burns itself down and then rises from the ashes of its former self. I absolutely love how it is capable of renewal and transformation. It's also a bit of a showoff, typically depicted as dying in a fierce show of flames and combustion, to then be reborn stronger than before.

I have spent the last years travelling the world and talking to organizations of all sizes who want to understand how to survive, and thrive, in times of radical change. Typically, they are corporates who want to understand new technologies and business models. And they're all trying to grasp what they can do when their market or business is disrupted. Most of them loved the Day After Tomorrow metaphor, and a lot of them chuckled at the 'Shit of Yesterday' concept. Most of all, because they completely recognized it as their own; they were dealing with the latter on a daily basis, and it kept them from really focusing on radical transformation.

Most companies didn't ACT on their Day After Tomorrow, though. They all loved the theory and wanted to be informed. Sometimes they even secretly liked getting a little spooked by stories of disruption, just like they did with horror movies and haunted mansions when they were younger. But the depressing truth is: at the end of the day, very few of the companies that heard my stories, changed anything.

I'm pleased to tell you that there were exceptions to this rule, too. These 'rarest of beasts' started to tackle the subject of disruption and radical transformation with both zest and intelligence. They mobilized the right people, invested in technology, and experimented with radically new ideas, concepts and business models. They toiled to create a new future for themselves, and their companies. Thanks to some of those, I had a front-row seat to the miracle that is the rebirth of a Phoenix, rising from the ashes of the old, and coming out stronger than ever before.

Don't get me wrong, I do have a lot of sympathy for the Unicorns. But what I want this book to convey is: "Don't give up on the dinosaurs, just yet."

That's why this is a book about the Phoenix. It's about understanding what is happening in a world of constant change. It's about observing and trying to learn from the Unicorns. But primarily, it tells the story of how you can REALLY act on your Day After Tomorrow, how you can apply innovation as an antidote to radical change. I won't just zoom in on WHAT you need to do in order to innovate, but also on HOW to make innovation a reality in your organization. I will share what I have learned from my global safari to hunt down the rarest of beasts – the Phoenix.

It is my dream that – if you are working in a traditional business, or in a traditional market – this book will offer you the inspiration, the guidance and the courage to transform, to reboot, and to become the Phoenix in your market. It is my dream that it will help you "Live long, and prosper", as the Vulcans would have it.

Ready?

Innovation is the New Normal

> If you don't take change by the hand,
> it will take you by the throat.
>
> — WINSTON CHURCHILL

My children function as the perfect lens to observe the future. While they help me see, at times this can be incredibly savage and harsh. Every time an 'old-timer' uses *digital* as an adjective, they roll their eyes at these tragic old farts, desperately trying to understand the world of today. To them, referring to a camera as digital is like calling the sea 'watery'. It's obsolete. And really dumb. Only on the rare occasion that something is NOT digital, will they add an adjective like 'vintage', 'analogue' or 'old school'.

When I wrote my second book 'The New Normal' in 2010, I had no idea how rapidly digital would indeed become a true commodity and basically lose all of its meaning as an adjective. Yet, I'm still regularly invited to companies that are proud to present their 'digital strategy'. I'm just as suspicious about this, as my children are about the old farts described above. You might be able to present your strategy for a digital world, but defining your strategy as digital only proves how little you understand about what is happening around you. I'm sorry to be harsh, but that's just the simple truth.

Next to the complete normalization of digital, we've also seen the momentous rise of ubiquity. Everything is 'Always On'. When I was still a kid, the dial tone on our fixed phone was the perfect way to check if the world hadn't fallen to pieces. If you picked up the phone and you got a dial tone, all was right with the world. Any old movie where the protagonists pick up the phone and the line is 'dead', you knew they were in deep, deep trouble.

That very same thing goes for the Internet access – especially wireless – today. My quality as a father is completely correlated to the quality of the Wi-Fi signal inside our house. If it's decent, then I'm an OK dad. However. When the tiniest bandwidth interruption occurs – one that causes just a millisecond delay in the streaming of Youtube or Netflix – my kids start questioning my degree in computer science.

We're all addicted to our New Normal. Tech is just a commodity and yet, every day we are challenged by it. Every day newsfeeds remind us about the potential dangers of Artificial Intelligence. They tell us that automation and robots could take our jobs, destroy the fabric of work and steal away the future of the next generation. Fear sells. The result is that a significant part of the population is starting to question the rate and value of technological progress. They are deeply skeptical about our capabilities as a human race to survive this onslaught of technologies stampeding into our future.

I think we have nothing to worry about.

Humans are remarkably good at coping with change. We have been around as the *Homo Sapiens* species for more than 350,000 years, so the last 300 years of human history represent only a tiny blip in the total picture. If we compress the total length of human history into one full day, then the last 300 years would account to the last two minutes of that entire day. From 23:58 till midnight.

And just look at what fundamental changes we've mastered during that tiny blip.

THE FRENCH REVOLUTION AND THE STATE

Three hundred years ago, we embarked on a revolution that changed how we organized our world in the most fundamental way. What started as a rebellion in Western Europe – with the French Revolution – ended up as a bonfire of the global societal structures of the day. On these ashes freedom and equality have become the fundamental mechanism through which we look at the world. Gone are the days of Kings and Noblemen who ruled entire countries. Power went to the people. The start of the French Revolution was truly disruptive. But it was also massively messy.

In 1789, the French Revolution overthrew the age-old monarchy in France and triggered a cascade of instabilities. Things only really settled down when Napoleon created a new order. We can safely say that his rule was nothing more than a dictatorship, but it did establish the idea of a 'Republic' as we know it now. More importantly, it provided balance and stability in most of Western

Europe, with brand-new systems, particularly of the rule of law and government, which are still in use today in many countries. The French revolution was one of the most significant events in human history: it triggered the decline of absolute monarchies, replaced them with the concept of democracy, and then spread all over the world like a virus.

The turbulence of the French Revolution was so huge that it took almost 150 years for the dust to settle. But with great turmoil, comes great impact. The way we run countries, organize democracies, enjoy the rule of law and operate a nation today, is pretty much the result of that tempestuous storming of the Bastille in Paris on that glorious day in July 1789. It gave birth to The State. And the concept of the Republic, which has become the 'Standard Operating System' that most countries use today.

THE INDUSTRIAL REVOLUTION AND THE FIRM

The second biggest disruption that occurred during the last two minutes of the human-history-day is the Industrial Revolution, originating a mere 150 years ago. Brand-new disruptive technologies like the steam engine, huge scientific breakthroughs in the field of electricity and chemistry, and the consequent mass industrialization changed the world completely.

This time around, the British were the ones to kickstart a new Revolution. Britain had been extremely efficient in expanding its reach all over the world, and it had treated its colonies as massive deposits of raw materials. These raw materials were then processed on home ground, before being re-exported to the world. To give you an idea of the power of Britain in those days: more than 80 percent of the world's goods were transported in British ships. As the British economy needed to process an increasing amount of materials into finished goods, technological disruption was about the only option to sustain the growth. So, textile manufacturing became the fertile ground in which industrialization first took root. The steam engine could exponentially increase the output of production, and soon Britain would become the 'workplace of the world'. In those days, at the onset of the industrial revolution, England pretty much played the role that China is playing in today's global economy.

By 1870, the full force of the Industrial Revolution came into play. Locomotives, steam engines and steamships neatly turned the world into a much smaller place. And Britannia ruled the industrial waves with its first-class engineers and mechanics. However, it did have a hard time catching up with the 'next big thing'.

Three waves of industrial innovation

1ST WAVE
GREAT-BRITAIN
The workplace of the world

An industrial revolution based on steam engines that turned the world into a smaller place.

Based on ingenuity of mechanics

2ND WAVE
GERMANY
Global leader in engineering expertise

An industrial revolution based on breakthroughs in electricity and chemistry.

Based on ingenuity of science

3RD WAVE
USA
World's dominant mass-economy

An industrial revolution based on efficiency, scale advantages, entrepreneurship and financial creativity.

Based on ingenuity of economics

SOCIAL REVOLUTION
→ the State

INDUSTRIAL REVOLUTION
→ the Firm

The **second wave of this Industrial Revolution** is where Continental Europe, and especially Germany, played a leading role. Companies on the continent had the advantage of arriving late at the 'industrial' party. And, without any legacy machinery holding them back, they were able to adopt the latest methods and innovations. The British, on the other hand, had a terrible time breaking loose from the 'first' industrial revolution technologies based on mechanical engineering and steam.

It was Germany's time to shine. Companies like Siemens thrived like elegant giants in the emerging disruptive technology of electricity; and organizations like BASF (Badische Anilin- und Sodafabrik) took over the world by taking advantage of the enormous breakthroughs in chemistry.

As Richard Evans points out in 'The Pursuit of Power', his excellent account of this period: "While the technological innovations that brought about the first industrial revolution had been achieved largely by the ingenuity of mechanics, the second clearly required the knowledge of scientists." Based on their belief in scientific progress, these companies grew like crazy. Werner von Siemens made his fortune by building telegraph systems that used needles to point to letters and thus basically made 'Morse Code' obsolete overnight. His company, Siemens, was to employ 75,000 workers in Germany by 1913, and another 24,000 outside the country.

The ambitions of these industrial giants to dominate the globe soared sky-high. The German firm 'Krupp' became the global supplier of rails, as well as axles and crankshafts for the railway engines that ran over them. Its ambition was to become the global supplier of all railway equipment, with railway lines "linking and crossing the great continents of Africa, America and Asia so that they will come to the status of civilized countries, and to connect the economies of the world to keep the industry busy until the end of the world." As a matter of irony, they added as an afterthought: "We will prevail as long as some windbag does not destroy our ambitions by developing air transport."[1]

Europe clearly dominated the scene of the industrial age. An amazing feat of engineering was the creation of the Suez Canal by the French entrepreneur Ferdinand de Lesseps. In a mere ten years – between 1859 and 1869 – he was able to join the Mediterranean Sea with the Red Sea, substantially reducing the time taken to transport goods and people between Europe and East Asia. Sadly, the mustached developer was not able to repeat his success when he set out to carve the Panama Canal. It turned out to be an unmitigated disaster. Eventually more than 22,000 men died from malaria, yellow fever and accidents until the money ran out in 1889. This was a tell-tale sign that the European domination in industrialization was on its last legs.

The United States, however, perfectly understood the enormous geopolitical importance of this Panama waterway. In 1904, President Theodore Roosevelt declared the Panama Canal of vital importance to the nation and mobilized all efforts to succeed. This time around, and thanks to American ingenuity in mass scale engineering, its enormous breakthroughs in heavy-duty machinery, and the advances in medical science (to overcome the debilitating diseases which were endemic to Panama), the US succeeded where the French had failed. And in 1914, they opened up the canal to the world.

But the **third wave of Industrial innovation** really took root in the United States with the advent of mass production. Henry Ford may have been the Steve Jobs of his time, but close follower General Motors would eventually grow even bigger than Ford's company. At that time Alfred Sloan – after whom the eponymous business school of MIT would be named – was the president, chairman and CEO of General Motors. And he was very much the Bill Gates of his time.

These massive technological disruptions would completely change the very nature of the countries where they reared their disruptive heads. Britain was transformed from a 'nation of shopkeepers' into the 'workplace of the world'. Germany evolved into a global leader in engineering expertise. And the United States became the world's dominant economy based on efficiency and scale advantages, matched with a heady combination of industrial innovation, entrepreneurship and financial creativity. Our planet became a global supply chain, and all of the above changed the pecking order of the world. The French social scientist Paul de Rousiers perhaps described it best: "Our French soldiers now carry canned meats, prepared in Chicago, in their knapsacks".

But, above all, the industrial revolution had a profound impact upon society. Before it took off, up to 70% of the population of countries like Britain or Germany worked in agriculture. At the end of it, less than 10% did. The industrial revolution sparked mass urbanization, as everyone wanted to live close to the factories. This profoundly changed the way lives were lived: it ultimately put more women in the workplace, unionized labor, and created a need to scale up education. A new social order emerged, with society's dominant class dwelling in the cities and towns of the industrial age, rather than in the countryside.

Where the Social Revolution had 'The State' as its most visible outcome, the clearest expression of the Industrial Revolution has to be 'The Firm'. How we manage companies today is still pretty much based on the Industrial Revolution's need for organizing large groups of unskilled labor. In 1904, Max Weber, one of the three founders of sociology (with Emile Durkheim and Karl Marx) was extremely passionate about the introduction of bureaucracy. He said: "Bureaucracy is superior to any other organizational form in precision, in stability, in discipline, and in reliability."[2] And indeed, today's standard 'Operating System' for large organizations is still based on this 19th century social set-up, developed to control and coordinate large groups of relatively unskilled workers.

THE TECHNOLOGICAL REVOLUTION AND THE EMPOWERED INDIVIDUAL

But there's another revolution to be dealt with. Today we are privileged observers of yet another fundamental transition. In these very last seconds of the human-history-day, we have seen the rise of the World Wide Web (since 1995) as well as other digital technology. This has fundamentally changed how we work and live. But in my opinion, we are merely at the very early stages of a seismic shift for humankind.

While the Social Revolution gave us 'The State', and the Industrial Revolution gave us 'The Firm', the Technological Revolution seems to be the onset of the age of 'The Empowered Individual'. The first two revolutions were all about the collective, but this one is giving a voice to the many facets of the individual. We see empowered consumers who have more information, more demands and a bigger reach than ever before, scanning barcodes, reviews, communities, social media and whatever else they can get their eyes on. We see empowered employees leaving comments on GlassDoor, or new recruits being taught about work ethics and company cultures before they even start a new job. From Uber Ratings to the controversial Chinese Social Credit Score system,[3] we are seeing the rise of empowered consumers, citizens and employees.

We're not there yet. Not even halfway. In the last 20 years, we've seen the transition from the world of the web to the world of mobile. And at the same time our initial enthusiasm about these technologies has dampened a little. Ah, remember those glorious days of the 'first Internet bubble' when we fantasized about 'eliminating the middleman'. It would be the end of the dominance of the retail industry: we would bypass those greedy dictators and go straight to the source. Twenty years on, and we've seen global platforms like Amazon and Alibaba taking over that 'middle' role, which we yearned to escape from. And they have more control, dominance and power than ever before.

Remember enthusiastically thinking that the 'information superhighway' would set us free from the mind control of traditional media like TV and newspapers? Remember imagining that social media could topple governments and set nations free from the shackles of corrupt dictators during the Arab Spring? And then, fast forward to our current society twenty years later. It's not exactly what we were rejoicing about back then, right? Today, we worry about whether Russia has meddled with the US elections to get Donald Trump elected. Cambridge Analytica became a household name for producing what would come to be called Fake News, at a global scale. And let's not forget about the sometimes sketchy platforms like Facebook, which are under scrutiny for everything from racism, extremism and government interference.

So, no, we're not quite there yet.

THE NEW NORMALS

But then again, we're only at the beginning. When I wrote 'The New Normal' to address the concept of 'digital', many companies were preparing their long-term vision in a neatly labelled '2020 strategic plan'. In those days I would be regularly invited to inspire audiences of large corporations who were deeply uneasy about conceiving their 2020 plans. The future seemed impossibly bright.

2020 is no longer the future. And the New Normal of digital has nicely settled in. Today, we have a new set of New Normals. Plural. There is no ONE New Normal anymore. There are eight.

■ Social Media

For my kids, Social Media have always been the most natural way of connecting, sharing and communicating. They have never known otherwise. It is how they find information, seek entertainment and distraction, are part of a community, or influence and be influenced. I shiver when I hear people talking about the 'digital natives', since I don't believe that the next generation can be categorized only by their ability to turn something on or off. What I prefer, is to look at this generation as 'network natives', for they have learned how to behave 'in the network'. They search in the network, reach out in the network, and connect in the network. Social Media is constantly evolving. New platforms rise and fall, but this is no longer a phenomenon that will erode. To the contrary, it has become part of the New Normal arsenal.

The New Normal Arsenal

- **SOCIAL MEDIA**
Is constantly evolving. New platforms rise and fall, but social media stay part of the New Normal arsenal.

- **MULTICHANNEL MARKETING**
Standard platform for understanding customers and trigger actions with desirable customer outcomes.

- **MOBILE**
Mobile devices have become our interface to the world, our source of information.

- **PLATFORMS**
Platform mechanisms have become the standard economic model for growth.

- **THE CLOUD**
Allows us to scale our computing needs almost instantly and only pay for what we use.

- **AGILE**
Has become the widespread philosophy to tackle all sorts of projects, in start-ups and large corporations.

- **BIG DATA**
Standard technology for understanding and predicting the behavior of customers in the New Normal.

- **API**
Application Programming Interfaces allow the quick building of applications by connecting to existing services.

Multichannel Marketing

Consumers are notoriously tricky to reach. And it gets more difficult by the day. They don't just live on the web alone, or in the mobile universe, but use myriads of platforms and systems. They are known to occasionally venture out in the real world as well (some more than others). The horror of all this is that the ways they can be reached just keep on growing. Even communicating with my own family members can be a living nightmare, forcing me to really overthink where my chances of success are the highest. I might still be able to reach my wife with a text message, perhaps connect to my son with Messenger, and maybe reach my daughter with an Instagram DM. And if I'm very lucky, I'll receive all of their attention on the family WhatsApp group.

In today's world, understanding a consumer's needs, behavior and preferences, and then orchestrating personalized communication with them, is no longer considered black magic. We want to tailor messages, personalize communications, and provide one-to-one intimacy. Multichannel marketing has become the standard platform for understanding customers. It's what helps us uncover where they are on their journey and how we can persuade them to choose for our offering.

Mobile

The iPhone was only introduced in 2007. Sure, the concept of a smartphone existed before that, but when the iPhone exploded onto the scene it revolutionized our behavior. Now, I wouldn't dream of leaving home without the comfort of this most personal of devices. Not only has it become our true source of information, dictating the rhythm of our lives, it is rapidly becoming our interface to the world. Asia has been a true forerunner in making mobile the 'standard operating mechanism' in their quest to unlock the world of services and interactions.

People spend fortunes on the latest Mobile device, gobble up wireless bandwidth at an alarming rate, and platforms such as Android and iOS have become global superpowers that control a significant part of our lives.

Platforms

Platforms are rapidly turning into the standard economic model of growth for the 21st century. Because of the scale reaction of digital and online as well as the 'network effect' – which can trigger a chain-reaction of exponential growth – we see the rise of 'network economies'. However, platforms are often under attack these days, primarily because we seem to have nurtured 'category kings' that have become dominant very quickly. You can have a lot of objections against Facebook, but honestly whyever would we join another social network if all our friends are there?

We're still grappling with their underlying economic mechanisms, but one thing is becoming very clear: platform mechanisms are the new economic normal.

The Cloud

I love the saying: "There is no such thing as 'Cloud Computing', it's just somebody else's computer". Nothing could be more wrong, however. True, when you use a cloud service, you're using someone else's infrastructure. But the Cloud is of course much more than just remote servers. It has allowed us to scale our computing needs almost instantaneously. In the past you needed to purchase expensive new servers if you wanted to increase storage or processing capacity. Today the true power of the cloud is its 'elasticity' and ability to expand or shrink depending upon your needs. That, and the incredibly tempting feature that you only need to pay for what you use.

In record time we've seen the growth of cloud providers like Amazon Web Services and Microsoft Azure. The economies of scale that they offer are truly unrivaled. And of course, they have become the true enablers of the startup age. Any kid with a credit card can 'shop' at AWS, be operational in about 15 minutes' time, and have more computing power at their disposal than the entire computing infrastructure of the Bank of America.

Agile

Not too long ago, developing applications was quite the Sisyphean labor. You would first take a very (very) long time thinking about what you (or your customer) and the end user – needed. Then you would very carefully (and just as slowly) design it, and then take eons to write the software. And in the end, you would come to the sad and frustrating conclusion that the result was not exactly what users wanted. And then you'd have to start all over again. It seemed like a brilliant plot to annoy users, but, frankly, there was no alternative.

And then the startup scene adopted the brilliant 'agile' movement. The truth is that startups just don't have the luxury, or the funds, to endure the tedious think-design-build-frustrate-reboot cycle. They just have to be much faster to incorporate user feedback. Enter the concept of the MVP (minimum viable product): this clever approach allows you to test your idea and assumptions with a very basic version of your product or service, receive immediate user feedback, and then rapidly adapt and steer it in the right direction. Agile spread very quickly. It is no longer just a mechanism for software development, but a more widespread philosophy on how to tackle all sorts of projects. Today, it has been adopted by every type of organization: from very small startups to the largest corporations.

Big Data

Once upon a time, we would store our information in robust databases. And that worked just fine until the World Wide Web happened. In the olden days we only needed to store limited amounts of information: the address and name of your customers for instance, or the orders they had placed. But the advent of the web – even more so in its mobile version – has unleashed a true tsunami of information, gushing out of all of our devices. Had the web had a voice of its own, it would have been chanting "Every click you take, every swipe you make. I'll be watching you". (No idea why, but I can actually hear it sing in South Park's Cartman's voice instead of Sting's.)

And then Big Data entered the game. Its technology was first developed by companies like Google to analyze the vast rivers of information flowing through their servers. Today it has evolved into the standard technology for understanding and predicting the behavior of our customers in the New Normal.

API

Some of you might be less familiar with the term, but the API – the Application Programming Interface – has also become an absolute New Normal. An API essentially allows anyone to build applications very quickly by 'connecting' to existing services. In other words, you no longer have to build everything from scratch yourself. It is the technological equivalent of Newton's infamous quote: 'standing on the shoulders of Giants'.[4]

Let me give you an example. The map of your Uber application is firmly 'hooked' into the Google maps function with the use of an API. And when you text or call your Uber driver, Uber will 'hook in' the API of Twilio, a company that specializes in providing these type of communications services. And if you, from your side, would like to build in a 'call an Uber' button in your application, you can simply 'hook it in' by connecting to the Uber API.

Safe to say that the concept of APIs has made the building of applications a lot easier, and has provided a framework where you can connect, click and snap all those services together.

So, 8 'New Normals', instead of just one. But why these 8? Simple. Every startup that is crawling out of an entrepreneur's head today, will take these New

Normals as a baseline. These 8 pillars are their 'ground zero', on which they will found their company. They will tap into the infrastructure in the Cloud, connect to all the relevant APIs, develop Platforms in an Agile environment, leverage Big Data to reach out to customers in the most Multichannel of ways, through Mobile and Social.

So what about you? If these 8 New Normal pillars are the 'standard baseline' for startups, and you're not leveraging all of them, chances are that you're probably already behind the curve. Could be high time for some soul searching. But let's leave that for the end of this chapter and first open up our perspective even more.

THE ERA OF CROSSROADS

When digital became the New Normal, a silo that used to be the safe dwelling place of nerds and geeks all over the world suddenly opened up to the mainstream. When I was studying computer science at the beginning of the nineties, most of my non-engineering friends had no interest whatsoever in technology. Now I see them casually talking about the impressive 12 Megapixel camera on their latest Smartphone or their AI-powered lawn mower robot. Technology is no longer the sole domain of the technologist. It is now the intersection of many different paths.

That's why I believe that we are living in an era of crossroads.

Technology meets economy

The most obvious crossroad is the one where Economy meets Technology. Sector by sector we are witnessing the impact of digital, the Internet and other Day After Tomorrow technologies on every single aspect of business. Technology used to be a mechanism for 'optimizing' an industry, but now it is fundamentally reshaping entire industries and markets.

Back in 2011, Marc Andreessen described this transition beautifully in his famous Wall Street Journal op-ed "Software is eating the world". As the founder of the brilliant but tragic Netscape, he became the poster-child of the first Internet bubble, who then reinvented himself as one of the most influential financiers in Silicon Valley. What he wrote back then in his op-ed, still stands strong: "Six decades into the computer revolution, four decades since the invention of the microprocessor, and two decades into the rise of the modern Internet, all of the technology required to transform industries can be widely delivered at global scale."[5] This transition is now happening at full speed. Amazon has transformed retail with software, Netflix has transformed television with software, and Uber has transformed transportation with software.

And we're just getting started.

When I was in my twenties, the brilliant 'Being Digital' by Nicholas Negroponte was one of the most influential books around. He was the founder of the MIT Media Lab, a forward-thinking interdisciplinary research lab at the Massachusetts Institute of Technology that encourages the unconventional mixing and matching of seemingly disparate research areas: from technology, to media, science, art and design.

Negroponte's book describes two types of companies: there are the 'bits' companies and the 'atoms' companies. 'Bits' companies deal with bits and bytes, data, information, ones and zeros. Banks are typically bits companies, since they essentially only deal with the information about the accounts of customers. Equally, insurance companies are 'bits' companies. Companies that haul cement from A to B are obviously 'atoms' companies as they physically move 'real' stuff around. Negroponte fundamentally believed that, in the end, every atom related business would come to be ruled by 'bits'.

And it seems that he was right. Take mobility: Uber is doing a pretty good job of transforming an 'atoms' business of physical cars into a 'bits' business of mobile platforms, APIs and Big Data. Uber does not own any cars. In fact, it doesn't own any of the 'atoms' that are part of its service. Yet, it has built incredible value in a very short period of time by 'orchestrating' the flow of bits in such a way that you can hail a ride from its mobile app. Uber was founded in March of 2009, and just 10 years later, it was floated on the New York Stock Exchange with a market capitalization of more than $70 billion.

Andreessen's 'software is eating the world' thesis was spot on in predicting what is unfolding in front of our very eyes. Information has become the core fuel of global platforms, some of which then turn into dominant 'category kings', that seem invincible.

Today, we're experiencing a backlash against this category king phenomenon. Platforms such as Facebook and Google are under increased scrutiny over the power they yield, the vast and deep knowledge they have amassed, and their consequent influence over consumers. As I stated earlier, we've gone a long way since thinking "Yeay, the Internet is going to cut out all middlemen from our transactions and the traditional media will no longer be able to control our sense of reality. We're free!"

Not so much. Twenty years later we're having some serious second thoughts about this evolution. Amazon grew out to be the most monstrous middleman we could have ever imagined: it knows exactly how to play us as consumers, and massively uses its economy of scale to pressure suppliers. Middlemen are back with a vengeance. Some of us even cherish nostalgic feelings of sympathy for the – in retrospect – limited influence of the 'old' media when we compare it to the highly manipulative power of a platform like Facebook. Not so long ago, a science fiction story where Russia influenced a Big Data company like Cambridge Analytica to leverage a global platform like Facebook to alter the outcome of the US Presidential elections would have seen absurdly far-fetched. But reality is much stranger than fiction nowadays.

■ Technology meets politics

We are at a crossroads. It's not just technology changing the economy. It's influencing geopolitics as well. The escalation of a new 'Cold War' between China and the US could have a profound impact on how the power balance of our planet develops.

I grew up in Europe during the 'old' Cold War. In the aftermath of the Second World War, Russia and the US were arm-wrestling for global domination. The stakes were high and driven by two vital technologies: nuclear and space. At first, the Russians seemed to be ahead of the game, continuously proving their technological and scientific superiority. The high point of their success was of course the seminal launch of the Sputnik satellite into an elliptical low Earth orbit on October 4th, 1957. That's when the Americans started to panic. They were truly and utterly flabbergasted that Russia had been able to launch the very first artificial satellite around the earth. Every American could turn on their radio and hear the (to them) ominous beep of the Russian Sputnik as it flew over US territory. That Russian beep was all it took to jolt the US into swift action.

Two very concrete measures of this panic-induced action plan are still extremely visible today. The first was the creation of DARPA, the 'Defense Advanced Research Projects Agency'. It received an almost unlimited budget to create 'breakthrough technologies for national security' and eventually helped the US win the Space Race. But it did a lot more than that. The Internet as we know it was a DARPA project, the Global Positioning System that guides our car navigation and Google Maps was a DARPA project, and even the Google Driverless Car was originally a DARPA project. It also allowed Silicon Valley to bloom into the global Mecca of technological innovation that it is today. In short, DARPA gave us the world of the New Normal.

The second swift action from the US Government after the humiliating Sputnik incident was the creation of the National Defense Education Act of 1958. The US realized that they did not have the scientific brainpower to battle the Soviets, or win the Cold War. So they initiated a dramatic increase in spending on education in science, math and foreign languages to build the right skillsets for the future. The result was that in the US, the percentage of people who transitioned from high-school to college would jump from 15% in 1940 to more than 40% by 1970.

It was exactly this massive spending and focus on technology, innovation and education that helped the US win the Cold War. There's a pretty good chance that we'll soon experience a remake of that movie, but with different actors: China and the US. The battlefields, too, have evolved. The new Cold War between the US and China has (mostly) moved away from nuclear and space technologies, and is instead played on cyber-security, artificial intelligence and the infrastructure for next generation networks, like 5G. The battlefields include robotics and automation, quantum computing, encryption, but also enormous advances in genetics and bioscience. This cold war is essentially a war on talent, with China producing almost 5 million STEM (Science, Technology, Engineering and Mathematics) graduates every year, while the US produces barely a tenth of that.

■ Technology meets biology

The geopolitical landscape of our world could be thoroughly reshaped by this new cold war. And yet, for me this isn't even the most interesting of the current crossroads. We are now rapidly moving into a world where 'disruption' goes way beyond the realm of digital. Take biology, for example. In the final weeks of 2018, two very cute and very special twin babies were born in China: Lulu and Nana. They had (illegally) been genetically modified with CRISPR-Cas9, a technology that had only been created a few years earlier. The simplest way to describe CRISPR-Cas9 would be to say that it allows to 'copy-and-paste' genetic material to modify the genetics of an organism. It's insane when you think about it: we only learned how to 'read' the full human genome back in 2001, and by 2018 we could already manipulate and 'copy-and-paste' genetic code. We are at the eve of our capability to start 'writing' genetic code. Soon, we'll be able to play God.

Now this is where it gets exciting: this disruption will spread beyond the digital domains into all sorts of new territories. Look at agriculture, and food. In the last couple of years, billions of dollars of venture capital have flowed towards entrepreneurs eager to use disruptive technologies to transform the food chain, and introduce vegan-based alternatives into our ecologically unsound eating practices. They will fully disrupt how we feed ourselves on this planet.

In my opinion, we are truly privileged to be a witness of such a massively transformational era. It must have been truly amazing to be part of the social or industrial revolution, but I'm sure our ancestors would have given up an arm or a leg to partake in the current shift. This is the era of disruption, the era of unbounded technological advancement, and it will completely transform our lives, our markets, and our society.

If you already thought that 'Digital' was impressive, brace yourselves, 'cause you're in for a helluva ride.

YOUR TURN

When I started writing this book, I knew that its theme and content would require it to be very pragmatic and executable. So I decided to end each chapter with some sort of 'homework'. In this case, I'll obviously not ask you to contemplate the last three hundred years of human civilization (tempting though that is), even if talking about the beautiful waves of the industrial revolution will serve you brilliantly at cocktail receptions.

What I *do* want you to do, is find out what **YOUR** New Normals are. If you look at your sector, your market, your business, what are the New Normals (plural!) that might not immediately be *your* baseline, but that any startup in your market would take for granted? If you would leave your company right now, and start all over again, what would your ground zero be?

There's more. There's very little use in doing this exercise just once. Everyone's New Normals change as time goes by. In fact, in a world where they keep evolving, we can safely say that we are entering a state of Never Normal. This is why you have to keep an eye on your New Normals and keep updating them. I think it's a very healthy exercise to do regularly so you can see where you should be as an organization, and which baseline is needed to stay relevant in this fast-changing world.

2

The Hourglass model

A PRACTICAL GUIDE TO THE DAY AFTER TOMORROW

> If we think long term we can accomplish things that we wouldn't otherwise accomplish. Time horizons matter. They matter a lot.
>
> — JEFF BEZOS

THE ORIGINS OF THE DAY AFTER TOMORROW

I came up with the idea for 'The Day After Tomorrow' a few years ago, during a masterclass in Barcelona. My partner in crime at nexxworks, Steven Van Belleghem, had organized a three-day workshop, and on the last evening I wanted to use a simple metaphor so that the group could go home with a clear final message and mission.

That's when I remembered an old diagram from one of my first professional activities as a young engineer at Alcatel, which was then one of the leading telecom equipment makers in the world. I was part of a team that had the mission to come up with a Video-On-Demand system, which would allow people to view movies whenever they wanted, in the privacy of their own home. It was basically a rudimentary prototype of Netflix. The biggest challenge in designing the system was that all the movies were essentially just a number of compressed video files on a very large hard disk and that, back then, it was quite difficult to have many users access the same file at the exact same time.

So, if a movie was very popular, say the latest Star Wars movie, and you had compressed it into a video file, only a limited number of users could access it simultaneously. As an engineer, you could do two things. There was the 'proper' engineering method, in which you would try to use all sorts of clever technological tricks & techniques to increase the throughput streams of the hard disk and to allow more users to access the same file. The 'other', much more practical engineering approach was just to copy the very popular movie-files, so you had multiple copies of Star Wars being watched at the same time.

A movie-based model

Needless to say, we opted for the latter. The result is that, as engineers, we had to understand which movies were very popular, and then make sure that we had enough copies of those. In the end, we came up with three categories: 'red hot' movies, that everyone wanted to see, and of which we needed a lot of copies, 'normal' movies that had a more average popularity, and 'esoteric' movies that were only occasionally requested, and formed essentially the 'long tail' of our video library.

The graph we used, looked pretty much like this:

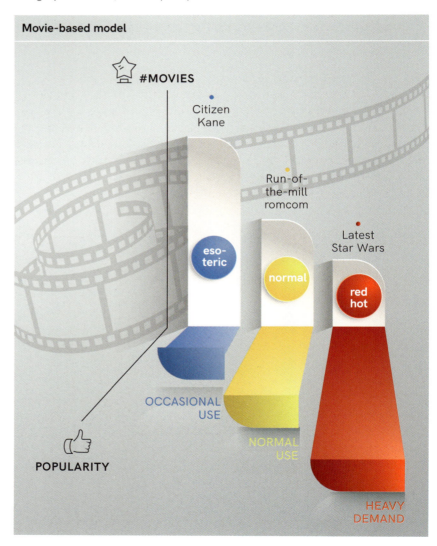

I loved the simplicity of this model, and how easy it was to explain. So that evening in Barcelona, I had the insight that we could apply this to our strategic horizons as well. I immediately put it to work and introduced the 'Day After Tomorrow' in the workshop the next morning, and it turned out to be an instant hit.

Three Horizons

A while later someone informed me that this 'Day After Tomorrow' model reminded him of McKinsey's 'Three Horizons Framework'. I had spent a year at McKinsey myself, as an 'Entrepreneur in Residence', during my forced sabbatical between my first and second startup. So it is entirely possible that I had encountered this model when I was working there, but, as I said, my true inspiration were the three types of movies described above.

McKinsey's 'Three Horizons Framework' is a mechanism that allows us to map out Value vs. Time in terms of strategic thinking, and it describes three distinct 'horizons'. The first horizon is the strategic framework that is used to maintain and defend your core business as an organization: Business as Usual. The second horizon is the one that allows you to focus on nurturing emerging business, often in the continuation of, or in the adjacency to, existing activities. The last and third horizon is the one where you create entirely new business for the firm, which is essentially the same as my Day After Tomorrow concept.

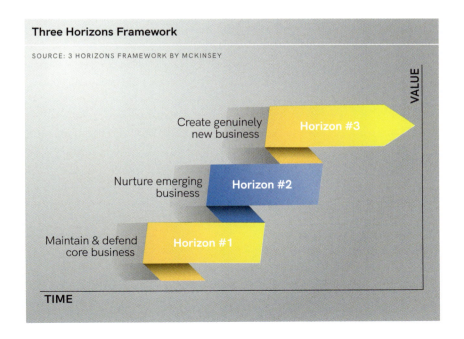

This model was first featured in the book 'The Alchemy of Growth', published in 1999 by Stephen Coley, together with co-authors Mehrdad Baghai and David White. Stephen is now a director emeritus in McKinsey's Chicago office. Back then, he uncovered a very dangerous bias inside organizations: being overly focused on the immediate future. This bias is extremely strong, as Horizon 1 carries the greatest immediate profits and cash flow. But in times of change and uncertainty, instead of focusing on 'securing' Horizon 1, companies must look further. The McKinsey model allows leaders to balance attention and investments in both current performance activities and opportunities for growth.

In essence, this has the same core as my 'Day After Tomorrow' model. In other words: how much time, effort, budget and resources are you prepared to allocate to your 'Today' (Horizon 1), your 'Tomorrow' (Horizon 2) and your 'Day After Tomorrow' (Horizon 3)?

With the final Day After Tomorrow model, I re-used this old 'Popular Movies' model, but now clearly with time in the x-axis, to clarify the boundaries between Today, Tomorrow and the Day After Tomorrow.

For me, the essence of the three 'buckets' consists of understanding what they each generate in terms of 'Value Creation' for the company. 'Today' thinking is very important to achieve your current targets and provides your 'current value'. 'Tomorrow' is important for your 'future value', but the Day After Tomorrow is essential to unlock the massive 'long term value' that new technologies, concepts or business models could generate.

Most companies have an extremely myopic view of the future, often merely extrapolating their 'todays' in the vague hope that tomorrow will be 'approximately' the same. That's why I love following the budgeting season in organizations: this annual sadistic ritual forces scores of employees to put 'fake news' into excel spreadsheets and then consolidate them into a mythical 'budget' (I can almost hear angels singing when I write this word) that almost NEVER materializes. However, I have recently met a number of companies that have abandoned the budget cycle altogether. They realized that it merely took up massive amounts of resources and energy, and resulted in very little. They were smart enough to see that in a fast changing world, with technology accelerating the pace of change faster than ever before, the concept of the annual budget becomes less relevant with each passing year.

When I started using the Day After Tomorrow model, it seemed to trigger people to start thinking about how they were looking at the (far) future and how they were appreciating value creation in their strategic thinking.

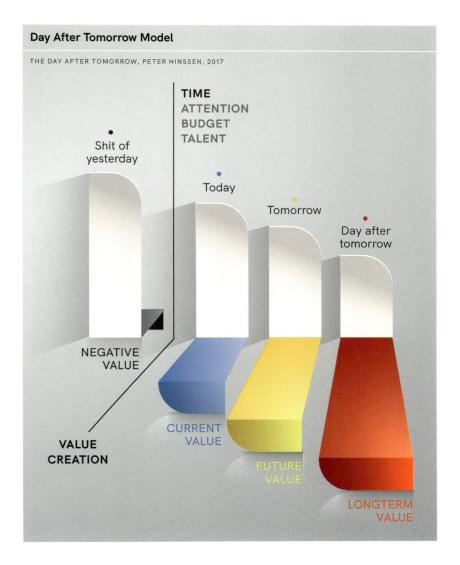

■ Fighting negative value

My absolute favorite part of the model is the 'Shit of Yesterday', though. It was one of our customers who added that bit onto what I had drawn on the flipchart. He told me that these very tenacious and sticky past problems added 'negative value' to his organization. His 'Shit of Yesterday' is what many companies would label as 'legacy': un-future-proof systems, processes, or even people that no longer add real value to the organization, but are dragging it down with a negative flow of value. And energy.

■ What is YOUR Day After Tomorrow?

However, the most important question is: 'what is the balance in your company between your Today, your Tomorrow and your Day After Tomorrow?' Ideally the Today would account for 70%, Tomorrow for 20% and the Day After Tomorrow for 10%. If most companies are honest, though, they'll have to admit that they spend the most time on managing Today and, even worse, cleaning up The Shit of Yesterday. So what about you? If the Day After Tomorrow or, God beware, Tomorrow have no firm place in your company, then what are you going to do about it? I want you to sit down (or stand up, or maybe run or cycle if they're your thing), and really think about that.

I think that the Day After Tomorrow model became so popular because of its simplicity. But it also left a lot of people with pretty big questions. A lot of them came to me after my keynotes or at receptions and then asked me something along the line of: "How can I MANAGE the difference between Today, Tomorrow and the Day After Tomorrow? How do I ORGANIZE these different futures? I understand the WHAT, but HOW do I steer towards the Day After Tomorrow?"

Clearly, the Day After Tomorrow model made people aware of the issue and the need to act on it (which I loved), but, in hindsight, I have to admit that it did not offer any guidance on HOW to do it. And that really bugged me.

So that's where the Hourglass model comes in.

THE HOURGLASS MODEL

It seems to be easy for me to spot those bits of the future that have arrived a little early. — WILLIAM GIBSON[6]

Just like with the brilliant 'Shit of Yesterday' concept, I have one of our customers to thank for this. Emile Piters is the Vice President of IT EMEA at Medtronic, the largest medical device company in the world, which improves the lives of two patients every second globally. You'll probably have heard of them as they are the world's largest medical technology company. It was founded in 1949 in Minneapolis and created the first battery powered pacemaker. Before that, cardiac patients could already be treated with electrical stimulation, but needed to be connected to the power grid. During a massive power outage over Halloween in 1957, large portions of Minnesota and Wisconsin lost electricity, resulting in the death of several cardiac patients. This triggered Medtronic's founder Earl Bakken to develop the first battery-powered, transistorized and wearable artificial pacemaker. Over the years, the company has grown massively and is constantly looking for their 'Day After Tomorrow' strategy. Especially in the fast-changing world of healthcare – where Big Data, sensors and mobiles are transforming the name of the game – it cannot afford to keep its horizon limited to "Tomorrow". The best example of how Medtronic is transforming its market, is the *Micra*, the world's smallest pacemaker which has disrupted the traditional technology by applying leadless pacing.

I had become friends with Emile when 'The New Normal' came out, and we would regularly exchange ideas about the latest evolutions in healthcare. When he started applying the Day After Tomorrow concept in his own business, the challenge was to structure IT resources according to the model's three buckets. A significant part of his team was managing the legacy, implementing large scale IT systems like SAP to 'run' the business. A company like Medtronic, which has more than $30 billion in annual revenue, must ensure that these systems run like Swiss clockwork. This meant that the majority of the budget, and his people, were managing the 'Today' thinking, and spending a lot of effort in cleaning up the SOY. No surprise that, when they *did* think of Tomorrow, it was almost always by extrapolating the current strategic framework.

At the same time, Emile realized that the world of healthcare was on the verge of a set of massive disruptive changes, moving towards a highly personalized form of medicine. The world of pacemakers could transform from a world of electronics into a world where data and digital platforms would become extremely important.

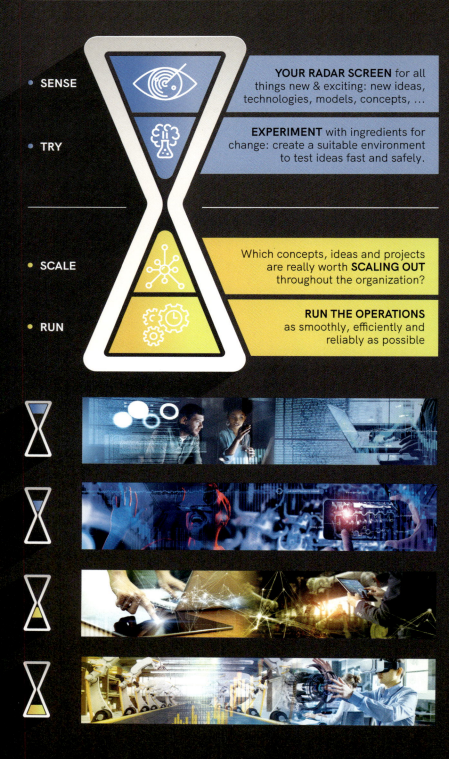

Gradually Emile started to align the two parts of his strategic framework – the existing and the emerging business – and began to allocate more and more efforts, budget and resources to the Day After Tomorrow. The metaphor that slowly emerged from this was that of the Hourglass.

I'm not sure how long it's been since you picked one up, but we all know that an hourglass has two parts. The TOP part of the hourglass is where the sand flows gradually downwards, through the middle section, slowly filling up the BOTTOM part.

If we apply this model to our strategic thinking process, the TOP part is composed of SENSE and TRY.

Sense

The SENSE element of the Hourglass model is our radar screen for all things new and exciting: new ideas, technologies, models, concepts, developments, you name it. In short, a way to spot "those bits of the future that have already arrived", to quote William Gibson.

We are experiencing the Never Normal, one of the fastest changing times in modern history. It is fired up by the non-linear dynamics of the network and a series of permanently interacting novelties. Basically, we need a better radar screen, a wider field of vision, and a deeper sensing network to keep up. We all need to be more alert, pick up signals faster – however weak and feeble they are – and continue to develop and sharpen our sensors for the next new things. Star Trek's The Enterprise sported a 'long range sensor scan', with which it could detect incoming starships long before they would show up on the visual monitors. That's the kind of technique that companies have to learn and develop. It's not enough anymore to attend the annual conference in your field to keep up to date. You have to scan for developments outside of your normal field of vision, understand adjacencies, developments in other sectors, and be extremely open minded for opportunities and serendipity.

■ Try

The second element of the top part of the Hourglass is the TRY segment. Once you have identified ingredients for change in your 'Sense' section, you need to experiment with them and create an environment where you can test ideas fast and safely. Startups have this modus operandi built in in the most natural manner. They are notoriously good at implementing Lean methods of experimentation, building Minimum Viable Products, and testing those with users.

Eric Ries was a young Silicon Valley engineer, who had experienced firsthand how tight budgets forced startups to work in a certain way. They 'naturally' applied a method of Lean development, testing alternate versions of a product with users to get early feedback, and learning from those findings how to quickly iterate to improve the product. It's quite simple: a startup has no alternative. They are in a constant race against the clock, permanently in fear of running out of cash before they hit sustainable revenue. Large corporations, on the other hand, do have that luxury, unfortunately. I say unfortunately, because the sad result is that whatever is being developed is often too late, and off the mark.

When Ries started working in Venture Capital, and advising many startups, he decided to write up his findings into his seminal book "The Lean Startup". It became an instant bestseller and has been widely adopted, not just in the startup world, but in many traditional organizations as well. The core element of Ries' method is to accelerate the feedback loop.

When startups build a product, they build a Minimum Viable Product or 'MVP'. The difference between a 'normal' product and an MVP is basically that the latter is just 'good enough' to be tested. A Viable product is the product that you would LOVE to build (and that's probably being developed by companies that are much better financed than you). A Minimum product, on the other hand, is an underwhelming – yes, maybe even 'crappy' – version of the concept that you want to test. It's in fact so bad that nobody would want to actually use t. The intersection of the two, the Minimum Viable Product, is the best possible version you can build for testing with early users: one that will bring you enough valuable input for your next iteration cycle.

According to Ries, this cycle is quite simple: Build, Measure, Learn, and then Start over. When you have built your MVP, you launch it and gather as much user feedback as you can. You then analyze these findings and deduct key learnings. That input should give you directions on how to quickly develop the next version of your product. And then you start right over.

Only once you have gone through a number of cycles of your 'Lean startup' routine, can you start fully developing your software or products. This approach has been widely adopted since first proposed, and just as much by corporates as by startups. It's also often used in combination with Design Thinking, which can help better understand and serve customers and help define the MVP's initial set of requirements.

This 'TRY' segment of the Hourglass can be an extremely powerful mechanism to experiment in a Lean fashion. With techniques borrowed from the startup world, companies can set up shop to test, decide what works, and then adapt or move forward.

■ Scale & Run

And so we have arrived at the lower section of the Hourglass, where we can 'SCALE' and 'RUN'. It's not hard to understand why this part tends to be best developed by successful traditional companies. This is where companies decide what is REALLY worth putting their money into by narrowing the concepts, ideas and projects of the experimentation phase through the bottle-neck between the top and lower half of the Hourglass.

When a concept, a project or an idea has percolated through the top of the Hourglass, and is considered likely to be a success, it needs to be SCALED out throughout the organization as quickly as possible. After that, it is crucial to RUN the operations as smoothly, efficiently and reliably as possible.

One could apply the Hourglass model for the very specific function of the Information Technology department, but some companies might have an appetite to use the Hourglass model on their entire strategic portfolio.

■ Top to bottom

When Google rebranded itself as 'Alphabet' in October of 2015, it seemed like a strange move for a company that had conquered the 'search' market so incredibly fast. They had not been the first mover in that field, though. It is relatively easy to conquer a market with a brand-new offering when you're the first, but in the search business, companies like Yahoo and Altavista had been around for quite some time. And Google killed them almost overnight.

But that was the past. Google knew it had to keep vigilant not to fall into the same trap of 'Kodak' or 'Xerox' and maybe even General Motors or General Electric: leaders that were once synonymous with a market, only to come crashing down after failing to reinvent themselves. As Google grew, it became clear to them that it was not easy to keep on innovating from the core, and they were terrified of turning obsolete in the same way their former competitors had.

Alphabet turned out to be much more than a cosmetic name-change. It was an elaborate exercise in strategic horizon planning. The high-growth, high-profit elements of the company (including search, Youtube and Android) became part of the 'core' offering of Alphabet: responsible for generating the lion's share of revenue, cash-flow and profit. In 2017, for example, 86% of Alphabet's revenue still came from search-related advertising. But next to this 'core', Alphabet made quite a few 'Bets', including Nest for home automation, Verily for their Healthcare activities or Waymo that handles the business of autonomous cars. And let's not forget the infamous 'Google X' lab, the most famous 'Bet'-factory of all.

When you look at this from an Hourglass model perspective, Alphabet's 'Bets' include daring concepts like connected contact-lenses or driverless cars. Alphabet recognized that these experimental ideas would NEVER survive if they were tried and tested inside their 'CORE' business.

■ Zero to One & One to N

One of the rawest accounts of the startup universe has to be the brilliant book 'Zero to One' by Peter Thiel. Thiel co-founded Paypal with Elon Musk, and has

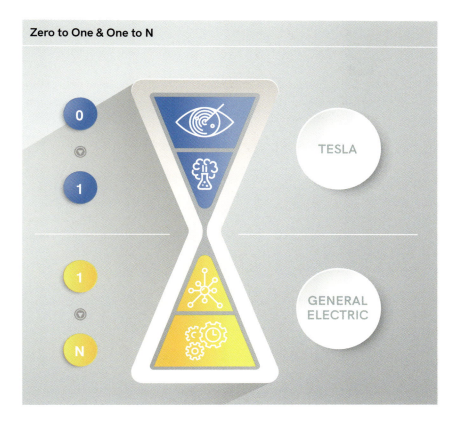

evolved to become one of the most influential investors in Silicon Valley. Based on his experience of running, and investing in startups, he taught a number of classes at Stanford and eventually turned this material into 'Zero to One'. Its premise is that creating Something from Nothing – zero to one – is the essence of a startup.

I would argue that this same dynamic is also the essence of the TOP part of the Hourglass. They're both about focusing a wide lens onto disruptions and opportunities, prioritizing, selecting, and then experimenting and testing. They perfectly match, just up to the point when a 'golden nugget' appears, which you then have to drop into the BOTTOM part of the Hourglass. We can call this second part of the process 'One to N'. This is where you scale and grow (going from one thing, to many) the business in the most effective way possible.

Very often the 'SCALE' part tends to reside in a project mode, with scores of nervous project managers trying to roll out brand-new concepts into the organization. The 'RUN' part, in its turn, is the beating operational heart of the organization: it's where we strive for bottom line results and apply traditional management techniques and Key Performance Indicators to achieve success.

One of my favorite quotes, attributed to Nelson Mandela, is this one: "I never fail, I either win or learn." For me, that is the true essence of learning from our mistakes. We all know 'Fail Fast, Fail often', a common mantra in the startup scene. Of course, the whole idea behind "fail fast, fail often," is not to fail, but to be iterative in how you learn.

▪ A LAT relationship

The top part of the Hourglass model - the Day After Tomorrow section - consists of being open for new things, failing fast and learning, and creating more clarity about where you need to place your bets. The bottom part is about producing the scale and bottom line as the foundation of your business. That's your Today, and your Tomorrow.

I have observed how Emile Piters gradually but very decidedly shifted his organization towards the Hourglass model. First, he made sure that his IT spending was pushed significantly towards the TOP part: it evolved from 5% at the top, and 95% at the bottom, to a situation where it's trending towards a 30/70 ratio. But he also knew that it was not just about moving funding from the bottom to the top: the two parts of the Hourglass required different skills, mentalities, cultures and leadership. And they had to be organized, managed and controlled in different ways. Above all, they had to be CONNECTED. They basically needed a perfect LAT (Living Apart Together) relationship. So Emile installed a mindset throughout the organization where the TOP part of the Hourglass was fully aware that they could not fulfill their potential without the Bottom part of the Hourglass, which generated the necessary funds, cashflow and scale. And the BOTTOM part of the Hourglass had to be fully committed to the top part of the Hourglass, and convinced that it was vital for remaining relevant in the Day After Tomorrow. Both parts were (and still are) interdependent to stay essential and relevant for the future.

I have observed many companies that have a brilliant bottom part of the Hourglass, but were unable to create the top part that would allow them to remain future-proof. But I have equally seen many companies that did develop that latter capability, but were unable to get the top and bottom parts of the Hourglass to align and create common objectives. Only if you manage to properly connect and align the zero-to-one AND the one-to-n will you have a solid formula for tackling your Day After Tomorrow.

I believe this could be the ideal recipe for the Phoenix: a mechanism to keep an open mind, understand new opportunities, and the possibility to bring innovations from idea to scale in a continuous process.

Apple is the Ultimate Phoenix. As some of you may know, I'm a fanatic collector of Apple memorabilia. And when I say fanatic, I *mean* fanatic: I have computers, software, advertising and virtually every single book ever written about the company. I even dedicated a museum to all the things I've collected over the years. But I'm digressing. Back to the essence: Apple went through a very near-death experience (at the time, some even said it had actually died) to come out stronger than ever, and eventually become the most valuable company on the planet.

But even before that *annus horribilis* and Apple's subsequent resurrection, its charismatic founder Steve Jobs had already predicted exactly this. In a rare interview with Playboy magazine in 1985 (yes, people *do* read the articles), just months before he was fired as chairman and thrown out of his own company, he was very open about the need to reinvent yourself as a company, in order to survive.

In the interview, Jobs said: "Companies, as they grow to become multibillion-dollar entities, somehow lose their vision. They insert lots of layers of middle management between the people running the company and the people doing the work. They no longer have an inherent feel or a passion about the products. The creative people, who are the ones who care passionately, have to persuade five layers of management to do what they know is the right thing to do."[7]

Jobs was absolutely right, and eventually that is what happened to Apple too. Layers of middle management turned the once fierce and vivid Apple into a bureaucratic monster, spitting out bland and uninspiring products which nobody wanted to buy.

Jobs probably had no idea he was about to be fired from Apple when he concluded the Playboy interview with: "What happens in most companies is that you don't keep great people under working environments where individual accomplishment is discouraged rather than encouraged. The great people leave and you end up with mediocrity. I know, because that's how Apple was built. Apple is an Ellis Island company. Apple is built on refugees from other companies. These are the extremely bright individual contributors who were troublemakers at other companies."

We all know the rest of the story. Jobs left Apple with a grudge, and poured most of his fortune into NeXT computers, which ended up a complete commercial and financial failure. But when Apple bought NeXT and brought Jobs back, it used the innovation and creative firepower at NeXT to reinvigorate itself. And so it happened that it emerged from the ashes to greatness, and became the most visible Phoenix of our generation.

YOUR TURN

When you think about the Hourglass model, I urge you to try to map how much effort, budget, people, governance and time your company as a whole, or your team as a part, would allocate to the TOP part of the Hourglass, and how much to the BOTTOM. How do you organize your "zero-to-one", and your "one-to-n"?

What is the balance in your context between 'Sense & Try', and 'Scale & Run'? How much time do you spend in management meetings, or board meetings, to discuss the TOP part and how much the BOTTOM part of the Hourglass?

And then, time to do some serious soul searching about whether you believe that this balance is preparing you for the Day after Tomorrow, or if you should reallocate your resources towards a new equilibrium. Maybe think about what the ideal Hourglass situation would be for you to future-proof your company, and then plan backwards from there.

Types of innovation

THE WHAT

> Without action, the world would still be an idea.
> — **GEORGES DORIOT**

I have noticed that many companies find it difficult to define innovation and, especially, pinpoint which type would work best for them and their situation. There are many, many ways to structure the types of innovation, of course. One way is to label it by 'intensity' level: from incremental to radical to disruptive innovation. I've written quite a bit about that in my previous books, so I won't repeat myself here. But I want to share an extremely simple framework that I've developed over the years, in order to help you map out your innovation challenges.

The model presents four main areas: there's Product, Market, Service and Model innovation.

Types of innovation

APPROACH / **REACH**

- service INNOVATION
- model INNOVATION
- product INNOVATION
- market INNOVATION

WHAT

SERVICE INNOVATION
Is a set of mechanisms to radically enhance the experience of customers, increase the service level but keep the same product mix and stay in the same market.

PRODUCT INNOVATION
The mechanism, environment, structures and processes that allow organizations to develop new offerings and solutions.

MARKET INNOVATION
You introduce a brand new idea or concept that goes beyond your own industry and you enter or create a completely new market.

MODEL INNOVATION
You fundamentally change the operational model of the company and learn how to cope with the transition to a new financial reality.

I PRODUCT INNOVATION

Don't find customers for your products, find products for your customers. — SETH GODIN

PRODUCT INNOVATION
The mechanism, environment, structures and processes that allow organizations to develop new offerings and solutions.

Product Innovation is what I call the mechanism, environment, structures and processes that allow organizations to develop new offerings and solutions. It can be an entirely new product or an improvement of an existing one, like adding a new feature. It's Apple launching a new version of an iPhone, Tesla revealing a new model, or Amazon Web Services introducing a new offering that adds to their cloud portfolio. It's J.Crew coming up with rumple-proof technology so that suits always look freshly laundered. Or LG designing a TV-screen that you can simply roll up. It seems easy and logical, but Product Innovation is not always a sure bet. Often it's a very risky business, and sometimes it can go disastrously wrong.

William Gibson taught us that "When you want to know how things really work, study them when they're coming apart". That's why Boeing's 'How not to' 2707 disaster story – with a cameo for a 'boring', less radical product innovation that would end up saving the day – is a great illustration.

The Boeing 2707 is at least two things. Firstly, it is one of my favorite Product Innovation stories. Secondly, it is the plane that almost killed Boeing, and with it, the entire city of Seattle.

■ Bye bye propeller

But first, a little history. After the Second World War, the world of aviation took off like crazy. The war had been greatly influenced by aeronautics. While in the First World War the effect of aerial combat had been marginal at best, the second time around it had been absolutely critical. One of the key reasons the Allied forces won was because they had been extremely cunning in weakening the German war machine with air power, and in particular, intense bombing.

Towards the end of the war, two brand new designs would entirely disrupt the world of flight: the German 'Sturmvogel' (Storm Bird) and the more stiff-upper-lipped British 'Gloster Meteor'. They changed the game because they were powered by Turbojet engines instead of the traditional propeller. Introduced too late in WWII to change the outcome, they would go on to be pivotal in the world of aviation at large.

We have British Royal Air Force (RAF) officer Frank Whittle to thank for the invention of the Turbojet engine, which makes virtually all air travel possible today. Whittle was a scrawny young boy who at first failed the medical exam to join the RAF, but persevered and eventually became an accredited pilot. He proved to have an exceptional engineering talent for airplane design, especially for their engines. In his thesis at the Royal Air Force College, he came up with an early version of the Turbojet engine. He then developed it further on his own, and eventually presented the idea to the British Air Ministry to see if they would be interested. They were not, and his ideas were labeled "impracticable".

Persevering as ever, Frank Whittle set up his own company "Power Jets" with extremely limited funds, in order to further the design, and then manufacture, his novel Jet Engine. It almost killed him. He was so obsessed and engrossed in his work that he worked 18-hour days with his team, and developed lethal habits. His smoking increased to three packs a day. He also started the habit of sniffing Benzedrine to keep him awake, and ingesting tranquillizers and other pills at night to allow him to sleep. Not a good idea.

But Frank Whittle was a technical genius and eventually developed a fully operational Jet Engine. However, he was no financial wizard, and by the end of 1939, his company 'Power Jets' could barely afford to keep the lights on. But when the British 'War Machine' kicked into a higher gear, the British Air Ministry finally understood the vital importance of Whittle's technology for winning the war. So the Royal Air Force commissioned the development of a fully functioning Jet Engine: it became the 'W1, the Whittle Supercharger Type 1", which eventually powered the Gloster Meteor, the very first British jet fighter.[8]

While Whittle developed his engine, on the other side of the English Channel, a German engineer was working on a very similar device. Hans von Ohain was a German physicist who had obtained a PhD in Physics and Aerodynamics from the University of Göttingen. Similar to Whittle, when he was still a student, he conceived of "an engine that did not require a propeller".[9]

It was actually Hans von Ohain who eventually got the first 'operational' Jet Engine up in the air, even though Whittle came up with the idea first. When the two men finally met, long after the end of the war in 1966, Whittle was initially very hostile towards the German, convinced that von Ohain's engine had been developed after spying on his design. But in time Whittle came to see that von Ohain had independently developed his ideas, and the two men eventually became very good friends. They would end up often touring the United States together, to give lectures and talk on the fascinating invention of the Jet Engine.

It is hard to imagine the world today without their contribution. I'm writing this book flying around the world, jetting from continent to continent. Whittle and von Ohain have dramatically shrunk the globe. But who would take their idea and turn it into true commercial success?

▪ A SuperSonic failure

Commercial aviation really took off after the Second World War. Turbo jets became commonplace, and so gradually preparations were made for the Next New Thing to appear. Then the world got terribly excited about the speed of the SuperSonic Transport airplanes. The lure of 'SuperSonic Transport' or SST was born.

One of my greatest personal regrets is that I am no longer able to board a Concorde flight, and cross the Atlantic in just a few hours. By the time I could have afforded a ticket, the service had tragically been dismantled. The reason: a fatal crash outside of Paris in 2003, with debris burning in a French farmer's field. It abruptly ended the dream of supersonic flight, at least for a time. Two new players are working on bringing the dream back to reality now, though. NASA is collaborating with aerospace company Lockheed Martin on "the son of Concorde", the X-59 QueSST airplane.[10] And Boom SuperSonic is designing an aircraft called Overture that will be able to reach speeds of Mach-2.2 (1,451mph), more than twice the speed of sound (Mach 1).[11]

But it's safe to say that they're not there yet.

When I mention flying faster than the speed of sound, probably only the Concorde pops up in your mind. Actually, there were no less than THREE competing radical 'Product Innovations' in the category of SuperSonic commercial aviation before Concorde was born: the Concorde, the Tupolev TU-144, and the Boeing 2707.

In my opinion it's an absolute miracle that the Concorde ever saw the light of day. Let me explain. The heart of the Concorde was its engine, the 'Olympus 593'. This contraption, a descendant of the genius prototypes of Frank Whittle, was the reason that the British AND the French actually built the Concorde together. In Britain, the Bristol Aeroplane Company (BAC) had the engine knowhow, but really lacked the engineering power. Conversely, in the South of France, in Toulouse, a company called 'Sud-Aviation' had been successfully building airplanes, and was also dreaming of SuperSonic machines.

After intense negotiations, on the 29th of November 1962, the British and French governments finally signed a collaborative agreement to develop an Anglo-French SST, which would become the 'Concorde'. The original scheme was to build a 100-seat long-range aircraft for transoceanic operations and a 90-seat mid-range aircraft for continental flights. Alas, the mid-range aircraft would never be built.

Airlines started to place orders to purchase Concordes as early as June 1963, with service deliveries originally expected to start in 1968. But that initial product launch estimate proved to be wildly over-optimistic. However, the Concorde eventually saw the light in 1971, when the first preproduction machine, the "101", performed its maiden flight from Filton to RAF Fairford on 17 December 1971. However, in the end, only 20 production machines were ever built, six for development and 14 for commercial service, with seven Concordes going into service with British Airways and seven with Air France.

It was an astounding innovation success, realizing the human dream of flying faster than the speed of sound, born from the collaboration of the British and the French. The head of the program, Morien Morgan, is claimed to have stated: "A combination of Gallic fervor and British phlegm produces pretty impressive results by any standards. At least in aeronautics".[12]

Obviously, the Russians did not want to be left behind, realizing that supersonic flight was essential in proving the superiority of Russian, over 'Western', technology. Their answer was the Russian Tupolev 144 (TU-144). Anyone who sees the pictures of the TU-144 immediately says: "It's a Concorde". The Russians claimed the resemblance between the Concorde and their SuperSonic jetliner was 'a mere coincidence'. Not entirely false, though. The TU-144 was pretty different from the Concorde under the hood, and quite an eccentric beast. It was also one of the last commercial aircrafts with a braking parachute. The prototypes were also the only passenger jets ever fitted with ejection seats... albeit only for the crew and not the passengers.[13] This may not have reassured the passengers.

No surprise, then, that the TU-144 was not exactly a commercial success. It only lived 6 months, flying a total of 102 scheduled flights, before it was removed from service. The reason was that the plane had not exactly been designed with 'customer centricity' in mind. It was extremely noisy, with sound levels frequently rising above 95 dB: passengers seated next to each other could hardly communicate, and those seated two seats apart had to pass hand-written notes as even screaming at the top of their lungs didn't work.

The design of the plane had been rushed to prove Russian supremacy, and of course this had majorly backfired. The TU-144 was constantly plagued by failures, and this became painfully obvious on a flight in January of 1978, when 22 of the 24 onboard systems would break down. Before takeoff, no less than 8 systems had gone into failure, but given the large number of VIP passengers – foreign TV and radio journalists and other foreign notables – it was decided to proceed with the flight to avoid the embarrassment of cancellation.

It turned out to be a tactical mistake. After takeoff from the Moscow Domodedovo airport, failures continued to escalate, and almost every single operational system of the plane began to malfunction. Because of this, an alarm siren went off almost immediately after takeoff, with sound and volume similar to that of a civil defense warning. The helpless crew could not figure a way to switch it off, so the siren stayed on throughout the remaining 75 minutes of the flight. Eventually, the stressed captain ordered the navigator to borrow a pillow from one of the passengers and stuff it inside the siren's horn. Needless to say, the foreign journalists were not impressed.

Whether it was a success or not, the Russians *did* manage to build the FIRST Supersonic aeroplane to break the sound barrier. Yet the Brits and the French disrupted the world of aviation by building the first OPERATIONAL supersonic jetliner. In the midst of the Cold War, this scared the Americans out of their wits.

The US had already been humiliated when the Russians had launched the first artificial Satellite, the Sputnik, in 1957. When the Russians, and even the French and British were starting to move into Supersonic travel, surely the mighty United States of America could not be left behind?

In a memorandum to the President of the United States after the announcement of the Concorde plans by the British and the French, the US Administrator of the Federal Aviation Authority, Najeeb Halaby, penned a pressing appeal to action. He wrote: "If the British-French consortium succeeds unchallenged in capturing the world market for supersonic transports, the U.S. will be forced to relinquish world civil transport leadership".

Moreover, he predicted that the US would lose out on more than 50,000 'high-tech' jobs per year in the development of these aircrafts. But the most powerful statement in his memorandum was undoubtedly the last one: "Not only would we become dependent on foreign sources to help our military take advantage of supersonic flight, but we would eventually have to tolerate that the President of the United States of America would have to fly on official business in a foreign aircraft!"[14] God forbid.

In the U.S., 'supersonic' fever kicked into high gear. At first, a wide selection of potential suitors wanted to build the U.S. SST dream-machine: companies like Lockheed, Douglas and Corvair. In 1963, President Kennedy announced the development of the U.S. National Supersonic Transport Program, with the aim to build a plane not only faster than Concorde, but also much bigger than what the Brits and French were cooking up. Ultimately, Boeing was selected to fulfill the American dream with their winning proposal: the Boeing 2707. This amazing vessel would seat up to 250 passengers (compared to 100 in the Concorde), and would fly at three times the speed of sound. It would make New York from London in less than 3 hours.

▪ When a boring hero saves the day

Unfortunately, these ambitious goals introduced some extreme technical challenges. One of them was the design of the wings. When the Boeing 2707 would take off or land, its wings would stick out at a 'normal' angle to the body of the plane. In supersonic mode, the wings would 'sweep backwards' to allow the plane to fly at Mach 3. Flying at that speed would heat up the exterior of the plane to several hundred degrees, which would melt any normal aluminum alloy, so the fuselage would have to be built out of Titanium.

Boeing was not deterred, though, and went all-in to save American pride. Initially airlines from all around the world started placing orders. TWA ordered 12, and PanAm wanted to use 15 of the Boeing 2707 flying wonders.

But during the 1960's, pressure mounted. Resistance against SuperSonic transport was rising, again, connected to the noise it produced. SuperSonic jets created a 'SuperSonic Boom': an extremely loud bang that could be heard up to 30 miles away. It was estimated that flying from New York to Los Angeles would startle up to 5 million people… every single flight. Even worse: it turned out that the 2707 – with its four massive jet engines equipped with extra afterburners – would consume insane amounts of jet fuel. When the techno optimism of the 1960s turned into the global Oil Crisis of the 1970s, those massive gas-guzzling flying boom-machines didn't seem all that great anymore.

So in 1971, President Nixon, pressured by economic and environmental concerns, pulled the plug on the Boeing 2707. When the aircraft was cancelled, there were 121 orders on the books. For Boeing, which had placed all its hopes on the 'Next New Thing', it was an absolute disaster. They had to let go of almost 20,000 employees. At its peak, Boeing employed more than 140,000 employees in Everett, just outside of Seattle. By 1971, fewer than 60,000 people still worked there. The situation in Seattle was so dire, that a famous sign was posted near Sea-Tac International Airport, which stated: "Will the last person leaving SEATTLE – Turn out the lights".

The "Boeing Bust" of the 2707 had almost meant the end for the company. The irony of the story is that while the 2707 was the plane that almost 'killed' Boeing, they would be saved by their 'Plan B', or Product B, if you will: the Product Innovation of the 747. They had conceived it as a 'stop-gap' solution while the company was transitioning towards supersonic flight. But the much more boring, yet ultra-reliable and extremely efficient 747 became massively popular with airliners. And it was the Queen of the skies for almost 40 years.

Seattle almost went under together with Boeing's supersonic dreams. The dream lives on, however, as the Seattle basketball team formed in 1967 was named the "Sonics", just after Boeing had just won the SST contract.

The story of the 2707 is the stuff of (bad) legends. Just imagine how its board of directors must have experienced this rollercoaster: being ecstatic when they were selected by the U.S. government to build the future, and then feeling utterly destroyed when they had to cut almost 70% of their workforce in order to survive. Only to be relieved as never before, when the 747 saved the day.

■ New (and not so improved) Coke

Another disastrous product innovation story is that of Coca-Cola's 1985 stunt: the 'New (and not so improved) Coke'. If you (binge) watched the third season of Stranger Things, you may have caught the reference: Lucas cracks open a can of New Coke and Mike asks "How do you even drink that?" with a horrified look upon his face. Ah, 1985, the year that brought us 'Back to the Future'. And the year that Coca-Cola wasn't so sure about its Future anymore. After the Second World War, it had dominated the carbonated soft drink market with a 60% share, but their challenger, Pepsi-Cola, was growing incredibly fast. By 1983 the market share of Coca-Cola had declined to a mere 24%. Pepsi was killing them with their "Pepsi Challenge" in which scores of consumers had been given a blind test, with two white cups: one containing Pepsi and the other Coca-Cola. The Pepsi advertising suggested that the good folk of America preferred the sweeter Pepsi over the classic Coke.

Alarm bells went off in the Atlanta headquarters of Coca-Cola and a top-secret project was launched to do the unthinkable: change the 'secret recipe' for Coca-Cola, which had remained untouched for 99 years. CEO Roberto Goizueta is said to have told his employees that there are no "sacred cows" in business. Oh boy, did he get that wrong. The top-secret project "Kansas" (after William Allen White, a journalist in Kansas photographed sipping Coca-Cola in Life magazine in 1938) came up with a sweeter tasting beverage, and instead of launching a new brand, the top management of Coke decided to go all-out disruptive and replace the 'Old' Coke with the all-new 'Coke II'. This "sweeter" Coca-Cola version proved a great success in taste tests: most preferred it over Pepsi and even regular Coke, even though 10%-12% said they wouldn't drink Coke again if this were the new flavor. What could possibly go wrong, right?

Soon after the launch in April 1985, the trouble began. Coke drinkers hated the new taste, and many of them reacted violently, writing scores of letters to the company to complain bitterly. The company received more than 40,000 calls and letters, the most famous one directed to CEO Goizueta Roberto… addressed to the "Chief Dodo, The Coca-Cola Company". There were reports about people stocking huge quantities of the 'Old Coke' in basements to last them through the next couple of years, and comedians and talk show hosts like Carson and Letterman would make a constant mockery of the stupidity of Coca-Cola. My personal favorite is that even Fidel Castro, top dog of Cuba and a long-time Coca-Cola drinker, lashed out – he saw New Coke as a clear sign of American capitalist decadence.

A group of disgruntled Coca-Cola enthusiasts were so disappointed that they organized themselves in the 'Old Cola Drinkers of America', and started a class action lawsuit against the company. This was dismissed by the presiding judge, who said he preferred the taste of Pepsi.

Time magazine put New Coke on the cover, with a big red cross over it, and called it 'one of the top 100 worst ideas of the 20th century'. It compared the marketing stupidity of New Coke to 'putting a miniskirt on the refurbished Statue of Liberty." No sacred cows, indeed.

Less than three months after the pompous introduction of the New Coke, Coca-Cola pulled the plug and recalled the product. They put the 'old' Coke back on the shelves and called it 'Classic Coke'. Ironically they sold more of it than ever before, and its stock skyrocketed. The madness had lasted only 79 days, but it made a permanent mark: when a new market launch is a complete disaster, it is now labelled the 'New Coke' of its industry.

Since then, many conspiracy theorists have argued that this may have been one of the most elaborate marketing stunts ever pulled. What if this whole 'New Coke' thing was just a way to reconnect their consumers with the nostalgia for the old product, and just an incredible way to boost sales volumes for Coca-Cola?

Don't let this innovation "strategy" inspire you, though. Making a New Product that customers hate SO much they will be glad to buy your OLD stuff is not exactly the best way to achieve success.

How innovation is key (Get it? Get it?) at Assa Abloy

A few years ago, I was invited to give a keynote presentation at long-lived (since 1907) Swedish company, Assa Abloy. It's the global leader in door opening solutions and a market leader in most of Europe, North America, China and Oceania. If you don't recognize the name, their acquisitions Yale or August might sound familiar. Now, I have to admit that I had rather low expectations about their level of disruption. I mean, how innovative can door locks get, right? Surprisingly, the answer turned out to be "very". Listed multiple times on Forbes' 'The World's Most Innovative Companies', it is one of the most beautiful examples of Andreessen's "software is eating the world". They moved from the atom world of locks to the Internet of Things, offering digitized access through smart locks. "We went from cassette tapes to CDs, and now we carry thousands of songs on our phones," stated Assa Abloy-acquired August Home's CEO Jason Johnson. "Likewise with keys -- we went from metal keys, to key cards and now that's being virtualized into the mobile phone."

In 1994 there were 4,700 employees in the Group, producing mainly mechanical locks. Today there are 43,000 staff setting the standard for innovative door opening solutions, including automated entrances. The company's transition has proved a huge success. New products launched in the past have exceeded their target of 25%.[15] They have scores of smart lock customers in the most diverse industries: from medical centers, psychiatric facilities, old people's homes and universities, to football stadiums, gyms, government offices, museums, city facilities, factories, shops, pharmacies, apartment blocks and many more.

Needless to say, this is not just a switch of 'materials'. When entrances go digital, there's a lot of concerns about (data) security and safety. Just imagine the security nightmare of someone hacking their way into a museum or hospital. Or; if students use their Apple watches to access a building... what happens to the information about which student is going where, and when? Just imagine how huge this switch must have been from the old "atoms" employees, to the new "bits" employees?

But Assa Abloy is not just investing in product innovation. It's simultaneously tapping into new markets as well (which is technically the subject of the next chapter, but I wanted to prove how disruptive a 100-year old lock company could be). For instance, it is working with countries around the world on the idea of a digital driver's license, and already has rolled out an electronic passport system in Tanzania. It's clear that innovation is deeply ingrained in the company's DNA: it has a global innovation council that represents various functions within innovation and design, as well as the various divisions in the group. Their product innovation process is based on a killer combination of Lean innovation principles and a clear obsession with the voice of the customer. Needless to say, it has a well-developed top of the Hourglass, forever investigating long-term social, political, technological and customer trends, market development, standards and regulatory development. Or as they describe it themselves, they are "influenced by the Voice-of-the-Customer, the Voice-of-Technology, and the Voice-of-Society". But the company also ensures that its experimentations with new products and even markets are carefully evaluated and tested against customer needs before moving into the engineering design phase.[16]

My personal favorite, though, is how Assa Abloy Shared Technologies holds innovation days twice a year in Stockholm, Gurgaon and Krakow. All employees are encouraged to participate in innovation that day, no strings attached: they have a full day and a half of free time to work on whatever they have been thinking of, or whatever they have been inspired by. Could be literally anything. What I really love is how these Innovation Days show that innovation is not just about wild, unbridled creativity and new ideas: it's just as much about learning new things, becoming inspired or even further developing the details of an "old" idea that never moved from ideation to testing. I found a clip online that showed three different employees with three very different interpretations of that day: a man who chose to 'enrich' and test an existing idea, another who was literally "starting from a blank paper" to come up with a new idea and a woman who chose to pick a book from the company library to expand her knowledge. Innovation is a highly complex game with very different subparts – learning, ideation, testing, filtering, implementation, scaling – that require very different talents and personalities. So it's great to see that Assa Abloy doesn't just focus on the ideation part, like so many companies tend to do with comparable Innovation Days.

■ Lessons learned

So what are some of the 'Product Innovation' lessons we can draw from these stories?

1. Don't get carried away by the 'Next New Thing'

Boards can be easily swayed by dangling shiny objects. True, we all become excited about new things, but the 2707 and New Coke stories show we need healthier radar screens to filter out the bias that comes with 'wanting to believe' so badly in the Next New Thing. It's realizing that sometimes, the Next Thing, is a boring but trustworthy product, rather than a futuristic superstar that fails to deliver.

2. The future isn't always faster

I'm travelling less and less in 747s these days, but my travel between London and San Francisco is still 10 hours by Jet Plane. In many markets we have seen 'exponential' growth (like computing power), but in other industries that just doesn't always pan out. Speeding up the 'atoms' business of transportation has proven to be tremendously difficult. Yes, new players are working on supersonic travel as we speak, like Nasa and Boom. And we all know that SpaceX and Virgin (and many others, apparently) are trying to make air-resistance-free and superfast Hyperloop travel possible. But we're far from there yet. I'm not saying that it won't happen but just beware thinking that 'better' and 'faster' are always synonyms. The future is a lot more complex than that.

3. Realize that innovation does not equal creativity

The Assa Abloy Innovation Days story shows us that innovation has many facets, and that each of these require very different skills, talents and personalities. A lot of companies still make the mistake of over-focusing on the creativity and ideation and they end up with a graveyard of beautiful ideas, put to rest forever because nobody took charge of developing, testing and scaling them. Innovation is not just about the top part of the Hourglass. Without the bottom part, it's actually pretty useless.

4. Don't put all your eggs in one basket

Boeing made the classic mistake of putting most of its focus, budget and talents on the 2707. It became their 'Bet the Farm' moment, and almost proved to be fatal. Many companies have fallen into this trap. Look at Apple when it introduced the Macintosh, massively believing that 'graphical' computers would render 'text-based' machines obsolete overnight. But it didn't. The Macintosh was initially an absolute flop in the marketplace, and it almost toppled Apple.

5. Have a Plan B

Imagine working on the 747 at Boeing in 1969, when all the noise and visibility went to the 'magical' belle of the ball, the SST 2707. Imagine putting all the long hours designing and building a plane that everyone else thought was slow, lame and boring. And then imagine the turnaround: realizing that you could be proud to have built the machine that would save the company. It's very much like the Apple II engineers who had suffered terrible scorn and contempt from Steve Jobs: he had believed that he and his Macintosh team were working on the nectar of the Gods, while the Apple II crowd were the plebeians working on the past. But just like the 747, the Apple II would remain the stable reliable workhorse that would lead Apple out of the financial abyss.

Product innovation might seem as the easiest of the four, but there are many challenges. Sometimes the available technology is not quite there yet, sometimes the customers just don't want what you made for them or sometimes your competitor is simply faster and cheaper. Just make sure that you avoid the pitfalls, and start your endeavors in an almost scientific way, like with Design Thinking[17] methods.

II MARKET INNOVATION

The only way to beat the competition is to stop trying to beat the competition. — W. CHAN KIM

MARKET INNOVATION
You introduce a brand new idea or concept that goes beyond your own industry and you enter or create a completely new market.

Market Innovation goes one step further than product innovation: you introduce a brand new idea or concept that goes beyond your own industry and you enter or even create a completely new market: sometimes close to your traditional business – what we call adjacent markets – or sometimes very far removed.

Now, the further you move away from your 'core' understanding of your traditional line of business, the scarier the innovation becomes, and the higher the potential risks and chances for spectacular failure. But when you do succeed, the impact can be huge.

Dr. Samuel West is a Swedish psychologist and innovation researcher, but he is also a collector of things that go spectacularly wrong when companies try to innovate. In that 'function', he is also the founder and main curator of "The Museum of Failure" in Helsingborg, which houses more than 100 innovations that ended up going horribly wrong in one way or another. He doesn't consider it gloating over the misery of others, to the contrary, he regards it as a splendid celebration of creativity.

■ Apple & the Apple Newton Messagepad

One of the objects in his collection is the Apple Newton Messagepad, which is also one of my personal favorites. For those of you who have never seen it, it looks like a chunkier, heavier version of an iPad. But the Apple Newton was introduced to the world in 1993, more than 25 years before the first iPad was ever launched.

After John Sculley had fired the Apple founder from the company in 1985, he was under intense pressure from the board to come up with a new North-Star for Apple, preferably one that didn't have 'Steve Jobs' written all over it. The

Macintosh had been a true revolution in the world of computers, but it was a PRODUCT innovation. People that bought 'classical' computers based on text, could perhaps be persuaded to buy 'graphical' computers like the Macintosh, that featured stunning crisp graphics and that you could easily use with the help of a mouse. But they were still 'computers'. Sculley wanted to create an entirely NEW market for Apple to invade: a fresh and quiet Blue Ocean[18] that he could navigate. Launching something in the traditional Red Ocean of 'computers' was far riskier. It was teeming with competitors, and major players like IBM were there waiting, wanting to eat their lunch.

Jobs had shared his admiration with Sculley earlier for what companies such as SONY and Philips had done for the world of consumer electronics, with the introduction of the Walkman and the Compact Disc: they had truly disrupted the world of music and entertainment. Philips had been trying to take the CD technology from the world of music into that of videos and applications. They had developed a technology that they called the CDI – the Compact Disc Interactive – which allowed consumers not just to 'consume' content, but to actively engage with it. Sculley convinced the chief engineer of Philips on that project, Gaston Bastiaens, to join him at Apple's headquarters in Cupertino.

Spurred by Sculley, Bastiaens created a division called Apple PIE, the latter standing for Personal Interactive Electronics. Soon Apple would market products such as compact disc players and digital cameras, and eventually it would even build a first generation gaming console called Pippin, an early embryonic version of the PlayStation or XBox. But the most revealing new concept that came out of Apple PIE was the Newton: the first Personal Digital Assistant ever.

It was to revolutionize the way we use information, take notes, schedule appointments, keep track of notes and to do's, read books or make sketches. It opened an entirely new market for Apple, focusing on the business user, and presenting the executive with an electronic assistant that would be able to boost productivity to completely new levels.

The Apple Newton was developed in a 'skunks works'[19] fashion, very similar to the Macintosh. Jobs had pulled the best engineers he could find into the latter team: true 'trailblazers' that cut a few corners here and there, but who were capable of pushing the boundaries of innovation further than any who followed the 'conventional' approach. Jobs had even put the Macintosh team in a separate building across the street, hoisted a Pirate flag, and treated them as 'artists': he showered them with all the perks and privileges of prima-donnas (as long as they performed, of course).

The Apple Newton was developed in a similar style. The team of developers led by the legendary programmer Steve Capps had to be incredibly creative to construct a Personal Digital Assistant with the limited technology that was available in the late eighties. But when it came out, it blew everyone's mind. You could hold the Newton in the palm of your hand, yet it held more computing power than any bulky heavy desktop computer of those days. You could write on it with a special 'pen', connect to a network using a modem, and to top it all, it would recognize your handwriting when you scribbled notes on it.

And that killed it. The Apple Newton wanted to impress the business world so badly, that they absolutely wanted to ship the Newton with 'handwriting recognition'. It was a revolutionary idea at the time, but it's so complex that even today's handwriting recognition technology is only just becoming relatively fool proof. And that was certainly not the case when the Newton came out, way back in 1993. Its handwriting recognition was insanely terrible. It was more than terrible; it simply did not work. What should have been Sculley's moment of glory, leading Apple into an entirely new Blue Ocean market, turned into one of Apple's worst PR nightmares.

Garry Trudeau was (and is) an incredibly talented, influential and occasionally incredibly sarcastic cartoonist. You may know him from his comic strip 'Doonesbury', which appeared in newspapers for over 45 years. He is notorious for taking on Donald Trump early in his career, when he was still simply a loudmouth real-estate tycoon. But in 1993, Gary Trudeau was also one of Apple's first Newton customers. He loved the product, but like most users thought the hand-writing recognition was an absolute dud. For weeks on end Trudeau would mock the Apple Newton in his comic: people doodling something on a Newton, and the machine interpreting it as absolute gobbledygook. When Mike, the main character in Doonesbury writes "Hello J.J. how are you?" on his Newton, and the screen displays the machine interpreting this as: "Hell jars, howard yoyo?", it was game over for Apple. It destroyed the reputation of the Newton irreparably.

Though the Apple Newton was a complete flop back then, you still have to admit that it was way ahead of its time. When Steve Jobs triumphantly returned to Apple in 1997, one of the first things he did was kill off the Apple Newton, rip out the Apple PIE division, and claim it had been a 'foolish' move. He was obviously still pretty scornful towards anything that had to do with his old nemesis John Sculley. But more than 20 years later he would introduce the world to the iPad, which according to many bore a striking resemblance to the Apple Newton.

Market innovation can backfire in a major way when you're too 'early' in a market: when you are introducing concepts that the world isn't quite ready for, and that consumers don't understand yet. And you can lose an enormous amount of money when you need to 'educate' a possible audience to warm up to an entirely new market.

The Apple Newton has its place in Dr. West's "Museum of Failures", but it is also a true celebration of creativity and talent, eager to explore new Market Innovations. Many of the people that worked at Apple PIE scattered out and ended up at some now almost mythical companies, one of which is General Magic. This is where early versions of the Smartphone were devised, that would ultimately become commonplace in today's New Normal.

■ Colgate & the Colgate Kitchen Entrees

Sometimes you can clearly become *too* creative. My #1 favorite piece in Dr. West's vast collection of 'innovation horror stories' is the story of Colgate and its attempt to corner a completely new market with the 'Colgate Kitchen Entrees'.

I'm sure most of you will associate Colgate with toothpaste, as it is the #1 manufacturer in the world. (Actually, Procter & Gamble took over that position from Colgate when it first introduced fluoride, but since then Colgate has re-claimed the top sales spot). Colgate is a part of the Colgate-Palmolive group, and has a long and rich history of product innovation. In 1896, Colgate was the very first company to sell toothpaste in a tube: the "Colgate Ribbon Dental Cream".

In 1982, Colgate did something very strange. Back then, it was one of the most well-established oral hygiene brands, selling toothpaste, toothbrushes, dental floss and mouthwash. And then suddenly, it decided to launch a full line of frozen food products, called 'Colgate Kitchen Entrees'. It was actually not such a bad idea to enter a new market for ready-to-eat meals, adapting to a world that was changing its habits with the mass adoption of microwave ovens. But,

SOURCE: RECONSTRUCTION COURTESY OF MUSEUM OF FAILURE

oh, the execution of it… One can only imagine the discussion in that Colgate boardroom back in 1982 when the go-ahead was given to launch the 'Colgate Kitchen Entrees'. Which board member in their right mind would have thought it was a good idea to launch a series of frozen TV-dinners with a brand that everyone associates with minty-breath dental products?

It's no surprise that Colgate did not want to have their 'Colgate Beef Lasagna' featured in Dr. West's Museum of Failures, standing next to amazing articles like Heinz's 'EZ Squirt' purple ketchup, or the Sony Betamax VCR system. So his museum sadly only displays a mock-up.

I believe we should regard these magnificent failures as learnings. Companies need to learn how to make large leaps to try new things, especially when markets move so fast. Instead of 'masking' failures, though, we should celebrate them. We should incorporate them and make sure they shine a light on a new future. We should let them inspire our people to keep trying.

▪ Amazon & AWS

One of the most brilliant examples of Market Innovation is the creation of Amazon Web Services: AWS. Amazon is the most well-known Unicorn of the e-commerce landscape, and the biggest online retailer in the West. But Amazon Web Services has become the largest Cloud Computing player on the planet, truly disrupting the global technology landscape, unsettling the status quo, and catching players like IBM, Microsoft and Oracle completely off-guard. AWS helped Amazon become a trillion dollar brand and it serves as an incredible example of the power of Market Innovation.

In 2006 Amazon was already the largest e-commerce retailer on the planet, happily supplying the world with books, CDs and DVDs with the convenience of online 'one-click' ordering. In that year, Amazon's annual revenue amounted to over $10 billion. And then it decided to launch its very first 'web services offering', basically offering customers access to the technology platform it had built to run its own e-commerce business. In a genius move, it decided to "recycle" its own technology and infrastructure as a sellable customer service, allowing anyone in the world to use the Amazon servers to run their online business. And so it was that AWS was born.

Back then, most people thought that founder Jeff Bezos was downright nuts. The October 2006 Businessweek put him on the cover with the headline: "Jeff Bezos' Risky Bet". Below, it continued: "Amazon CEO Jeff Bezos wants to run your business with the technology behind his website. But Wall Street wants him to mind the store." Most analysts thought Bezos had lost his marbles and many would have seen it as the technology equivalent of "Colgate's Lasagna". They all turned out to be completely wrong. By 2018, Amazon Web Services had grown into a $25 billion business, generating more than $7 billion in Operating Revenue. It had truly become the beating heart of the Amazon Empire.

I've had the pleasure to do some presentations together with Werner Vogels, the Chief Technology Officer of Amazon, and the chief architect of AWS. I vividly remember how he introduced himself to the board members of Philips with the line: "I'm the system administrator of an online bookstore."

That pseudo-humble understatement of an introduction reflects the essence of the birth of AWS. Back in the early 2000s, Amazon was an e-commerce company growing like crazy, and struggling to support the hyper-scaling of its online businesses. These growing pains forced the company to build some incredibly sophisticated internal technological infrastructure, to cope with its explosive growth. This laid the foundations of what would become AWS.

In the early 2000s Amazon had experienced such amazing multi-directional growth, with all sorts of businesses inside the company building their own systems, databases and applications that it had become somewhat of an architectural IT-spaghetti disaster. Andy Jassy, who later would become the CEO of

AWS, was the chief-of-staff of Jeff Bezos in those days. He realized that they needed to clean up their own systems if they wanted to scale even further. The growth of Amazon needed a set of common infrastructure services everyone could access without having to reinvent the wheel every time. So that's precisely what Werner Vogels set out to build. And when they had, they realized this could open up a whole new market for Amazon. No one on the planet had such intensive experience in developing the infrastructure to build hyper-scale digital businesses. As Vogels puts it: "There is no compression algorithm for experience." In other words, they had an incredible head start on anyone else in the tech business.

So, in an executive retreat in the house of Jeff Bezos in 2003, they laid out the contours of their offering. Initially, Amazon had planned to build out 'Merchant.com', where other third-party merchants such as Target or Carrefour could use the Amazon online technological platform. But in that famous retreat in Bezos's house, they realized they could attack a much larger market. Not just retailers, but any company on the planet that needed an online platform.

Still, from that moment, it took three years to launch AWS into the world. But when it was, Amazon had succeeded in developing an operating system for the Internet generation, allowing anyone to run their applications on top of the AWS platform. In very little time, every startup out there would start using the AWS infrastructure to build scalable applications. When I was still forming technology startups in the first Internet bubble, back in 1999, I literally needed millions of dollars just to get started. I needed to buy servers, infrastructure, networks, backup systems, power systems, software, databases and on top of that hire really expensive experienced engineers to administer all of it. Today, any startup with a credit card can be up and running on AWS within 15 minutes, and have more computing capacity at their disposal than NASA.

It changed the world of technology. And it caught the 'traditional' players like Microsoft, IBM and Oracle by surprise. The lead that AWS had built up, their years of experience, gave them an enormous head start. Even 'new' tech players like Google were playing catch-up. Andy Jassy was candid about its explosive success: "I don't think any of us had the audacity to predict it would grow as big or as fast as it has."

The launch and growth of AWS is typical of the 'Day One' mentality that runs deep inside a company like Amazon. The 'Day One' mantra is Bezos' reminder that they all need to stay on their toes, be open minded for new ideas, concepts and markets, and above all to avoid complacency.

The term goes back to an interview that Bezos gave back in 1997 when he was still a very young, and somewhat naïve entrepreneur. When asked about what was happening in those crazy heydays of the first Internet bubble, he responded: "What's really incredible about this world of e-commerce, is that this is just Day One. This is the very beginning. This is the Kitty Hawk[20] Stage of electronic commerce."

In a famous Amazon all-hands employee meeting twenty years later, Bezos got a question from someone in the audience: "What does Day Two look like?" After his characteristic deep laugh, he gave his employees a rare peek inside one of his most profound beliefs: "Day Two is stasis. Followed by irrelevance. Followed by excruciating, painful decline. Followed by death. And that is why it is always Day One at Amazon." The audience went wild.

This is the very heart of how Amazon innovates, and looks at the future. Day One is the mechanism that allows Amazon to keep thinking like a startup. It means that Amazon is obsessed with the customer, has a constant focus on results over process, understands the world better than their competitors by embracing external trends quickly, and can react faster than their competitors by making high quality decisions very quickly.

There's a number of idiosyncrasies of the Amazon culture that you'll have probably heard about. Like the 'two pizza rule", or the 'read the memo in silence method'. The 'two-pizza rule' was the (not so) silent agreement that every internal team should be small enough to be fed with two pizzas. It was a typical Amazon mechanism focused on two aims: efficiency and scalability. The 'two pizza rule' keeps teams modest in numbers. Because smaller teams spend less time managing timetables and keeping people up to date, and more time doing what needs to be done.

The 'memo' spiel is another one of those mythical narratives. Most board retreats and management meetings of traditional companies have become an avalanche of PowerPoints, with people droning on and on over their slides, until 'Death by PowerPoint' occurs. Not at Amazon. In his 2018 letter to his shareholders, Bezos revealed that he was banning PowerPoint presentations from meetings. At the start of each meeting at Amazon, each participant reads a narratively structured six-page memo. For thirty minutes everyone sits in silence to read the memo, and absorb the ideas. Then, they start the meeting by jumping straight into the discussion.

These are the wonderful quirks of a very unique company culture. But it's not limiting pizza orders to a maximum of two, or banning PowerPoint, that makes you a Unicorn. The true cultural differentiation is the absolute belief of Bezos in 'Day One': the necessity to be fast, open minded, externally focused and obsessed with the customer. That 'Day One' mentality is why he saw the opportunity for Amazon Web Services. Day One is the reason he was confident to create an entirely new Market Innovation in the world of technology that the traditional players like IBM or Microsoft had ignored and overlooked.

SpaceX & Starlink

It would have been easy to dismiss Amazon Web Services as mere 'Lasagna' in 2006. In fact, people, in a certain way, did. It took guts and the entrepreneurship of the Amazon management to pick up the opportunity, realize the potential, develop and then execute the strategy. One of the most controversial entrepreneurs of our time, Elon Musk, also has an absolute fascination with Market Innovation. He embodies the very soul of 'Day One' in attacking entirely new markets over and over again. He started PayPal in the (back then) blue ocean of electronic payments. Tesla was trailblazing in opening up an entirely new market of electric vehicles. And SpaceX broke ground creating an entirely new market of commercial space transport from scratch.

I've had the pleasure of visiting SpaceX on a number of occasions, in their headquarters in Hawthorne, just next to Los Angeles Airport. It is a truly impressive organization. The first thing you notice when you enter the building is a sign that states: "Gravity is a Bitch." That mission statement tells you exactly what they are fighting against: the gravity that pulls us back down onto this blue planet.

SpaceX has known amazing growth since it was founded in 2002 by Musk. Musk saw that he could dramatically redraw the economics of lifting cargo into space, by reusing the rockets: in doing so, they could cut the launch price by a factor 10 for their customers, and still keep a healthy 70% gross margin. This approach revolutionized the business, but in essence, it was 'Product Innovation'. Musk and his merry band of engineers had built an incredible new and much cheaper product that could land itself safely back on the earth after liftoff. As such, SpaceX excels at Product Innovation, with stronger and stronger rocket systems coming out of the factory: the Falcon Heavy rocket, which had its maiden launch in 2018, provides the highest payload capacity of any currently operational launch vehicle on the planet. Characteristically, Musk

PHOTO BY STUART RANKIN ON WWW.GOODFREEPHOTOS.COM

showcased its potential by launching a bright red Tesla Roadster (with a 'Don't Panic' sticker on the dashboard), in a one-million-year orbit around the sun. It may come back in a few million years to collide with earth, or even with Venus (if it's still whole), but until then, it will have been a glorious marketing stunt.

In the same year that SpaceX launched the Product Innovation Falcon Heavy, it started a massive journey towards Market Innovation too. In 2018, it had negotiated the launch of up to 11,927 satellites in Earth's orbit with the U.S. Federal Communications Commission. The aim of these was to provide Internet connectivity to millions of users through the combined network of satellites.

In May of 2019, a Falcon Heavy successfully deployed the first 60 satellites as part of SpaceX's disruptive broadband Internet system 'Starlink'. A formidable example of radical Market Innovation. Ultimately Starlink should have two groups of satellites in orbit: one batch of 4,409 satellites located between 500 and 1,000 kilometers in space, and a second batch of 7,518 satellites, flying slightly lower in altitude. SpaceX plans to keep on sending up satellites in batches of 60 in the years to come, with the aim of launching between 1,000 and 2,000 per year.

It wasn't IBM, Microsoft or Oracle who invented Cloud Computing, it was an online retailer who saw the Market Innovation opportunity, and developed Amazon Web Services. Vodafone, T-mobile or China Mobile didn't launch a network of space satellites to disrupt global telecommunications, it took a space cowboy like Musk to develop Starlink. When you would have presented Cloud Computing at an Oracle board meeting in 2003, or Starlink at a Vodafone board meeting in 2018, you would very probably have been laughed away with your ridiculous 'Lasagna'.

So is it impossible for a traditional player, an incumbent, to create radical Market Innovation in their own 'conventional' market and business landscape?

The horrible truth is that traditional players are often so addicted to the margins in their established business and so accustomed to the conservative patterns of business transactions, contracts and processes, that most of them are systematically blind to opportunities outside of their immediate field of vision. In other words: they suck at the top half of the Hourglass model. And when you're not paying attention, someone can catch you completely off-guard.

■ Alibaba & ANT Financial

Look at what is happening now in the financial services industry. Those of you who have had the chance to visit China these last few years, will have witnessed the remarkable rise of electronic payments: players like WeChat and AliPay allow the Chinese to pay for basically everything with their smartphones. In cities like Shenzhen, even the homeless have a QR-code on their beggar's cups. I kid you not.

China is rapidly becoming a cashless society, and this 'disruption' has infected the entire Asian continent. WeChat has basically become the operating system of China, and by extension the standard Operating System of the New Silk Road, one of the most ambitious infrastructure projects ever conceived. It envisages the creation of, among other things, a vast network of railways, energy pipelines, highways, and streamlined border crossings, both westward and southward from China.

WeChat is much more than a payment processor. It started out as a messaging system and a communications tool, but now it's a services platform that you can use for pretty much everything: from ordering lunch, to booking a taxi, or checking into a hotel. The payment function was actually more of an afterthought for WeChat. But it is rapidly transforming the market in financial services, and not just for payments.

Alipay is an offering from ANT Financial, which is in turn an affiliate of Alibaba Group. It was spun out of Alibaba when the parent company realized it had 'accidentally' opened up a whole new market with their payments application. What originated simply as a way of paying for goods purchased on Alibaba (the same way that PayPal was started to pay for goods on eBay), has become a financial services platform offering payments, banking and many other financial services too. If you buy a bike via Alipay for example, you can not only pay for the bike within the Alibaba platform, you will also receive the option to insure your brand-new bike, all in the same platform.

The valuation of the company has skyrocketed. In 2015, Ant Financial raised $4.5 billion, at a valuation of $45 billion. By 2018, the company raised an additional $14 billion, at a valuation of $150 billion. It was hailed as "the biggest-ever single fundraising globally by a private company" which turned Ant Financial into the highest valued FinTech company in the world, and China's most valuable unicorn.[21]

The banks didn't see it coming. They were caught out of 'left-field' by platform companies that 'accidentally' seized the Market Innovation opportunity in payments and banking. The race is not run globally, and yet there are still massive opportunities everywhere. The US, for all its other glories, is a particularly good example. The payment system is massively antiquated and the opportunities for Market Innovation are wide open. With the Chinese now so accustomed to their fast, fluid and seamless smartphone payments, when they land in the U.S. and see Americans still using non-contactless credit cards and writing out cheques, they must laugh their heads off.

▪ Lessons learned

So what are some of the 'Market Innovation' lessons we can draw from these stories?

1. Don't dismiss Lasagna

When you read the Colgate story, it is easy to chuckle at the enormously naïve executives who thought they could move the 'dental' brand to the emerging new market of frozen TV-dinners. I regularly attend board meetings about disruption, and when companies present their 'Day After Tomorrow' plan, I often have a knee-jerk reaction – a 'Lasagna alert'. But when Jeff Bezos saw an opportunity to position Amazon as the undisputed leader in the totally new field of Cloud computing, Businessweek was all too happy to dismiss it as "Lasagna" too. In the case of Colgate, the answer could have been as simple as just using a new brandname, not in any way attached to mouth hygiene. But regardless, just don't dismiss 'lasagna' because you never sold it before.

2. Don't be too early

The biggest challenge in Market Innovation is being right about new market opportunities, but wrong about the time. The Apple Newton was way ahead of its time, 25 years to be exact. Sculley had the right vision to create an entirely new market, but the consumer wasn't ready, the market was not mature, the context was not ripe and, above all, the technology not up to par (certainly the handwriting software). They had been off by a few decades. And, when you feel that you've made a mistake, pivot quickly. New Coke was dismissed after only 79 days, but in those days you had Fidel Castro to tip you off.

3. Don't get caught off-guard

If you're an incumbent you have to work extra hard not to be surprised. Others could eat your lunch, invade YOUR market, and create a value proposition you would have never thought of because they actually have a completely fresh view of your customers' needs. IBM could have been the 'natural' leader in Cloud Computing, and HSBC could have been the 'natural' leader in payments in Asia, but they weren't. They were caught off-guard, attacked by a Market Innovation coming out of left-field.

4. Keep the 'Day One' spirit

The main lesson is to keep 'fresh'. To build a better 'radar-screen' for Market Innovation, and to keep your lens in the TOP part of your Hourglass as wide as possible. I like the Amazon 'Day One' spirit: focus on the customer, results over process, pick up external trends quickly, and make high quality decisions as quickly as possible.

III SERVICE INNOVATION

Your most unhappy customers are your greatest source of learning. — BILL GATES

SERVICE INNOVATION
Is a set of mechanisms to radically enhance the experience of customers, increase the service level but keep the same product mix and stay in the same market.

Service Innovation is the set of mechanisms to radically enhance the experience of your customers, dramatically increase the 'service' level of your offerings, but basically keep the same product mix, and stay in the same market. To put it bluntly, it's about using technology to 'pimp up' your service and customer experience. This is an area where incumbents can absolutely, and often do, excel.

■ Faster fast food: McDonald's Kiosks

To me, one of the best examples is the transformation of perhaps the most established restaurant icons in the world: McDonald's. Love them or hate them, but many of us have enjoyed McDonald's comfort food in dozens of cities all over the globe. It's the familiarity that does the trick: all burgers taste the same, wherever you sample them. The brand has even become an indicator for economic development: using the 'Big Mac Index' (published by the Economist newspaper), you can calculate how long the average worker in a given country has to work in order to purchase a Big Mac.

My experiences at McDonald's have dramatically improved since they introduced the 'Kiosks', one of the finest examples of Service Innovation. It has nothing to do with new burgers (although they are constantly changing their range of offerings) as 'Product' innovations, or with new 'Market' innovations like Lasagna, but rather with a simple and extremely effective way of using technology to make the lives of their customers easier.

Have you ever experienced the stress of queuing in a crowded McDonald's with small and very 'picky' kids? Maybe one doesn't like mustard, the other hates pickles, and the third can't stand the sight of ketchup? These minor, but highly explosive and tantrum-stimulating dislikes, are solved through the simplicity of the Kiosks: your orders are always 100% correct, modifications and trimmings nicely incorporated. Or try to order a 'Big Mac without cheese' in a

non-English speaking foreign country, as I have done so many times. Now I can just switch any Kiosk to English and neatly type my order in.

Kiosks don't just improve the ordering, customizing, paying and queuing experience of customers, they also enhance the efficiency of the restaurants' operations. The associates placing the orders have a much simpler job to do, are more effective, and the 'information' from the Kiosks flows straight into the systems that tell the cooks which burgers have to be cooked, with which customizations.

Obviously, this doesn't come near the level of complexity of building a new SuperSonic airplane, or launching a whole new world of Cloud Computing. But it does make a lot of McDonald's customers a lot happier. Wall Street was certainly enthusiastic. They hadn't been "lovin' it" for a long time. Having seen very little innovation in the fast food chain, Wall Street had started to think that maybe McDonald's was a relic from the 20th century, that wouldn't or couldn't survive the current day and age.

But the Kiosks changed all that in a spectacular fashion. And this is why: those who click through their selection receive gentle suggestions from the Kiosk for an extra beverage, a desert or something else. The result: McDonald's raised their 2018 'same store sales estimate' from 2 to 3 percent. That doesn't sound like a lot, but when you multiply that over the vast number of restaurants out there, you'll understand why Wall Street giddily raised the price target for McDonald's shares from $140 to $180.

Things became even more upbeat for McDonald's when they decided to collaborate with Uber Eats. This fast-growing Uber-based food delivery service allows customers to order takeaway food from local restaurants. At first the business grew on 'boutique' specialty foods from local eateries and pubs, but when companies like McDonald's joined, this hugely boosted the growth of Uber Eats. McDonald's could have developed a delivery service on their own, of course. They could have created their own platform and app and developed their own logistics network of local delivery couriers carrying your Big Macs – with and without cheese – straight to your doorstep.

But they chose something else. They joined the existing Uber Eats 'platform', without any of the hassle of having to develop something on their own and created 'McDelivery' virtually overnight.

It turned out to be a major hit. Sure, many Uber Eats customers had an intense craving for a Crushed Avocado & Poached Free-Range Egg on Organic Sourbread toast. But a lot of them just wanted to munch away on their Big Macs, Chicken McNuggets and French Fries, without having to leave their comfy couch.

But this isn't the end of the McDonald's Service Innovation Journey. In March of 2019, they acquired the Tel Aviv-based startup 'Dynamic Yield' for $300 million. It was quite a big sum for such a relatively small company in the field of AI-based dynamic personalization. The fledgling company already worked with many brands across e-commerce, travel, finance and media – like IKEA and Hallmark – to create what's been described as a data-based "Amazon-style personalized online experience". Does that mean that McDonald's will now completely base its pricing and service offering on Artificial Intelligence? Hardly. Personally, I'm not convinced it was such a bright acquisition and I'm really curious as to how it will throw this into the mix of their service offering. After all, spending $300 million on an Israeli startup is the equivalent of 110,701,170 Big Macs. That's a lot of extra Big Macs to sell if you want to recuperate that investment.

Service Innovation is certainly NOT just about acquiring new technology. It is a process of really understanding the CHANGING customer needs, and essentially using technology to enhance your service offering for them.

As McDonald's illustrates, incumbents CAN do this really well. But sometimes they don't.

■ Breaking Banks: TransferWise & Revolut

We've talked about the evolution of financial services, already: with emerging Chinese platform players like Alipay and WeChat that have created 'Market' Innovations, which took traditional players off-guard.

But where I live, in Europe, banking has remained a pretty slow moving industry. After the global financial crisis in 2008, most Western banks focused on survival, rather than innovation. They concentrated on the 'basics': getting their balance sheets in order, and making sure they could be resilient should another 'banking crisis' come along.

However, after the calamity of 2008, a great deal of startup funding and venture capital went into the area of FinTech services. Many venture capitalists thought this would be the Next New Thing, where new entrants could potentially become the next Google or Facebook, but of banking. This dream absolutely materialized in the East with players like ANT Financial. But it did not in the West. At least, not yet.

What DID happen is that a number of new players emerged, who focused on Service Innovation to improve the experience of banking users. I myself became a very happy user of those Service Innovators, with TransferWise and Revolut as my two favorites.

In May of 2019, TransferWise was valued at $3.5 billion following a $292 million second funding round.[22] In doing so, it became one of the (quite rare) European Unicorns in FinTech innovation. What they essentially do is help you transfer money from one country to another.

If you've ever transferred funds between countries with a 'normal' bank, you know what a horrible, difficult, and terribly annoying process this can be. You have to understand exchange rates and you have to understand 'SWIFT BIC CODES'. You have to accept the fact that you have NO idea when your counterpart in the other country will actually receive their money. Plus, you'll have NO idea which ridiculous fees your bank will charge you to make the transaction possible. In short, it's a painful nightmare.

Enter TransferWise.

This is a perfect 'Service Innovation' case study that takes all the hassle out of cross-border payments and makes them simple, transparent, efficient and even fun: you know exactly what it will cost, you see how much you save versus using a traditional bank, and your counterpart will know EXACTLY when they will receive the money. Once you've used their service, you will never again want to transfer international funds via your traditional bank.

In the world of FinTech this happens all the time. Many FinTechs offer 'sweet spot solutions' that focus on one particular customer pain-point and try to radically improve the service offering.

Personally, I've stayed with the same 'traditional' Continental European bank for almost my entire adult life. It was my parents' bank, where they opened an account for me when I became a teenager, and I never thought twice about it. As my needs grew, so did my relationship with the bank: all my personal, private and professional banking has remained with this exact same institution, because my parents gave me that bankcard when I was sixteen years old.

Only recently, I wanted to experience a new digital FinTech service innovator first-hand and I signed up with the 'neobank' called 'Revolut'. Now, I'm well aware of the controversy, and turmoil that this startup has caused in the press. Like Uber, that grew so quickly that their management culture was not in line with their responsibility as a global icon of entrepreneurship, Revolut has suffered equally damaging reports about some of their practices and behavior as they experienced hyper-growth. You might question the company, but honestly as a customer I absolutely LOVE their service.

In essence, a startup like Revolut does NOT offer you Product Innovation. You sign up with the neobank, get an account, get a credit card and you can use that to pay for goods, meals and services. There's no 'Product Innovation' here at all. I've been using credit cards for most of my adult life, but the Service Innovation of Revolut is quite spectacular.

Let me give you an example. When I recently landed in the United Arab Emirates to give a lecture in Dubai and took my phone off 'airplane' mode, I received a warm welcome message via my Revolut app, including the local exchange rate: "Welcome to the United Arab Emirates! Right now 100 Euros gives you 416.49 Dirham. Enjoy your trip!" Talk about a smooth service.

When I arrived at the hotel, my old credit card from my traditional bank turned out to be 'blocked' but my brand new Revolut card saved the day. When the hotel staff swiped my card, my app sent me a message, stating how much money had been used by the hotel. I spent the next 22 minutes making a long-distance call to the bank in my home country and when I finally got someone on the phone, they told me they had blocked my credit card... because they did not know where I was. This is the moment when you think: "Why isn't my bank as smart as Revolut, and why can't it implement this Service Innovation?"

When our daughter went off to college, she needed a credit card. Out of habit, I suggested to use my old bank, since they had known our family for ages. We filled out an online application for a credit card together, and one week later they mailed her to say that her application had been rejected, since "she could not guarantee sufficient funds" to cover her card payments. If my bank had ANY idea what I – its loyal customer – had been doing for the last 25 years, they should have understood that I would back up my daughter's account. But nope. They didn't even call me to check. So the neobank saved the day, again. I signed her up for a Revolut card and till this day, she's extremely happy about that. This is one customer that is never going back to the service of a traditional old bank. Oh well, their loss.

■ Streaming convenience: Netflix

Service Innovation can happen in your core business, but it can also be an extension of your service offering.

Netflix is a great example of a radical Service Innovation that stuck to the core offering, but completely changed its operational service. As many know, it originally started out as an online DVD-rental business. In 1999, you could go to netflix.com, type in 'Dances with Wolves', and order the DVD with Kevin Costner. Some person in the Netflix warehouse would find it, ship it to you in an envelope and you would watch it and then mail it back when you were done. But when the bandwidth of the Internet exponentially increased, it became possible to deliver the same film, but online. I can almost imagine the conversation back in 2000 when some IT guy from Netflix came up from the basement, and said: "Why don't we just stream it?" Today Netflix has become a verb. It's still essentially the same as "Watching Movies and Series". Its service offering was greatly enhanced by the service innovation, but its core has pretty much stayed the same. Of course, Netflix also creates its own content – and so is heading into the world of Market Innovation. Here it is dragging the entire industry along for the ride – with Disney set to launch the Disney+ service over 2019 and 2020. It goes to show that service innovation can even allow you to build new service lines very fast... And move the entire market.

■ Building the future: IKEA

But sometimes, the service innovation is an 'extension' of the current offering. A great example is IKEA acquiring startup 'TaskRabbit', an online platform where you can find people to help you out with household chores. If you have to hang up a painting on your wall and you have two left hands, you can find 'a guy' on TaskRabbit to come and do that for you. Allergic to grass and need someone to mow your lawn? Ask TaskRabbit. In fact, in 2017, it turned out that their number #1 search term was: 'IKEA furniture'. Apparently, many people don't really fancy putting all the separate parts together or (in the case of a kitchen or bathroom) install them. This brilliant insight inspired IKEA to acquire TaskRabbit, a perfect example of Service Innovation by 'extending' their offering towards customers.

▪ A stranger in the house: Amazon

As we learned earlier, it's always Day One at Amazon. So it should not come as a surprise that it's investing in very different types of innovation all at once, not just market innovation like with AWS. Sometimes it's about making enormous and daring waves, and sometimes it's just about little ripples of change that make the customer trust and like them even more. Its In-Home Delivery service is a really good example of that. When you order a package, it's not always possible to wait at home until it's delivered, and in some cases it's not possible or not practical (if it's a heavy object for instance) to have it delivered to another location. The In-Home delivery completely solves that problem. Now, a lot of us won't really feel comfortable with a stranger entering our homes while we're away, but Amazon has an answer for this trust-issue as well. Just before your driver arrives, you will receive an "Arriving Now" notification and you can – almost voyeuristically – watch the delivery happening live once he unlocks your door via the Amazon handheld scanner (so no special codes or keys are given to the driver). This is the type of innovation that makes people fall in love with Amazon over and over again.

▪ Facing friction: Lufthansa Group

If you travel as much as I do, you can really (really) appreciate a fast and frictionless experience at an airport. Ah, the underestimated bliss of not having to flash your boarding pass and passport for the umpteenth time. It's like a breath of fresh spring air. Lufthansa Group's automated kiosks with facial recognition offer exactly that fresh spring air at the Los Angeles International Airport. It identifies passengers, cross-checks them in the Customs and Border Protection database and boards them on a plane within a few seconds, roughly halving total boarding time. You neither need to present a boarding pass nor a passport, and the airline staff can focus on preparing the aircraft for departure and solving last-minute challenges. This is the type of service that frequent flyers are willing to sell their first-born for, as it addresses one of the most annoying and time-consuming parts of flying.

■ Lessons learned

So what are some of the 'Service Innovation' takeaways we can draw from these examples?

1. Develop your radar screen

When you run a business, you might think that you know all about your customers and their behavior. But today that can change very quickly. We're now in a transition where 'attitudes' adapt faster than 'behaviors'. This means we can – and have to – pick up and address evolving attitudes faster than ever before, before they turn into behaviors and habits. A great example is in the food industry: an increasing number of people have a positive attitude towards non-animal products (from cashew 'milk' to the plant-based impossible burgers), but this does not massively translate into a changed shopping behavior yet (they still buy a lot of animal products). But when it does shift, food industry players will have to be ready. FinTech is another excellent illustration: banks should understand that customers who have used the neobanks, or new services like TransferWise, really love them, and expect the same from their bank.

2. Boost customer centricity to the extreme

The extremely customer centric kiosks at McDonald's and Lufthansa are a great example of relentlessly focusing on the customer experience. Understand the mechanics of delighting your customers. Constantly strive to improve the experience. Minimize friction. And maximize effectiveness and experience. Loyalty will follow automatically.

3. Service Innovation can be brutal

Can you imagine the board meeting at Netflix when the IT guy suggested they would stream the content instead of shipping the DVD? Can you imagine the decision to focus everything on this next customer experience, and to fully endorse this radical Service Innovation? Service Innovation can be logical, easy and incremental, but it can also be brutal and require a complete remake of your operational fabric.

4. Service Innovation is rewarded

Wall Street loved McDonald's when they focused on transforming their service. The Kiosks and the partnership with Uber Eats lifted this company out of a stock-market lull, and helped it become hip (well, you know) and future-minded. If performed right, Service Innovation tells a story on commitment to the customer and to the future. And this is definitely honored by the financial markets.

IV MODEL INNOVATION

You never change things by fighting the existing reality. To change something, build a new model that makes the existing model obsolete. — **BUCKMINSTER FULLER**

MODEL INNOVATION
You fundamentally change the operational model of the company and learn how to cope with the transition to a new financial reality.

The last innovation mechanism I want to write about is 'Business Model Innovation'. This is the really exciting stuff: you are fundamentally changing the way you make money, dramatically altering your company's operational model and learning to cope with the transition towards a new financial reality. It's also by far the most difficult, the most daunting and the most disruptive of the innovation patterns. But it's my favorite part of innovation.

■ The day traditional music models died – iTunes & Spotify

During the last decades, a lot of people felt sorry for those poor miserable individuals who had to work in the sinking music business. The amazing appeal of the roaring sixties, rocking seventies and new wave, punk and hip-hop fueled eighties and nineties gave way to a completely new landscape, dominated by technological disruption. Selling music used to be easy. You would just 'peddle' the carrier: that could be tapes, vinyl records or CDs. Then lightning struck when the mp3 was introduced. Virtually overnight music became synonymous with a 'file', and not the carrier. An entire industry went from atoms to bits. And since bits are easily transferred over networks, the music industry started falling into a lethal tailspin.

Napster was probably the most visible culprit of that entire episode. In 1998, the total revenue from U.S. music sales and licensing amounted to roughly $15 billion. Bloated by the vast profits of the CD business, the industry was rolling in cash. But in 1999 the young nerd Shawn Fanning had created an application that linked computers together over the Internet and offered mutual access to other's mp3 audio files. Shawn was the technical genius, and he met his business counterpart Sean Parker on a webchat channel. They hit it off, and Napster was born. Within no time the concept had gone viral. More than 80 million users had downloaded Napster and started to widely share mp3 files. The genie was out of the music industry bottle and it would never be contained again. Napster ran into enormous legal troubles, and filed for bankruptcy in 2002, but the damage was done. In the wake of the Napster crash, a myriad of similar tools – like LimeWire – evolved and people kept downloading and sharing music in a monumental way. In the space of a decade, the U.S. music industry's revenue had more than halved.

Out of the ashes of the old music industry, a new world order would appear. In probably one of his most defining business deals, Steve Jobs single-handedly pushed the entire music business in a new direction with the iPod.

He sat down with the major record label executives in 2003. At that point, the industry was in complete disarray, record sales were plummeting, and despite the enormous damage the Internet music piracy had had on their companies, execs were too busy crying like reflux-ridden babies to begin to understand the technologies themselves. No wonder that the flabbergasted and totally desperate industry executives accepted Jobs' offer. It truly transformed the industry.

While Jobs positioned his new music player, the iPod, as the vehicle for change, the real engine of disruption was the iTunes platform. The iTunes store was released to the world on the 28th of April 2003, and it became an instant hit. Users loved that they could buy just one song for $0.99 instead of being manipulated into buying an entire album with maybe 9 other songs, which they hadn't wanted in the first place. The music industry had to gobble down a massive business model shift, as well as an incredible loss of revenue. It was a simple choice, really: follow Apple and getting "something", or be disrupted by Napster clones and getting nothing.

Ironically, lightning did strike twice in the music industry. Not even 10 years after the restructuring of the music business landscape by iTunes, it would happen again, this time through the technology of streaming. Spotify was launched in Sweden in 2008. In 2009, Sean Parker was connected with the Spotify-founder Daniel Ek, and a year later invested $15 million in the nascent company. After Napster, Parker had gone on to become president of Facebook, but he had kept following the music industry closely. Spotify wanted to shift the business model for music once again, by offering a subscription model: an 'all-you-can-eat' formula for unlimited use in return for a fixed monthly charge. It turned out, customers wanted this as well. In 2011 Spotify reached its first million users. By 2019, it had more than 200 million active paying users. The real twist is that Apple, the company that had disrupted the music business in the first place, was now being disrupted by Spotify. It had to change its course and introduce its own version of the streaming music service called Apple Music. In 2019, it finally pulled the plug on iTunes, realizing that it had become obsolete, despite having been the music business' disruption and savior, less than two decades before.

It is fascinating that the music industry had to absorb two major disruptions in such a short time. It teaches us a lot about the cause-and-effect ripples of disruption. Streaming might not have happened without the catalog buildup of players like iTunes. And the latter might not have materialized without the digitalization of the industry thanks to the mp3 format. But it would have been very hard to predict this long-term evolution when you downloaded that first rickety metallic version of 'Eye of the Tiger' back in 1999.

Today, the music industry isn't dead, though. To the contrary, it is now getting back to its pre-Napster levels. It has 'survived' disruptions, a fundamental restructuring of itself as well as two business models shifts, and has emerged stronger and more resilient than it ever was before. This 'rebound effect' from disruption gives us valuable insights, and perhaps it would be better for us to learn from these lessons in disruptions, than to feel sorry for the people who work in those businesses.

■ Redmond, we have a problem – Microsoft rising from the browser ashes

Today, we are witnessing a very similar situation in the world of computer software. It's a market that has been around for decades and now is undergoing a systemic shift in business models. And Microsoft is at the very heart of it. In my opinion, this Redmond based software giant is perhaps one of the most visible potential Phoenixes on the planet.

To understand the roots of this disruptive Model Innovation in software, we have to go back to the Great Browser Wars of the end of the 20th century.

On August 9, 1995, Netscape went public. Its Initial Public Offering would go down in the history books. The company had been around for only a little over a year, but its web browser, the Netscape Navigator, was red-hot, and used by everyone who wanted to surf the World Wide Web. Despite this, the company couldn't demonstrate a hint of profitability, although its shares - listed at $28 a piece - sold like hotcakes. The Netscape stock skyrocketed as high as $74.75 per share on its first day of trading and then landed at $58.25 when the market closed. The latter valued the web browser company at around $3 billion. By the end of 1995, Netscape shares were trading at $174.

Netscape was the brainchild of Marc Andreessen, a chubby computer scientist from Iowa. He had happened to work at the National Center for Supercomputing Applications in Illinois when he stumbled on the concept of the World Wide Web, which had been developed by Tim Berners-Lee at CERN. Marc then developed the first usable browser, Mosaic, together with fellow programmer Eric Bina, and the pair then teamed up with Jim Clark, the founder of Silicon Graphics. Netscape was born in 1994, and their first product became an absolute hit. Everyone who wanted to connect to the information superhighway essentially had to use their browser.

In hindsight, now that browser software is an absolute commodity, their plan might seem pretty naïve. But back then, when the Netscape IPO became headline news, and set off the global fireworks that would mark the 'dot-com-era', it sent shivers down the spine of the then most important software company in the world: Microsoft.

Microsoft had grown from very humble beginnings to becoming the dominant player in the software industry. They had a quasi-monopoly on the market for IBM PC compatible computers, supplying the operating systems like DOS and Windows, as well as the bulk of the most important applications like Word, Excel and PowerPoint. Users didn't like Microsoft very much in those days: the expensive software was seen as the 'Microsoft tax' that you had to pay if you wanted to get anything done on your computer. But the installed base of IBM PC compatible computers was so big that Microsoft was basically printing money with Windows and Office.

But then Netscape joined the game. And Microsoft realized it might very well be in a lot of trouble. This 'browser' thing was not so harmless, since it allowed people to connect to the Internet, and access websites and applications from anywhere in the world. Back in 1995, the browser was still primitive. But it held the potential that one would no longer use a LOCAL copy of an application like Excel on a computer, but one would just connect to the web, and use a browser like Netscape to perform calculations and make graphs. And that 'harmless' little detail, could end up killing the Microsoft monopoly.

Bill Gates understood the fundamental shifts, and the great potential danger to Microsoft. He wrote a lengthy memo in 1995 to his top executives called 'The Internet Tidal Wave'.

In this wonderful document, he sharply described the disruptive powers of the Internet and the browser. He wrote: "The developments on the Internet over the next several years will set the course of our industry for a long time to come. I assign the Internet the highest level of importance. In this memo I want to make clear that our focus on the Internet is crucial to every part of our business. The Internet is the most important single development to come along since the IBM PC was introduced in 1981."

Bill Gates had been surfing the Internet, and had become fascinated by the creativity of the web and the ease of use of the browser. He remarked: "Amazingly it is easier to find information on the Web than it is to find information on our own Microsoft Corporate Network." He clearly understood the danger of the rise of fledgling startups like Netscape, when he observed: "A new competitor "born" on the Internet is Netscape. Their browser is dominant, with 70% usage share. We have to match and beat their offerings."

So there was a Red Alert at Microsoft's Redmond headquarters. Their response to this disruption is well known: they eventually demolished Netscape by releasing their very own – completely free – browser, the 'Internet Explorer'. And so they kicked Netscape out of the market. It was a nasty war. The first versions of Explorer were extremely poor products, but Microsoft put all its effort into creating a better one. When they released version 4 of the Internet Explorer, a number of Microsoft employees had hoisted a giant model of the Internet Explorer logo onto the back of a truck, brought it to the Netscape offices and dumped it in their corporate office's fountain. That seems hardly sympathetic but it's a perfect illustration of the harshness of the competition between them. By 1999, the market share of Internet Explorer had skyrocketed to 80%, and Netscape had lost.

But Gates was wrong about one thing. He had erringly thought that the Browser was the root of the evil that could topple his empire. He understood the importance, when he wrote that, "there will be a lot of uncertainty as we first embrace the Internet and then extend it. Since the Internet is changing so rapidly we will have to revise our strategies constantly. The Internet is a tidal wave. It changes the rules." Well, A++ for installing a 'sense of urgency'. But killing the browser would prove to be insufficient.

After Netscape was sold off to America Online, leaving Marc Andreessen to go on to become one of the top venture capitalists in Silicon Valley, Microsoft believed the war was won. The truth was, they had only won the battle for product innovation with Netscape, while the business model innovation combat had only just begun.

This was much bigger, much more disruptive than 'just' a browser. The Internet was becoming an operating system of its own. More and more applications became web-native: a trend that would later be coined 'Software-As-A-Service'. It didn't matter if you used a Netscape browser or an Internet Explorer browser, but what DID matter was whether you used a provider like Salesforce to manage your customers.

It was the biggest shift in the world of software ever. Previously software was 'sold' and installed on your computer, or on the servers of your organization. IT departments would buy, install and manage huge datacenters, which housed large numbers of servers, databases and networks that would run all sorts of applications and software. But now, this model was becoming obsolete. Instead of buying all that expensive computing power and expensive software, you 'used' applications from providers like Salesforce, or 'used' computing power from cloud providers like Amazon. And you only paid for what you *actually* used.

Ten years after the famous memo by Bill Gates ordering the Microsoft army to march into battle and start the Browser Wars, a new cry for help was launched by Ray Ozzie. Ray had become the Chief Technology Officer at Microsoft, after he had previously worked at IBM developing Lotus Notes. Ray was an incredibly bright technology thinker, and he saw the second wave of disruption coming, knowing it would be bigger than the previous one. He wrote a memo in 2005 called 'The Internet Services Disruption'.

He remarked: "It is now 2005, and the environment has changed yet again." It was not about the browser, but about the core business of how Microsoft made money: software. Ray Ozzie continued: "Businesses are increasingly considering what services-based economics of scale [i.e. the Cloud] might do to help them reduce infrastructure costs or deploy solutions as-needed and on subscription basis." In other words, customers no longer wanted to pay *up-front* for software. They wanted a *subscription* model for using software services.

He concluded: "This model has the potential to fundamentally impact how we build, deliver, and monetize innovations." He ended the note: "As much as ever, it's clear that if we fail to do so, our business as we know it is at risk."

But whereas in the first Browser Wars Microsoft acted very quickly, very decisively and extremely aggressively, this time around they did not. I would argue that in the first alert raised by Bill Gates, it was clear what to do: build a better browser than Netscape. It was Product Innovation, and that was very much embedded in Microsoft's DNA. They knew that inside out. And at that moment, the legendary founder himself had still very much been the captain of the ship.

But this time around, Bill Gates had already moved on to his philanthropic work. Ray Ozzie was absolutely spot-on in his strategic assessment, but Microsoft was not geared up to act in battle-mode. Run by Steve Ballmer – who was a sales-person first and foremost- the company had become stale and complacent. The 'machine' of Microsoft was not ready to fundamentally re-invent itself in the light of this massive Business Model Innovation at the very heart of its market.

It took a complete change of leadership – with Satya Nadella as the new CEO – in 2014 to really tackle the 'Cloud' and the 'Services' business model revolution head on. And it was almost too late.

I have to admit that I was skeptical when Satya was introduced as CEO, but I have since become a big fan of the massive transformation he introduced at Microsoft. He chronicles this journey of change in his book 'Hit Refresh', published in 2017. In the first pages, he describes the culture of the company that he was chosen to lead: "Innovation was being replaced by bureaucracy. Teamwork was being replaced by internal politics. We were falling behind."

Not just Microsoft was falling behind, actually. Everyone in the software industry was going through the biggest change in the history of their profession. One of the main rivals of Microsoft, Oracle, is an equally good example. Its founder Larry Ellison was a notorious 'Cloud-hater' when the trend first surfaced. Some of that must have been based on technical grounds, but the main reason was that he pretty much hated Marc Benioff, and Salesforce. Benioff had been the youngest vice president at Oracle, an incredible salesman, and when he left Oracle, he had founded the 'Software as a Service' success story Salesforce, along exactly the paradigmatic and disruptive fault line that Ray Ozzie had warned about. Salesforce was using the slogan "The End of Software" to market their ideas, selling users on the idea they did not have to BUY software, but only PAY for what they used. When companies had many users, they would pay a lot, but when you only used a little, you never had to overpay your provider. On top of that, the software that users consumed was always the latest version, and always up to date.

Larry Ellison had made his fortune selling software licenses, getting paid up front, whether a customer would use the software or not. On top of that he made a lot of money selling pricey upgrades. Needless to say that he thought

Benioff was a fool. Ages ago, I used to visit the big Oracle sales convention in San Francisco, the Oracle Open World. Ellison used to warn his audience that "the Cloud was evil". A few years later, however, he changed his tune and acknowledged that the Cloud had its role, under certain circumstances. And even further down the line, that very same Ellison would preach the Cloud gospel and predict that "The Cloud is the Future". I have not observed a more telling reversal of stirring rhetoric since "Four legs good, two legs bad" by Snowball in George Orwell's Animal Farm...[23]

By the time that Nadella took the helm at Microsoft, the company had almost lost the race. He put transforming Microsoft into a Cloud based company as the top priority, and urged his employees to develop all the applications of Microsoft in a 'Software as a Service' model. He realized they had little time left. Companies such as Salesforce were taking the 'Software as a Service' market by storm, and in their own backyard in Seattle, Amazon Web Services had been quietly growing into a world giant. And it was starting to attract all the best talent away from Microsoft.

They embarked on a similar all-out combat mentality as they had done during the Browser Wars. Only this time, they went beyond Product Innovation: it was Business Model innovation. Instead of receiving the full (and sometimes bloated) license fees up front, they would have to re-engineer their financial flows, as money would trickle in from customers on a per-use, per-user, per-month, basis. To me, this is one of the greatest transformations of our time: under Nadella, Microsoft is proving to be one of the most clever and decisive Phoenixes of all. But most impressive of all is probably that they were able to completely reinvent themselves without disturbing their market capitalization. Instead, during that period of intense business model transformation, they would briefly become the world's most valuable company on the stock exchange.

Later in this book, I'll also discuss the cultural aspects that are required to pull off such a massive evolution. Microsoft's accomplishment is obviously not just about technical, operational and financial engineering. It is just as much a transformation of culture and leadership.

In 'Hit Refresh', Satya Nadella cites John Batelle, one of the founding editors of WIRED magazine, who wrote: "Business is humanity's most resilient, iterative, and productive mechanism for creating change in the world."

That is precisely what I adore about this last mechanism of Business Model Innovation. It provides an excellent mechanism to see who will SHIFT their business model to cope with changes, and embrace new opportunities, and find out who will do everything to PROTECT their old model, with their old margins and value propositions. Only those in the first group can become a Phoenix. The latter is destined to become roadkill on the journey of disruption.

■ Lessons learned

So what are some of the 'Business Model Innovation' experiences and morsels of wisdom we can draw from these examples?

1. More change in 10 than in the last 50 years

When the full force of 'Business Model Innovation' hits an industry, that's when the real storms are unleashed. Holding on to old business models and margins won't help, and is actually dangerous. Mary Barra, the brilliant CEO of General Motors, (more about her in the industry case that follows) once told us: "There will be more change in the 10 years ahead, than we've seen in our industry in the last 50 years." Are you prepared for that? Is your company?

I believe that we might start to notice a few dark clouds over the horizon in many sectors, like Finance or Healthcare. And they *will* introduce a world of Model Disruption. Most of us haven't even felt the first raindrops yet. But when they start to fall, be prepared to radically rethink the future. The trick is to look at this as an opportunity, and not a threat.

2. Learn from rebounds

Some sectors have already weathered the storms, some even twice. We can learn from some of these 'survivors', like the music industry. Some media sector players for example, came out stronger of the ordeal. One of the newspapers I read most is the Financial Times, founded way back in 1888. It has not just survived the digital transformation of its sector, but it has more subscribers than ever before. And more than 80% of its business is now 'digital'. We really don't have to feel sorry for those 'disruption victims'; we have to draw inspiration from those that were able to rise again, Phoenix-like, from the ashes of their industry.

3. Much more than finance

Business Model transformation is the full operational overhaul of an organization: you have to question EVERYTHING, and anything CAN change. The way you operate, the way you make money, the way money flows, everything is capable of being disrupted. As Microsoft shows, you need clever financial and operational engineering just to make it happen. But being successful in these Business Model innovation journeys, goes WAY beyond finance. This type of evolution is about culture, attitude, behavior, skill and leadership. In the next chapters, we'll focus intensely on how to prepare and leverage these characteristics.

4. Prepare when you have the means

It's too late to think about fundamental change when you run out of money. It's important to start PREPARING for such fundamental shifts BEFORE the Shit of Yesterday hits the fan. But the problem is that most companies don't. Luckily Microsoft was still extremely flush when Satya Nadella came on board: he still had the mechanism, and the funds to pull off his radical transformation. Don't make the mistake of waiting until it's too late. As Nadella mentions in his book: "You don't have to invent the wheel, but you should adopt it quickly."

V AN INDUSTRY CASE: ACING INNOVATION IN THE AUTOMOTIVE SECTOR

Ten to 20 years out, driving your car will be viewed as equivalently immoral as smoking cigarettes around other people is today. — MARC ANDREESSEN

When it rains, it pours. The music industry has now seen the storms of disruption pass through their market and wash away their models and margins several times. The software industry is right in the heart of the hurricane, and cloudburst season is sweeping their models away. And today the automotive sector is beginning to feel the first drops of rain. Industry players are realizing they may well be about to face a massive thunderstorm.

Four fundamental trends are currently colliding in the world of mobility, and they are characterized by the acronym ACES: Autonomous, Connected, Electrified and Shared.

■ Autonomous – a new market

AUTONOMOUS driving made the media headlines when Sebastian Thrun won the 2005 DARPA Grand Challenge – a 130-mile driverless car competition held in the Mojave Desert – with his robot car Stanley. He was subsequently hired into Google to further develop this groundbreaking technology. Since then, Google has spun off this division as a separate company called Waymo which is currently providing driverless-taxi services in test areas like Phoenix, Arizona.

Autonomous vehicles without traditional chauffeurs will truly disrupt the market. Autonomous transportation is not merely a brand-new market for Google, it will also potentially disrupt and invade many other markets. I abhor short flights across Europe. Traveling from Brussels to Frankfurt, comprises of just a one hour flight and yet, the whole journey to the airport, with all the security, check-in, waiting, and other inconveniences, amounts to more than four hours in total. I could drive to Frankfurt in that time.

And if I were to have the opportunity to sit out that journey in a driverless car – watching Netflix, taking a nap, or reading a book in the meanwhile – I would choose that option over the airplane in a heartbeat. Even better, instead of flying to Frankfurt and checking into a hotel to be there early for my first meeting, I could hire an autonomous sleeper-car for the night and arrive well-rested in the morning. This market innovation has the potential to not only disrupt the airlines, but many others, like the hospitality sector.

■ Connected – a new service

The easiest disruptive innovation in that list is probably 'Connected', because it is essentially a SERVICE innovation. Today's vehicles have evolved into computers on wheels, whizzing us from A to B. Their sensors, electronics and software are orders of magnitude more complex than the rocket that took Neil Armstrong to the moon. But the user doesn't always see that 'invisible' technology under the hood, or appreciate its intricate complexity. But what the user DOES see has to be in line with the 'New Normal'.

I love to sit in traffic and watch my fellow congestion victims in their cars. Most of their vehicles have plastic contraptions stuck to their dashboard or ventilation ducts, displaying their smartphones as one of their main interfaces. It's incredible how quickly the 'satellite-navigation' and 'GPS' systems of automobiles became completely antiquated, only to be replaced by our Google Maps and Waze powered smartphones. And why would you still build in a radio, CD-player, or mp3 player in your car, when all you do is stream your music via Spotify? The next generation of cars will probably abandon all these obsolete systems, and position our New Normal smartphone as their connected heart.

But it goes beyond navigation and entertainment. Tesla was the industry pioneer, allowing cars to 'update' themselves, developing new features or possibilities from the moment that the 'software' of the car was downloaded and updated. Cars will also signal to their maintenance partners what needs to be replaced, and will automatically 'order' spare parts to arrive in the garage long before the driver even sees a blinking light on the dashboard.

In essence, CONNECTED is all about SERVICE innovation, providing a better customer experience for the driver, but essentially preserving the standard 'product'.

But that is just the tip of the iceberg.

■ Electric – a new product

Tesla was the disruptive startup that initiated the avalanches of change in the automotive sector. Their focus on ELECTRIC was the first of many evolutions. This is clearly about PRODUCT innovation, about building a new product. One that is not based on carbon fuels, but on clean, efficient and practical electrical energy. True, Tesla was not the first. There have been many attempts over the past 100 years to jumpstart the uptake of electrical automobiles, but Tesla was the disruptor that really ignited the flame. Over the last couple of years, every single car company has been planning, producing and launching electric vehicles. And many countries have put very clear deadlines on when it will no longer be acceptable to have fossil-fuelled vehicles on the roads.

■ Shared – a new business model

The last one in the list is SHARED. In this age of 'access over ownership', why should we own a car in the first place? Uber has transformed the world of mobility by focusing on 'using' mobility instead of owning vehicles. Now, as wonderful as the flexibility of 'mobility as a service' is to a customer, it's a complete business MODEL innovation for the manufacturers. Instead of selling you a car, they will allow you to use a vehicle, probably under a 'subscription' model. I personally would love to use a small sporty BMW during the week, and then a larger model when I travel with my family on the weekend. And during the holidays, we might very well want to use an SUV when we take a trip to the mountains. That is why, in 2019, Daimler and BMW teamed up to create a 'Mobility As A Service' offering that would allow them to completely change their operating model.

When you look at Autonomous, Connected, Electric and Shared, this 'ACES' cocktail of disruptive Product, Market, Service and Model Innovations could be cooking up a real gale-force tempest in the world of automotive. Imagine what it means to lead a car company today, and to have to navigate it through this ACES superstorm.

■ Mary resurrecting General Motors

One of the leaders I most admire, who is navigating these tempestuous automotive waters, certainly is Mary Barra, the CEO of General Motors. GM is an icon of American entrepreneurship, firmly woven throughout the fabric of the U.S. economy. But it also was horribly mismanaged at the end of the 20th and the beginning of the 21st century. GM ignored the changing tastes of their customer base. It had seen more and more of its market shift towards more reliable, efficient and cheaper Japanese rivals, and instead of innovating, it had been waiting for the storm to pass. Big mistake.

General Motors eventually ran itself into the ground and declared Chapter 11 bankruptcy on June 1, 2009. This biggest industrial bankruptcy in the history of mankind marked a pitch-black moment for the American economy. Not so long before, in 2007, GM had celebrated its position as the worlds' largest carmaker, for the 76th consecutive year, and was sitting on more than $25 billion in cash. Eighteen months later it was bankrupt, pushed over the edge by the financial crisis of 2008, and had to be bailed out by the American taxpayer. In an article titled 'A giant falls', the Economist wrote: "No one believes that GM will ever return to its former glory."

There are many reasons why General Motors failed. They didn't try their best to understand customers, who, it turned out, might want different things from a car. They did not pick up on the signs of changing tastes. Finally, they didn't adapt their operating mechanisms fast enough. It took them way too long, for instance, to realize that the Japanese could not only make better cars, but also could do it far more efficiently. They were too slow to respond to changing gas prices, and didn't act quickly enough to build vehicles that were much more fuel efficient. But what ultimately killed them off was the enormous cost of labor. After the Second World War, GM had been growing so quickly that they needed to secure a steady flow of new employees. So they agreed on labor deals with the United Auto Workers union that, over time, would turn into an insupportable burden. The cost of retired workers' health care for example, diverted billions of dollars from developing new models: every single car that drove off the assembly line cost $1,400 more than those made in Asian plants because of this.

So when Mary Barra became the CEO of General Motors in 2014, she was faced with one of the toughest challenges in corporate America. Barra was a GM lifer, having started her career as an intern at the company in 1980, when she was only 18 years old. She graduated from Kettering University (originally the General Motors Institute of Technology, actually), with a degree in electrical engineering, and rose quickly through the ranks. She ran manufacturing, headed up Human Resources, and eventually became head of Product Development. When she was chosen to become the CEO in January of 2014, she was the first woman ever to run a Detroit automobile manufacturer.

Her job was to no less than restore GM to its former glory. Not only did she have to deal with the massive 'Shit of Yesterday', but she had to steer the company towards a new future, with the ACES typhoon on the horizon.

When she became the chief executive, she predicted that she "expected to see more change in the world of transportation in the next 10 years than we have seen in the past 50." Five years after her appointment, she remarked: "Today, that pace of change is only accelerating. In this rapidly changing world, General Motors must earn the right to exist."

She embarked on a mission to completely rethink and remake General Motors. The vision of the company is now centered on a future of transportation that is characterized by Zero Crashes, Zero Emissions, and Zero Congestion. For her, the ACES trends are the 'mechanisms' to unlock the possibilities of that vision. When she took the helm, she quickly realized that GM did not own all the ingredients to fully unlock the ACES potential, and so she invested $500 million in the shared transportation company Lyft. At the time, this seemed like an awful lot of money to shell out for a company that just recovered from bankruptcy thanks to a government bailout. However, it proved to be quite a good investment: two years later Lyft IPO-ed and the value of the GM stake had doubled. But it also provided an excellent top of the Hourglass radar screen for Barra to understand the world of the collaborative economy.

She also acquired an Autonomous Driving San Francisco based startup called 'Cruise Automotive' in 2016, for the all-in price of $581 million. That too may seem like a big chunk of change for a startup that could not even present a working prototype at the time. But it gave GM excellent insight into the world of autonomous cars. In fact, GM did a great job at keeping the startup independent without its own 'machine' squeezing the living daylight out of it. Cruise has since become the #1 competitor of the Google division of Waymo. It was also, in hindsight, a really smart financial move. Investments in Cruise in 2019 from Japan's SoftBank Vision Fund and Honda boosted its worth to almost $15 billion. But apart from the financials, the acquisition of Cruise gave GM an active – top of the Hourglass – interface into the innovation ecosystem of Silicon Valley.

The transformation at GM continues to be brutal. It is not just about investing in the future, but it is also about letting go of the legacy of the past. Since she became CEO in 2014, Barra has not just been dropping cash in Silicon Valley. She also had to shut down production plants and eliminate unsuccessful and money-losing models. And of course, she had to lay off thousands of GM employees, who were not 21st century proof.

'Time is not our friend' is one of her favorite statements. Change is brutal, and this definitely is not just about technology. It is just as much about culture, leadership and skills. Transforming a company like GM is the same process as transforming the workforce. Barra noted a list of 10 critical 'jobs' that would be essential to the future of General Motors, and its capability to respond to the ACES disruption:

1. Electrical engineers – to explore and develop electric vehicles
2. Analytics experts – to create algorithms to enable smart data to help drivers
3. Interaction designers – to ensure that information and technology within the car can be accessed safely and intuitively
4. Web programmers – to develop software that allows the next big thing to easily connect to the vehicle and its occupants

5. Autonomous driving engineers – to develop advanced sensor and radar systems to make these vehicles and those that follow a reality
6. Customer care experts – to connect with customers directly and almost instantaneously via social channels
7. Sustainability integration experts – to help us find ways of using less of everything to keep our planet green
8. Industrial engineers – to challenge engineers to build complex vehicles in ways that are sustainable and efficient
9. 3D printing engineers – to help us innovate and build faster, often allowing us to have more affordable options to test
10. Alternative propulsion engineers – to refine and develop new ways for cars to move[24]

It is fascinating to see this list and think that half of these jobs weren't even around as a 'job' when General Motors filed for bankruptcy in 2009.

General Motors isn't out of the woods, of course. Plus, it's only starting to drizzle in its industry, since the full impact of ACES hasn't even begun. But Mary Barra is preparing her company for the biggest, most fundamental changes the industry has ever seen. As she puts it herself: "We are in the midst of nothing less than an absolute transportation revolution."

CONCLUSION

In his "museum of failures", Dr. West prefers to talk about the 'celebration of creativity'. I wholeheartedly agree. Whether your company is facing Product innovation, Market innovation, Service or Model innovation – or all of the above at the same time – it will be up to you, and your team, to fully take up the challenge, and let creativity, passion and innovation reign.

During my many years as a keynote speaker, one of the (most predictably) recurring questions has probably been "Could you show us an example of a traditional company that has performed such a transformation successfully in our market?" I hate that question. It is a sign of what I call the 'HBR-bias'. Over the years, and especially in the last part of the 20th century, we have seen new concepts and ideas surface time and time again. But then we all patiently wait around for the definitive 'Harvard Business Review' article to appear, so that we could apply its 'seven steps for success'. The truth is: these HBR articles are the grown-up equivalent of the safety blankets from our childhood: extremely comforting, but very inadequate in the case of actual problems, like wild bear attacks, fire or a hurricane.

In today's fast-changing 21st century world, characterized by the Never Normal, you won't have time to wait for these 'final and definitive' HBR articles. By the time that they have surfaced, you might have run out of gas. In this age, you have to ACT in the now, to conquer the Day After Tomorrow.

Even so, there are future-driven companies that I greatly admire, obviously, so I don't want to deprive you of their bright and shiny beacons. Just don't expect to be able to copy them in "X steps", to reinvent yourself for the future. The two examples that I want to provide are going through massive transformations, they are simultaneously faced with ALL four dimensions of innovation, and seem to be doing a really good job at managing their consequent reinvention. One is a Phoenix, the other a Unicorn.

■ The Alphabet of innovation

Let me start with the Unicorn, and talk about Google. Many people still see Google as a relatively 'young' company, and true, it was only officially launched back in 1998. The two founders Sergey Brin and Larry Page had met three years before, when Brin was asked to show Page around the Stanford campus. They hit it off, developed a web crawler and search algorithm originally called 'BackRub', and were about as surprised as anyone that their search engine became so incredibly popular. They went into hypergrowth after 2000, and by 2004 – when they filed for their initial public offering – the company was already valued at $27 billion.

Today, the company has been renamed 'Alphabet', and has more than 100,000 employees. In 2018 it generated more than $100 billion in annual sales, just 20 years after it was founded.

But like every other company, even the 'magical' Google needs to reinvent itself.

Google is very transparent about their need to continuously improve, challenge themselves, and discover their 'next new thing'. The profitability of their core business is so vast, that they have the luxury to do this with more intensity than anyone else. But everyone at Google realizes that disruption can be just around the corner, and that innovation is not a luxury but an absolute necessity to secure their Day After Tomorrow.

Let's start with the easy one: Product Innovation. Google is an incredibly creative organization, filled with talented and bright individuals, who are given the 'creative freedom' to experiment and try out new ideas. Some of the Product Innovations at Google were triggered by the fabled 80/20 rule, which allowed its employees to spend 20 percent of their time on creative side projects. This for instance led to many interesting new products, one example being Gmail. But after such enormous growth, maintaining the 80/20 rule wasn't so easy.

But Google is still a 'machine' for Product Innovation. Some of them are 'radical' new Products, like the introduction of Google Glass back in 2012. Sergey Brin was constantly spotted wearing a pair, and all of a sudden in 2013, everyone wanted one. But when the product was finally launched, it turned out to be quite unusable: it had a very limited battery time, tended to become very hot and emitted significant radiation very close to your brain. On top of that, from a functionality and experience point of view, it proved to be quite the disappointment. But it also triggered massive interest for the world and opportunities of Augmented Reality. Google was not afraid to launch radically new Product Innovations. Even if they failed in the marketplace. Sometimes you can launch too soon, but I still believe that the concept of Google Glass has a lot of potential, and that they learned a lot from this failure.

My favorite Product Innovations at Google might be the 'smaller' ones, though: the incremental innovations in their products. A great example is the autocomplete function in Google Search. If you are old enough, you'll remember that you used to have to type in a complete search query, and then press 'Google Search'. But in 2004, Google implemented the 'autocomplete' function, which suggested a number of possible ways to complete a query after one has started typing. Google had learned to 'finish your sentence for you'. I remember a Google presentation a few years ago, when one of the executives told us: "If you make a typo in your search query, we consider it OUR problem." As a company, it is systematic in these incremental Product Innovations, as it wants to continuously improve the user experience.

Though Google is the home of most of the Product Innovations, its parent company Alphabet is the place where many of the other types of innovation patterns reside.

A great example of Market Innovations is Alphabet's research organization Verily, which is devoted to the study of life sciences. Google has been very intensely involved in healthcare and biotech since the very beginning. One out of 20 searches on Google are health related, and an entire generation has grown up searching for symptoms and treatments on 'Dr. Google'. But Verily goes way beyond that. Originally founded in the 'incubator for radical new ideas' inside Google, the fabled X lab, it was spun out as an independent subsidiary of Alphabet in 2015. It has attracted a large number of researchers, combining the art of data science with the field of biology, and is entering the completely new market of personalized healthcare. In 2019, Verily announced that it was forming alliances with some of the largest pharmaceutical players in the world like Novartis, Sanofi, Otsuka and Pfizer. These partnerships are primarily to work on clinical trials, to help develop the breakthrough drugs of tomorrow, powered by data and new ways of using medical information.

Google is constantly looking at new market opportunities, but is also constantly tinkering in Service Innovation. Perhaps the greatest tribute to that is Android, the mobile operating system that has become a global standard. Android was actually an acquisition. It was not developed by Google, but by a young technical genius called Andy Rubin in 2003. He wanted to build an operating system that could power digital cameras but then pivoted to mobile phones. Android was acquired by Google in 2005, probably without much strategic insight, as this was two years before Apple launched the iPhone, and ignited the smartphone explosion. But Android thrived within the Google ecosystem, grew exponentially, and since 2013, it has become the most popular mobile operating system on the planet. By 2017, there were more than 2 billion active users of Android, and it commanded a market share of more than 87% of the worldwide market for smartphones.

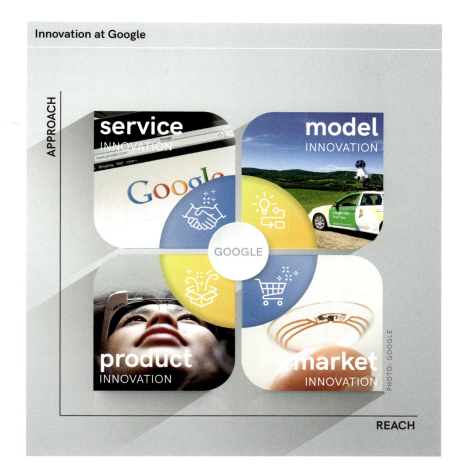

Innovation at Google

And they all use Google to search. Imagine that Google had NOT bought Android, and decided to keep focus on its original idea, search in a web browser on desktop computers. Today, the bulk of the $100 billion in revenue streams through their Android channel into the company. Customers shifted from their computers to their phones, so Google HAD to follow with their Service Innovation to keep the customer experience flawless and fresh.

Finally, we've already discussed the great leaps of faith that Alphabet makes in Model Innovation. When you look at the driverless cars of the Waymo division, these are massive new Business Model Innovation opportunities where hopefully one day Alphabet's NEXT $100 billion of revenue will come from. Many of those ideas come from their X lab, which has as its mission statement: "We create radical new technologies to solve some of the world's hardest problems."

It is comforting to see that even the God of Unicorns, Google, a company that has gone from nothing to $100 billion in revenue per year in just 20 years, still feels the pressing need to keep pushing itself to continuously and relentlessly reinvent itself. Google sees this not as a burden, but as a true celebration of creativity and an absolute brutal necessity.

I'm sure that some of you are thinking something along the lines of "Ah, well, that's easy when you're making $100 billion." Or, the "Sure, but they're Google, they're still wet behind their ears. Show me an example of an OLD company that was able to accomplish this."

▪ It's an innovative world after all

Ok, I will. I'll tell you about one of my all-time favorite companies in the whole world, which, for many of us, played a big part in our childhoods: Disney. Today, this global entertainment player is nearly 100 years old. And it has gone through some really rocky rollercoaster-esque moments during its lifetime.

Walt Disney grew up in Kansas City. He was a true creative talent, who became the cartoonist of the newspaper of the McKinley High School he attended. After a number of jobs working as an apprentice artist, he decided to make his own fortune. His first venture 'Iwerks-Disney Commercial Artists', with the legendary artist Ub Iwerks, failed to take off. His second venture, the film studio 'Laugh-O-Gram Studio' became a real business hiring animators and producing cartoons. But eventually they ran out of money, and filed for bankruptcy in 1923.

After this failure Walt Disney moved to Hollywood in July 1923, to join his brother Roy. The two brothers started to collaborate, and the 'Disney Brothers Cartoon Studio' eventually grew into the 'Walt Disney Studio' in 1926. That's when the business really started to take off. This happened first with a cartoon series starring 'Oswald the Lucky Rabbit', but Disney soon came up with the idea of a mouse character named Mortimer. His wife Lillian hated the name, so they changed it to 'Mickey Mouse', which was stylized by his faithful creative genius Ub Iwerks. When the first Disney film with sound, called 'Steamboat Willie', came out, it starred Mickey Mouse, and was an instant smash hit. It was one of the very first cartoons to appear with a synchronized soundtrack; an absolutely radical Product Innovation for the time.

As the Disney studio kept growing, Walt Disney developed a strong appetite for pushing the boundaries of technology in his productions. His masterpiece was the creation of 'Snow White and the Seven Dwarfs': the very first full-length

Innovation at Disney

cell animated color motion picture in history, which came out in 1937. Something of this scale and complexity had never been done before, and it was a massive risk. His brother and business partner Roy tried to talk him out of it, as did Lillian. In Hollywood the endeavor was ridiculed as 'Disney's Folly'. He had to mortgage his house to get the film produced, at a cost of almost $1.5 million, which was a massive sum for a feature film in 1937.

It paid off. Massively. 'Snow White and the Seven Dwarfs' was a smashing success. The audience loved it, and the film would make almost $8 million in its original run. Walt Disney and the seven dwarfs even appeared on the cover of Time magazine. And the success would endure for decades. In 1994, the film was released on VHS for the first time and raked in another $430 million for the Disney Company. The DVD version, released in 2001, would bring the combined home video and box office revenue to a staggering $1.1 billion.

PRODUCT INNOVATION

The success of 'Snow White' gave Disney wings. The company went to the stock exchange in 1939, and this gave way to a string of innovative and financial successes such as Pinocchio, Fantasia, Dumbo and Bambi. They all turned out to be classics. After the Second World War, Disney entered the new and exciting world of television.

There is still a knack for technological Product Innovation running deep through the Disney Company's artistic veins, and it was deeply embedded into the personality of Walt Disney himself. He loved new exciting concepts, and was eager to understand how technology could improve his products and enhance the experience of his audience. After Walt died in 1966, the company went through a relatively long period of success, still fueled by the momentum of his legacy and vision. In 1984, Michael Eisner was appointed CEO of Disney. The management of the company went through a massive change, announcing the resurrection of a whole new Disney.

There is much debate about the massive change of the 'Eisner Era'. The company grew, significantly, but according to many critics the extremely controlling leadership style of Michael Eisner inhibited efficiency and progress. Eventually, his reign would drive Disney to the verge of collapse. One of the most vocal opponents of Eisner was the last remaining Disney family member on the board:

Roy E. Disney, the son of Disney's co-founder Roy O. Disney. He was the one who kept the initial spirit of his Uncle alive, and when he was ousted, he accused Eisner of running the company into the ground. Roy E. Disney blamed Eisner for micromanagement, accusing him of failing to revitalize the television activities and the theme park business, and told the world that Eisner had turned Disney into a "rapacious, soulless company."

At that time, Disney's own animation studio, the original heart of the company, had failed to keep up with time, and had struck a deal with Pixar (owned by Steve Jobs) to bring to the market such amazing successes like Toy Story. It was no longer Disney that was the creative innovator, but the genius of Pixar, and Disney became merely a 'distribution' mechanism. Not surprisingly, Steve Jobs and Michael Eisner did not get along at all. And in 2004, the relationship between Pixar and Disney fell apart. Pixar started looking for another distributor for when their 12-year contract with Disney would end. The fear of losing Pixar, as well as a number of high-budget Disney films completely flopping at the box office, announced the end of the Michael Eisner era.

Enter Bob Iger and the complete disruptive revitalization of Disney. This is the era where Disney would become one of the most visible Phoenixes of our generation. Bob Iger was a television man: starting out as a local weatherman, he joined the American Broadcasting Company (ABC) in 1974, with the hope of one day becoming a news anchor. It turned out quite differently, though. He rose through the ranks, and became the head of ABC Entertainment in 1989. In 1996, Disney purchased the ABC company, and eventually Iger would be appointed president of Walt Disney International, the business unit that oversees Disney's international operations. And then, in 2000, he became the COO of the company.

PHOTO BY LITTLELOSTROBOT ON FLICKR.COM

When Michael Eisner fell, Disney announced that Bob Iger would become the CEO, and he grabbed the opportunity to "save Disney" with both hands. Iger understood the importance of maintaining the lead in animation – their core Product offering – and he decided to acquire Pixar Animation for $7.4 billion in an all-stock transaction. Steve Jobs, the main shareholder of Pixar, thus became Disney's largest individual shareholder, with a 7% stake, and caught a seat as a board member.

This strategic move totally revitalized Disney. Iger understood that this acquisition could majorly backfire, if Disney were to 'strangle' the creativity and artistic freedom of Pixar. Instead, he named the creative genius at Pixar, John Lasseter, as Chief Creative Officer of the entire Walt Disney Animation Studios. Iger then embarked on a number of brilliant acquisitions to strengthen the core Product Innovation capabilities at Disney: he bought Marvel Entertainment for $4.24 billion in 2009, and Lucasfilm, the company behind Star Wars, for $4.05 billion in 2012.

Some say that Disney had to 'buy' their Product Innovation, in order to reinvent themselves. True, but there is no harm in reaching outside when you realize that the potential for Product Innovation inside your company has run its course. The credit goes to Iger for not seeing those acquisitions as 'buying' innovation, but for using it as a mechanism of change, a 'transfusion' of new blood to revive the company.

If the clever acquisitions of Pixar, Marvel and the Star Wars franchise fall under the 'Product Innovation' category, the enormous theme park business of Disney clearly falls under the 'Market Innovation' category. The latter would never have happened if Walt Disney himself had not been so incredibly stubborn in wanting to build his own 'Disneyland'.

As a kid I grew up close to Anaheim, where the original Disneyland is located. I loved visiting it as a child: walking through the park truly felt like entering another world. That was exactly what Walt had dreamt off when he started to fantasize about building a novel 'themed' amusement park. He used to take his daughters to carnivals and fairs, but found them messy, loud and ugly. He became obsessed with a vision to create something entirely new and different: a 'magical park' where children and parents could have fun together. He wanted to build rivers, waterfalls, and mountains. He had a vision of flying elephants, giant teacups, a full-sized fairy-tale castle, a railway and a rocket to the moon.

His brother called him nuts. Roy Disney was very loyal to his brother, but Walt was the dreamer, and Roy had to deal with the operations and finances of the Disney Company. A typical Disney movie would cost them about $1 million to produce in the 1950s. Walt's radical vision for a 'magical park' would probably amount to more than $10 million. Ultimately, when the 'Magic Kingdom' would open, it had cost more than $17 million to develop. And Roy was not willing to take that risk.

The curious story about the biggest 'Market Innovation' in the Disney history, is that Walt was so convinced about the potential for his 'magical park' that he

MARKET INNOVATION

decided to bankroll it on its own, without the financial support of the Disney Corporation. He mortgaged all his assets, including his homes, and took out massive personal loans. He entered creative contracts with sponsors like Pepsi and the then fledgling ABC network. Walt Disney set up WED enterprises (for Walter Elias Disney, his full name), and this company undertook the gargantuan task of building a completely new 'magical land' from scratch in a 65 hectares (160 acres) plot of orange groves and walnut trees in Orange County.

It got off to a very shaky start. The opening day was an absolute disaster: record heat, a 'Magic Kingdom' that was not even remotely finished, a plumbers' strike that had left the entire park without drinking fountains, there was not enough food to feed the hungry guests, and the asphalt melted into people's shoes. More nightmare than magic.

Still, the customers loved it. Disneyland became an instant hit, growing into a symbol of American creativity with a true global appeal. When the leader of the Soviet Union, Nikita Khrushchev visited the United States in 1959, he only had two requests: to meet John Wayne, and to visit Disneyland.

By 1965, ten years after its opening day, 50 million visitors had entered through the gates of Disneyland. It became clear to the Disney Company that Walt had been right all along about this massively risky 'Market Innovation'. So, in 1965, the Walt Disney Corporation acquired WED Enterprises, realizing that the theme parks were now both core and integral to the future of Disney.

The second Disney theme park opened in 1971 in Orlando in Florida, and was a much larger undertaking than the original California venture. Walt had already passed away by then. EPCOT was opened as a tribute to the future in 1982, and since then Disney has opened up parks in Paris, Shanghai, Tokyo and Hong Kong. Roy Disney had thought that Walt was 'crazy' with his idea of a 'magical park', but by the early 1980s, the theme parks were generating 70% of Disney's income. Walt Disney once said: "Disneyland will never be finished as long as there's imagination left in the world."

Disney has become brilliant at maintaining Product Innovation and realizing the potential of Market Innovation. But in my opinion, today it is first and foremost a champion at Service Innovation: constantly trying to improve the experience of its customers in every possible way.

One of my favorite examples in this area would be the concept of the Magic-Bands, introduced for the first time in the Disney World theme park in 2013. These MagicBands are simple RFID bracelets for park guests, which greatly enhance their stay. When you check in, every family member gets their own MagicBand, and from then on, you can use them for pretty much everything. You can unlock your hotel room door by just swiping your MagicBand. It serves as a 'ticket' to enter the park. And you can buy anything you want with it – a hat, a T-shirt or a burger, you name it. The MagicBand conveniently replaces your keys, credit cards and wallet.

SERVICE INNOVATION

Of course, the MagicBand is an amazing source of information for Disney. They know exactly where you are in the park, what you do, where you spend your money, and which attractions you enjoy. And every guest is happy. If you're wearing your Disney MagicBand to enter a Disney restaurant, a host will greet you at the door and already know your name. As my colleague Steven Van Belleghem says: "No one complains about privacy in Disney World. They don't call it privacy. They call it magic." As the science fiction writer Arthur C. Clarke famously remarked: "Any sufficiently advanced technology is indistinguishable from magic."

The wristbands may seem like simple technology, but retrofitting the entirety of Disney World cost a massive $1 billion. Talk about dedication to the customer experience and to Service Innovation! But the payback for Disney has been huge. As anyone who's been to Disney World knows, you truly enjoy the simplicity of the MagicBands during your entire stay, but tend to be a 'little' surprised when you sign off on the final invoice when you check out. They are so easy to use that you lose track of how much you spend. But hey, it's magic!

The final element of the innovation patterns deployed at Disney is Model Innovation. The world of content consumption has been dramatically changing as a result of technology. The rapid rise of players like Youtube, Amazon Prime Video and Netflix is transforming how we look at video, follow media and consume content. Disney was one of the founding partners of HULU, a subscription

video on demand service that was founded by a multitude of partners like AOL, Universal, Comcast and even Facebook. When Disney acquired 21st Century Fox, including its 30% stake in Hulu, it wound up having a controlling 60% interest in the company. But it wanted full control, and it was hungry for even more.

In order to compete with Netflix, it released Disney+ in the US in 2019, and will start targeting Western Europe and Asia-Pacific countries in 2020. Disney aims to take the full spectrum of its content universe to streaming: from 'Snow White and the Seven Dwarfs', to all the movies of the Disney franchise all the way to the Marvel, Pixar and Star Wars assets, to the Simpsons and National Geographic. It has launched its vast library of more than 7,000 television episodes and 500 films (as well as content produced exclusively for Disney+) into a 'subscription service', as a true example of radical Business Model Innovation.

One of my favorite Disney words was originally coined by Walt himself: the fabulous 'Imagineer'. It is the crucial combination of 'imagination' and 'engineering' that is necessary to unlock the potential of ingenuity and turn innovation into a celebration of creativity. Sheryl Sandberg is one of Disney's former board members, and she summed it up beautifully when she said: "There are a lot of companies that focus on content and a lot of companies that focus on technology, but I think Disney is one of a few companies that do both equally."

In January of 2015, Bob Iger appeared on the cover of Fortune Magazine, with the headline "Empire of Tech." The subtitle was: "How Bob Iger brought the coolest innovations from Lucasfilm, Pixar, Marvel and ESPN into the Disney Galaxy." I believe he did much more than that. Bob Iger 'saved Disney' and turned it into the most visible Phoenix in the world of entertainment. He cleverly combined Product, Market, Service and Model innovation to reinvent a company that is almost 100 years old. Iger has truly turned Disney into a Phoenix, a true Empire of Tech.

YOUR TURN

In this fast changing world, innovation has evolved into a core necessity. Most companies will never be a Unicorn, but as Google has shown us, even Unicorns have to keep reinventing themselves. Companies such as Microsoft, Assa Abloy and Disney show us that even 'traditional' players, that have been around for a long time, CAN reinvent themselves and become a Phoenix.

I hope their stories will inspire you to think about how you can reboot your business. Ask yourself how you can turn Product, Market, Service and Model innovations into weapons of mass disruption to unlock your Day After Tomorrow. Ask yourself which one of these you ought to experiment with, to keep your company relevant for the coming years.

But the sad reality is that this 'WHAT' of innovation, these patterns, might be the 'easy' part to figure out. The trick to successful transformation and the true recipe for success to become a Phoenix, is probably less driven by the 'WHAT' than by the 'HOW'. So stick around, as I'll discuss this in the next part of the book.

The anatomy of a Phoenix

THE HOW OF INNOVATION

> Set up a situation that presents you with something slightly beyond your reach.
> — BRIAN ENO

VORSPRUNG

In 1982, Audi hired the British advertising legend Sir John Hegarty to help it sell more cars. During a visit to one of its manufacturing plants in Ingolstadt, deep in the heart of Bavaria, Sir Hegarty spotted a slogan written on an old and faded poster hanging on the wall. It read: "Vorsprung durch Technik." He immediately recognized the power of the slogan, and convinced Audi to take this rather difficult to pronounce tagline, and turn it into the Audi global advertising baseline. The Audi strapline is now one of the most famous and long running in the history of advertising.

Loosely translated, "Vorsprung durch Technik" means "Advancement through technology." Today, technological innovation is at the very heart of the most fundamental and radical changes in almost every sector, but obviously in itself alone, it will NOT give you an advantage. True, many (disruptive) technologies have become New Normals, and we may have entered the era of Never Normal, but in my opinion the 'technological' side of innovation is a MUST, not an EDGE. In other words, understanding technology, recognizing the power of disruption, and investing in the right skillset to cope with technological shifts is a NECESSITY, but will never set you aside from the pack. Today, "Vorsprung durch Technik" no longer applies. It's simply not enough.

When Audi started to market their top of the line Audi A8 model they introduced another tagline: "The Art of Progress." And that is what I want to talk about in this part of the book.

I have come to believe that technology is essential, innovation is no longer a luxury, and that it is vital that you understand the WHAT of innovation. But if you want to unlock the 'art of progress' in your company, the HOW of innovation will be even more important.

I have broken this part into five elements: How to focus on customers in the age of disruption, how to operate in the world of platforms, how to unlock the cultural aspect of disruption, how to remaster your organization and how to structure it for agility and innovation.

I CUSTOMER DISRUPTION: EXTREME CUSTOMER CENTRICITY IN THE AGE OF 'ME'

Whatever you do, do it well. Do it so well that when people see you do it, they will want to come back and see you do it again, and they will want to bring others and show them how well you do what you do.
— WALT DISNEY

▪ Milk (for) the customer

I'm often invited to speak at many exceptional events, for many wonderful customers, all around the world. But sometimes I am asked to talk about certain subjects or markets that are a real challenge to me, leaving me to ponder how I will address the concept of disruption on that particular occasion.

One of my favorite encounters over the years was with the top executive team of one of the largest dairy companies in the world. I won't name the company, but they are a global player in the world of dairy products, and have been around for a very long time. And they wanted me to come and talk about disruption.

Now, I have done quite some work for the food industry in the past, and understand the complexity of the relationship between the suppliers and the retailers, the tensions between the two in terms of data and 'owning the customer', and the enormous role that 'digital' plays in that dialogue. So I was really looking forward to discussing disruption with this company. When I had the chance to do a prep-call with one of the company's senior managers, and asked what their top priorities were, the answer I got was quite interesting: "1. Milk, 2. Cheese, and 3. Yoghurt".

Luckily, I have worked with Brian Frank on many occasions in Silicon Valley on the riveting topic of the future of food. Brian is a serial entrepreneur, and a bit of a foodie, and he now focuses on the emerging venture capital scene around the future of food. At this moment there are lakes of money being poured into food-startups, ranging from egg-white-without-chickens, to meatballs-without-meat, or completely plant-based meat replacement like the Impossible Burger. So I called Brian Frank and he suggested I take a look at a fledgling startup called PerfectDay.

PerfectDay is a company that produces Synthetic Milk. That is, milk without the need for cows. It was founded by two brilliant young scientists who loved to drink milk, but were getting seriously concerned about the impact of all those farting cows on our environment. So they set out to create a new kind of milk, completely synthetic, but with the same taste and texture as its traditional counterpart.

This is a really great example of a diverse group of talent – chefs, food developers, scientists, engineers, and marketers – setting out to solve a pretty big challenge in our world: they allow us to enjoy the foods we love while making the world a kinder, greener place.

PHOTO CREDIT: PERFECT DAY

'Dairy Without Compromise' is their main tagline and their website explains how they use microflora and fermentation techniques to develop the very same dairy protein that cows produce. Their creative mindset and approach is clearly reflected on their website, where their clever copywriters talk about "A Smaller Hoofprint," and my personal favorite: "Join the Moo-vement." Their bottle says it all: "Animal-free milk, brewed with love in San Francisco."

When they proved they could do the science, PerfectDay teamed up with Archer Daniels Midland, one of the largest agricultural processors and food ingredient providers, to help them scale in a massive way.

When I talked about this beautiful example to the team of the global dairy company, an extremely interesting debate unfolded. Some of the executives thought: "Great, we should buy this company! We already have all sorts of 'vegan milk' from 'almond milk', 'oat milk' to 'rice milk' to 'soy milk'. So if the customer tastes are changing, and they now want 'Synthetic Milk', we should provide this!" They also knew that consumer attitudes change faster than consumer behaviors, but wanted to make sure that they would be ready to capitalize when the 'mindset' of customers regarding ecology would translate into their buying preferences.

But a number of other executives were not so sure. They thought about the cows, and about the large number of farmers that depended on them to bring their natural products to market. Some of those farmers are eighth generation farming families that have worked incredibly hard to bring pure and unspoiled milk into the hands of consumers. Surely, the company couldn't just abandon them and introduce a completely 'synthetic' product?

This is actually one of the most basic and age-old questions when it comes to innovation: "Do you focus on the cow, or do you focus on the customer?" Or even better yet: are you making milk for your customer, or milking your customers? Think about YOUR own situation, here. And be honest: how often are you truly discussing the point of view of your customers and their changing needs? And you know that talking about your market, your products, your services and products is not the same as talking about your customers. How often have you been taking 'the cow' in your business for granted? How many times did you (because it's just so much easier) extrapolate from the 'cow', because "that's the way we've always done things"?

■ Is Tech the answer?

But surely, technology will be able to help here? Surely, in today's age of the Never Normals, technology should allow us to 'sense' customers better than ever before? Surely with Big Data and Artificial Intelligence we should be able to copy from the playbook of the Googles and Facebooks of this world and EASILY understand the needs, wants and desires of our customers better than ever before? Marketing should be a breeze, right?

Not quite. I'm not so sure we're making as much progress as we'd like.

Let me point out the issue with a personal anecdote. In 2018 the entire Internet – to this day I still have no idea which behavior of mine triggered its obsession – seemed to believe that I had to buy a pair of Mahabis.

What are Mahabis? Well, I'm glad you asked: they are a brand of slippers that ironically target "the man who doesn't wear slippers." They were the brainchild of the boyish barrister turned entrepreneur Ankur Shah, who founded the company back in 2014 in order to market a new concept: trendy woolen $99-a-pair slippers that could be transformed into outdoor shoes by stepping into detachable rubber soles. They were supposed to 'disrupt' the slipper market.

Ankur Shah had previously started a social media advertising company that he had sold to Experian. I can only presume that's where he learned the art of bombarding users with targeted online ads. Mahabis became quite famous for their massive online campaigns, and I can truly vouch for their tenacity. For almost six months, Mahabis' ads stalked me absolutely everywhere and constantly. I would open up my Facebook: Mahabis. Open up my Instagram: Mahabis. Read a tech article: Mahabis. It was a mahabysmal campaign. There were plenty of other 'neo-slipper' companies out there, but Mahabis was by far the most aggressive.

You might not believe it, but I eventually became so fed up with the stalking that I decided to buy a pair over the Christmas period. To my complete surprise they were out of stock. Later I realized that the company had actually been placed into receivership at exactly that point in time. Initially the company seemed to be doing well, selling more than $30 million' worth of the trendy woolen slippers in 2017. But in 2018 they might have spent a little bit too much on online advertising, and went belly-up.

The always hard-core and witty Andrew Hill of the Financial Times coined the term Slipper-freude: "Mahabis' woes have triggered a substantial amount of what you could call Slipper-freude: the hand-rubbing glee of people who, over the four years since its launch, have found it hard to escape the avalanche of online ads its founder Ankur Shah unleashed."

But surely, in today's day and age of ultra-smart technology, there should be better ways to understand, and target consumers online?

And yet, how many of you have had this experience? You book a hotel room in Bilbao on a site like booking.com and you HAVE the reservation secured. But for the next two weeks, every time you check your favorite news site, weather site or Facebook, you're bombarded by ads trying to sell you that very SAME hotel in Bilbao! How is this type of Artificial Stupidity possible when we also have Artificial Intelligence that can train itself to beat the best GO[25]-player in the world? Go figure.

Perhaps we haven't gone far enough. Remember when Europe unleashed GDPR (the General Data Protection Regulation) in 2018 to 'protect the online privacy of citizens'? There was an enormous amount of agitation about these evil online players that were supplying us with 'free services', but in exchange were also 'stealing' our private and confidential information and selling it off to advertisers.

But honestly, I wish I could give these online players MORE information about me so that they could present me with BETTER targeted advertisements! I would LOVE to share with Facebook and Google that I did already book that hotel in Bilbao, and that they should not waste my time by showing me what I already have.

The current state of affairs doesn't always feel like "Vorsprung durch Technik" to me. It feels more like "Frustriert durch Technik" sometimes.

If I look at the future of technology supporting the evolved understanding of customers, I see four major trends:

■ I. Relevant

I think we can all agree that the 'average' consumer died a violent death in the 20th century, and that we are now in the age of 'personalization'. We all want to understand the consumer, focus on his or her UNIQUE characteristics, and tailor our offerings and communication accordingly. All with the absolute ambition of staying RELEVANT to the consumer: in our communication and in our offerings of products and services.

I would have absolutely no problem to share MORE of my personal information, tastes, habits and quirks to allow everyone out there (from platforms to retailers and from hotels to car companies) to truly address the market of ME, the only one that truly matters (to me).

■ II. Smart

We make and capture so much Big Data. But what are we doing to filter and transform that raw data potential into true value in a SMART way? And for whom do we provide that value? For the company that owns the data, or do we let that value flow back to the consumer?

Like I've told you before, I've been with the same bank for ages. That bank is sitting on a goldmine of information about me. It knows I should probably change my mobile provider because I'm overpaying. It knows I should probably shift my electricity provider, because I'm not getting a good enough deal compared to my peers. It knows so much about me. So why hasn't my bank been able to turn that raw information into value, and give me some of that value back?

When we talked about Disney's MagicBands, we said that no one complains about privacy there. Disney joyfully captures this information and analyzes the behavior of their customers in order to optimize the rides, merchandising and its food and beverage operations. But it also provides that information back to the user. If you indicate that you want to go to Space Mountain at 15:00 in your app, your MagicBand will tell you exactly when you should head over there, based on your current location. That's a really SMART way to turn information into value, and not just value for Disney. It brings real value to the END customer of the park.

▪ III. Timely

There's this running joke that Amazon will ultimately know what you want BEFORE you know it yourself. They are in fact so good at understanding your tastes and behaviors, that they will already start shipping the goods to the nearest warehouse, because they KNOW you will order it soon.

There is no point in knowing everything about your customers AFTER they have left your website, you have to start to know what they want BEFORE they act. This transition from responsive to proactive will allow you to delight customers, instead of frustrating them with your lack of understanding.

▪ IV. Connected

Finally, the last bucket is 'connected'. Clever companies understand that everything is networked and that this hugely influences cause and effect. When I ask my phone about the weather, it knows where I am, so it will first inform me about the LOCAL weather. Our phones understand what we're doing, where we are, why we ask things, and what they could 'piece together' from the various 'clues' that are out there.

Again, I would love to offer my mobile providers even more data. I would love my phone to really understand all of the engagements, appointments and travel schedules in my calendar. I would be thrilled if my phone would tell me – when I'm packing my suitcase – what the weather will be in the next three cities that I'm travelling to. Or that it would alert the hotels about possible delays since it KNOWS which flights I'm taking. There would be an enormous improvement in our customer experience if our applications would understand the context of the networks of information in which they operate.

I would wholeheartedly and immediately sign for future systems – that cater to me as a consumer – to become more relevant, smarter, timelier and more connected. And if the latter would mean that I would have to give up some of my privacy, I would gladly allow it.

But I'm an engineer.

When I wrote 'The Day After Tomorrow', I started working very intensely with my business partner and friend Steven Van Belleghem, and he followed up on my book with his own brilliant 'Customers the Day After Tomorrow'.

Steven is one of the most brilliant marketing experts out there and he understands customers and marketing far better than I ever will. That's why I asked him to offer his view on the future of customers: how companies that want to reinvent themselves as a Phoenix should look at customers, and how technology could make our customer experiences so much more enjoyable.

Enjoy his insights! I know I did.

How Phoenixes can create an 'offer you can't refuse' for their customers.

BY STEVEN VAN BELLEGHEM — keynote speaker, author and partner at nexxworks and Intracto

■ The age of complexity

The average service level has, in the past two decades, risen sharply. In virtually every company and industry, social media has increased the urgency to put the customer first. Social media are essentially a communication tool but, within companies, they have generated a customer-led culture. Company directors are, all of a sudden, fearful of assertive and critical customers. Over the past decade, the relationship between customers and companies has been changed even more dramatically by social media and mobile apps.

Customers just expect more these days. Everything has to be faster, more authentic and easier to use. These changes and improvements have gradually become part of the daily lives of customers. If you compare the service levels of 2020 with those of 2000, the difference is truly spectacular. It's been a great ride. This time frame also saw the emergence of 'big tech'. The influence of these mega companies on the world in general, and on customers' expectations in particular, has been huge. They have served as beacons for companies around the world, demonstrating how they can make the lives of customers easier and better.

Despite these spectacular changes, I foresee even bigger challenges in the next twenty years. The 'easy' years of customer experience are behind us. Just to compare, developing a communication strategy for Twitter is a whole lot easier than conceiving a proactive service, based on the smart analysis of customer data. Similarly, an app to easily execute orders is far simpler than an automated system whereby the consumer no longer has to worry about his or her purchases. The challenges will only increase in the years ahead.

In the mobility industry, road maps have been digitized over the last twenty years. That is, of course, fantastic, as we're all smoothly guided to our destination, each and every day. If there's a traffic jam, we're told how to neatly avoid it. That technology is now 99% reliable. This evolution has been important and I wouldn't want to travel without it, but it's a whole lot simpler than the challenge for the next twenty years: getting driverless cars on our roads.

The same can be said of healthcare. For the past 20 years, the consumer has been discovering 'Dr. Google'. As soon as someone gets a headache, they're on Google, asking: "What's wrong with me?" Consulting Google about an odd physical twitch has become a human reflex. But this was just the beginning of healthcare digitization. Over the next twenty years, healthcare will undergo a much more major transformation thanks to the gene editing technology CRISPRcas9 and genome engineering.[26]

Consider the ambitions of some big-name companies. The challenges, when setting their goals, are bigger than ever. In the early years of Amazon, Jeff Bezos had no interest in the delivery and warehousing of products. These days, Amazon is busy building one of the world's biggest logistic fleets. Similarly, in Starbucks' vision of the future, I see unprecedented challenges ahead. Starbucks' CEO is planning a new growth phase, fuelled by mobile commerce. In the future, we're told that Starbucks' customers should have access to their favorite drinks, anywhere and at any time. Just think about this for a moment, and you'll realize the logistical complexity of that vision. We're talking about the supply of (mostly) hot drinks. The concept of next-day delivery is obviously not fast enough for this service. Even a delivery within the hour won't cut it.

In this specific context a consumer orders a coffee in which (s)he expects that drink to magically appear a few minutes later. Fulfilling this ambition will require a completely new way of working. In the description of the strategy, Starbucks' CEO draws on the way of working in China, where this logistics context is already the norm. It's striking how more and more companies and industry experts are looking to China to 'preview' the complex future of customer experience in action.

The near real-time delivery that Starbucks is evolving towards is, in China, almost a reality now. For over ten years now I've been tracking the list of the most innovative companies in the world, published annually by the magazine 'Fast Company'. Between 2008 and 2018, the top-3 companies almost always came from Silicon Valley. In 2019, for the first time ever, the top two places were taken by non-US companies. For years on end, the top three places were filled by the almost obvious names: Apple, Tesla, Google, Amazon … Then, suddenly, in 2019, the Chinese company Meituan Dianping topped the rankings. Many Western people hadn't, until then, even heard of this company. Be that as it may, it has over 600,000 employees. The vast majority of them ride around Chinese towns on electric mopeds in yellow jackets. Meituan is the world's most advanced logistics company. They cooperate, very effectively, with both the end consumer and with their various business-to-business partners (restaurants, small local traders …). These days, they're succeeding in delivering orders in less than 30 minutes to a consumer's current location. It's this kind of service that Starbucks, in the coming years, also intends to launch in the West, in order to create a whole new 'customer experience'. Imagine the growth opportunities suddenly available to a 'love brand' like Starbucks if they pull this off.

▪ The end of the 'Unique Selling Proposition'

The new digital and logistics possibilities are more complex, but create the opportunity of an unprecedented level of customer service. This will lead, in turn, to a significant rise in customer expectations.

This continual rise in customer expectations will sound the death knell for classic marketing principles. Anyone who's been on a marketing course will have surely heard of a company's USP (or that of a product). What is your USP (unique selling proposition)? Which unique element or aspect of your company manages to convince the consumer? Marketing theory suggests that if you excel in one aspect, an average score on all the rest will do. A single 'nine out of ten' is enough to offset all the 'sixes'. If you worked in retail, you could win by having the best location, the lowest prices or the friendliest service. Service compensated for price and a lesser location. Location could compensate for price or a limited product range.

These days, though, I'm finding that consumers expect both good service and a competitive price. The Internet has made 'location' a lot less relevant. This trend was started by the 'Unicorns'. Companies like Booking.com or Amazon have an infinite product offering, their prices are competitive, location is irrelevant, and their service is better than the market average. If you observe the 'screen time' of the average consumer, you'll also see that over 80% of the screen time is spent on the sites of disruptive tech startups. So that they, once again, are setting the bar for the next level of customer expectation.

▪ Three levels of customer expectations

Customer expectations are rising and the challenge to meet them is growing. Customer expectations can be grouped into distinct domains.

1. Time is a scarce commodity

Time is probably the most socially equal asset of a society. Everyone has 24 hours in their day. Never more. Never less. Most people have too little of it, though. Combining a hectic professional agenda with family life is not always that simple... And virtually every retired person that I meet also complains about being very busy. Even children have to combine their homework with after-school activities and a budding social life. Most people are short of time. Consequently, how you – as a company – aim to deal, respectfully, with the precious time of consumers is the first key question.

2. Personal dreams, ambitions and bucket lists

Your customers all have different personal dreams and ambitions. Some are saving up for their first home. Others want to book that dream holiday to Peru. For others, the main challenge is to get to the end of the month with a positive bank balance. Pretty much everyone has dreams, challenges and aspirations. Many of those dreams are linked to commercial industries. How you – as a company – can help realize the personal dreams of consumers, is the second key challenge.

Three levels of customer expectations

SOURCE: THE OFFER YOU CAN'T REFUSE BY STEVEN VAN BELLEGHEM

3. An uncertain and demanding world

Lastly, many consumers are anxious. Transnational movements raise many significant issues, and these can cause widespread anxiety. The climate movement has a broad base; nobody really knows what the impact of global warming will be. Most consumers are aware of climate policy and climate change, but also are very keen not to have to pay more for daily purchases, energy and air tickets. The new 'cold war' between the United States and China, Brexit and other macroeconomic conflicts raise serious questions, but there are few easy answers. Companies, however, can offer answers to some of these issues. The third challenge for companies is to help tackle some of these issues, and to involve the consumer more actively.

■ Three strategies to meet today's expectations

To meet these needs of the modern customer, there are at root three major strategies. Combining these in novel ways can lead to a robust customer relationship.

1. The evolution towards INVISIBLE transactions
2. The why of the CUSTOMER comes first
3. Let's save the world TOGETHER

1. The evolution towards INVISIBLE transactions
Time is the customer's scarcest commodity. The big technological unicorns have been the best at freeing up time for their customers. Amazon is successful largely because it takes up the least of the customer's time. The 'one click order', the 'dash button' and the automated 'Amazon Go stores' are just a few examples of how Amazon saves significant amounts of time for its customers.

In the coming years, customer interfaces will become increasingly invisible to the customer. Companies used to "score well" with a well-conceived (human) interface. But what matters most now is an excellent self-service app or website. In the very near future, these will evolve into perfectly working 'digital butlers'. Amazon's Alexa and Google Assistant are currently in the first phase of their evolution into this role. The existing virtual assistants are, perhaps, what the Blackberry was to the first iPhone. They have their flaws still, but with a little imagination, we can all see how the next generation of these AI-assistants will become a common aid in daily life. They will become the dishwashers of the 21st century, ensuring that people need to invest less time in the things that they HAVE TO GET DONE, opening up time for the things closest to their hearts.

Looking further into the future, the next step will be the evolution of these assistants into automatic and invisible interfaces. These invisible interfaces will take decisions and execute commands without the consumer even needing to ask. It will all be done automatically. If you look carefully, there is evidence already, here and there, of such 'invisible interfaces'. I myself, for example, am a big fan of the app of KBC, my Belgian bank. My favorite part of the app is the automation of multi-storey car parks. Thanks to the KBC app, I don't have to intervene at all when I enter a Belgian car park. The car park instantly recognizes my car and raises the barrier. On leaving, the barrier opens automatically, once again. Meanwhile payment has been taken care of, with no effort or interaction on my part. I think this is great! It's a great example of a completely invisible interface.

When the 'Waze' traffic app works out a new navigation route for me, it's also fully automatic. For the user, it's invisible intelligence with a tangible advantage: time efficiency. Every organization should be asking itself these questions: "Which customer interactions can we render invisible?" and "Which aspects of the process still require a relatively big effort, by the consumer, and how can we use his or her time more efficiently."

2. The why of the CUSTOMER comes first

For years now, Simon Sinek has been travelling the world with his fantastic story. 'Start with Why' has become standard terminology in the global world of business. Every self-respecting company has one or more discussions a year about their 'why'?

Organizing a 'why' session in your company gives direction. If done properly, it establishes a common goal and shared vocabulary among staff. The limitation of the 'why' exercise is that it emanates from within the company itself. What are WE going to do?

Filling in the 'why of the customer', on the other hand, is often largely virgin territory. Every customer has aspirations, worries and dreams. Organizing yourself – as a company – to help realize these is perhaps the biggest opportunity of our era. Some banks have, for example, devised tools whereby consumers can 'save up' their change in order to make their dream trip to New York possible. These can be 'fun', but they are often just tools on the sidelines. Gimmicks.

The key question is: how can you become a true partner in the life of the consumer? The more you understand their context, the better you can see things from their perspective. Data will play a crucial role in this. Think, for example, of the enormous opportunities in healthcare. The data from our smartwatches, our smart digital scales or a scanner in our phone (to monitor our dietary intake) are just a few examples that generate an increasingly complete snapshot of the consumer's health. This consumer data can turn every company into a personal health coach.

Recently, I had the pleasure to visit the Chinese company iCarbonX. Their goal is to keep their customers' quality of life as high as possible, and for as long as possible. They've been going to great, and surprising, lengths to achieve this. If you join their program they insist, for example, that you install a smart toilet in your home. Every time someone uses the toilet, a stool sample is taken and the results of that test are kept on file. Thanks to this (and several other data sources) they can make accurate predictions about the evolution of your body. This provides consumers with information to take decisions and to stay healthy for longer.

3. Let's save the world TOGETHER

Many companies have started projects to help make the world a better place. It's encouraging to see how investments in sustainability and social projects have risen sharply over the past decade. However, these projects are often doubly disadvantaged. They are not part of the core business, and customers rarely know the nature and extent of a company's efforts. To alert customers to a company's efforts, customers need to be actively involved. If the customer feels that (s)he is helping create a better world, then there is a whole new level of engagement possible. For example, many consumers are proud to buy clothing from the Patagonia brand because they know that it is very sustainable, and even second hand clothes get a second life in their used-clothes market.

Another angle on this is Tesla. The first Tesla drivers were primarily tech-lovers, but they also often liked to stress that 'riding electric' is the future and how proud they are to have done their bit already. Organizations that manage to get consumers to join a movement to save the world (in some small way), add an extra layer to their customer relationship.

■ The offer you can't refuse

Companies that manage to combine these three strategies effectively create a product (or service) offering that customers will love. In fact, it becomes "an offer you can't refuse", to borrow a phrase from The Godfather. The combination of transactional perfection, helping to realize people's dreams and personal ambitions while, in the meantime, helping to solve a global problem is a robust proposition. Let me finish with an example of a company that succeeded in building such an offer: the Swedish company Spotify.

Practically everyone is a fan of Spotify, and they have grown exponentially in recent years. When the company was founded, the illegal downloading of music and films was still normal behavior. People went, in droves, to sites like 'The Pirate Bay' to grab their favorite music for free. When Daniel Ek and Martin Lorentzon launched the company, it looked a lot like a Don Quixote mission. Who, in God's name, would be prepared to pay a monthly fee to gain access to a music library if you could download whatever you wanted for free?

The two founders were convinced that 'speed' could outweigh 'for free'. If, back then, you wanted to download a song, you had to wait a while before you could listen to it. Spotify's objective was to have the music playing inside 200 milliseconds. They chose 200 milliseconds because, to human brains, that seems 'immediate'. They wanted to give people an interface in which all the music of Pirate Bay became (apparently) immediately accessible, for a small monthly fee. The ultra-fast interface was what attracted the first users.

As a later addition to the platform, playlists were introduced. With its smart algorithms, Spotify was a partner in the smart structuring of music, but also in the discovery of new songs in a chosen genre. Many music fans were instantly addicted to the playlists. Spotify was, thus, a partner in their organization and discovery of music.

Last but not least, consumers could overcome their latent feelings of guilt, via Spotify. No longer do they need to 'steal' from their favorite artist. Now they could listen, lawfully, to their favorite music in a user-friendly way. Spotify offers the consumer the chance to make the world slightly better.

The combination of these three levels of customer value offers customers a fantastic deal. They can gain very user-friendly access to a product, the company also becomes a partner in their daily life and, together, they make the world slightly better. Those three layers create an 'offer you can't refuse'.

II PLATFORM DISRUPTION: OPERATING IN THE AGE OF PLATFORMS

Amazon doesn't think like a retailer, it thinks as the retail industry. — SIMON WARDLEY

■ GE's uncomfortable platform journey

In September 2001, Jack Welch retired from General Electric, and handed the keys of what was then the most valuable company in the world to his hand-picked successor, Jeff Immelt, who had been working at GE since 1982. The company, famously co-founded by Thomas Edison to develop the business of incandescent light bulbs, had greatly diversified over the years. It was no longer associated with just one industry or one product, but with industrial innovation itself. It was an icon of business, and an icon of what managerial excellence could achieve.

During Welch's tenure at GE, the company's value had risen no less than 4,000%, and this had made him an extremely wealthy man. The market cap of General Electric stood at an all-time high of more than $600 billion when he announced his retirement. But by 2019, however, its market cap had fallen to less than $90 billion. In fact, GE did not even rank in the top 50 global market caps anymore. Its glory days were clearly over.

Jack Welch's nickname was 'Neutron Jack', a name he thoroughly despised. He had earned the moniker when he was appointed as GE's CEO in 1981. Within five years he had cut 118,000 jobs, or 25% of the workforce. So his nickname referred to the 'neutron bomb', as he seemed to master the detrimental ability of removing "bodies" from his organization while leaving the buildings standing.

Nobody embodied the 20th century management style better than Jack Welch. He was named the 'Toughest Boss in America', becoming famous for forcing the company's top management to either fix, sell or close its wide range of businesses. He introduced the world to the management practice of 'six sigma', the relentless and continuous drive for process improvement. Jack Welch was a ruthless improver, constantly trying to optimize, and he hated bureaucracy with an unwavering vengeance.

In the annual report of 2000, he wrote: "Bureaucracies love to focus inward. It's not that they dislike customers; they just don't find them as interesting as themselves." As well as "In a digitized world, the internal workings of companies will be exposed to the world, and bureaucracies will be seen by all for what they are: slow, self-absorbed, customer insensitive – even silly."[27]

That annual report shows a smiling Jack Welch next to his successor, glowing with a resolute belief in the digital future: "Digitization is transforming everything we do, energizing every corner of the company and making us faster, leaner and smarter even as we become bigger."

They had just acquired Honeywell, one of the major industrial conglomerates in the world, and 2000 had been a remarkable year of record-breaking business performance. Net revenues had grown to more than $129 billion, and 15 of the top 20 businesses within GE had posted double-digit earnings increases. The future was bright, and they were ready for change.

In Welch's words: "We've long believed that when the rate of change inside an institution becomes slower than the rate of change outside, the end is in sight. The only question is when. We strive every day to always have everyone in the organization see change as a thrilling, energizing phenomenon, relished by all, because it is the oxygen of our growth."

It seemed that his successor Jeff Immelt had been handed a poisoned chalice, though. First there had been the 9/11 catastrophe (only four days after he took the helm as CEO), and a few years later GE had been hit hard by the financial crisis of 2008. Over the years, much of its business had veered away from the core industrial, manufacturing and energy operations into insurance and financial services, through its GE Capital arm. Those businesses turned out to be extremely sensitive to market turbulences and the 2008 crisis nearly left GE insolvent. In fact, the company only survived the crisis thanks to a massive $139 billion in loan guarantees from the federal government.

Immelt wanted to steer GE back to its industrial roots and radically transform it into a visionary leader using digital. He envisioned a bold somersault from the industrial businesses into the age of platforms. Companies like Uber had been making waves by growing incredibly fast and generating massive revenues, just by leveraging data and owning virtually NO assets. Immelt talked up the analysts about making GE a "top 10 global software company." So he created GE Digital, an ambitious effort aimed at building a global 'digital platform' to handle the torrents of information created and captured by next-generation industrial machines.

It made a lot of sense.

Take plane engines. General Electric is an absolute world leader in jet engine manufacturing. If you fly in a Boeing 787 Dreamliner, the chances are very high that it is powered by two powerful GEnx engines (General Electric Next-generation) that cost about $25 million. These engines hold the power equivalent of almost 30 Formula-1 racing cars. But they are not just marvels of mechanical engineering, they're digital miracles as well.

In the good old days of Frank Whittle, turbojet engines were all about hydraulics, combustibles and high-grade precision mechanics. But today, these engines are filled with a myriad of sensors, measuring every aspect of an engine's performance and operation, and generating gigantic amounts of information.

The first wave of digital disruption was focused on consumers and it gave rise to the well-known platform-players such as Facebook and Google who took advantage of the exponential rise in information to fundamentally rewrite the business models and their marketing and communication.

Business-to-Business always seems to experience a certain 'lag' with respect to Business-to-Consumer, but it was not long after the rise of the 'consumer'-platforms, that companies like GE started to dream about what platforms could do to transform their own industrial businesses. Jet engines were 'streaming' information by the busloads: what if GE could harness that flow of information, and turn it into value?

▪ The same, but digital

So General Electric became the champion of 'digital twins'. This concept is to create a virtualized replica of an actual facility or plant, or in this case, an aircraft engine. The digital twin of the GEnx engine is a 'carbon-copy' that is based on all the information that streams from the sensors of the real engine. These twins are used to monitor the 'real' engine, and to optimize and maximize performance. Companies like GE can use them to understand their products better, by modeling different scenarios, with a goal of making proactive instead of reactive decisions.

They also could radically transform the business model.

Instead of 'selling' an engine, General Electric could sell 'Power by the Hour' to aircraft carriers. Airlines could essentially 'use' a GE engine, and only pay for the time that they actually powered a flying airplane. For the aircraft carrier, the option is extremely financially tempting. Instead of shelling out $25 million for an engine, they would use the option to consume the 'Engine-As-A-Service'.

But for General Electric, it could provide an incredible advantage as well. It has more than 30,000 aircraft engines powering airplanes on the planet. With the combined data streaming from this vast array of engines, GE is sitting on a goldmine of information: it could easily optimize the output and efficiency of those engines and provide an economy of scale in terms of information that no one else in the world could ever approach. True, they would no longer receive their $25 million up front, but over the lifetime of an engine, they could optimize their insights to generate a lot more bottom line from the turbojet. Today, every jet engine that GE produces – 70 percent of the world's total – has a digital twin.

Jeff Immelt, and many analysts, had high hopes for GE Digital. He believed it could turn around the business and transform GE into a more technologically focused enterprise. The concept of the digital twins resulted in their industrial platform called Predix. However, it turned out to be a daunting and complex challenge that faced costly delays and technological issues.

■ A GEar too slow

But it turned out to be too little too late. The tragic part is that the vision of the digital transformation of the industrial world, and the rise of platform thinking based on data, was absolutely brilliant. But the first tangible results of Predix and GE Digital were too slow to materialize, and in the meantime the problems in GE's legacy businesses kept growing. By the time Immelt retired in 2017, more than a half-trillion dollars in market value had been wiped out since that all-time high 18 years earlier. That's about the Gross Domestic Product of Belgium, or roughly the market value of Facebook, that disappeared into thin air. Poof. Just like that.

Then poor, poor John Flannery took over from Immelt. Had he been in Star Trek, he would surely have owned a Red Uniform. Let me explain: the 'real' Trekkies noticed that the red-uniformed personnel surrounding the main Star Trek characters tended to suffer quick and violent deaths. Those wearing yellow or blue seemed to have a lot more luck. But not John Flannery. Nope. He lasted less than 12 months as CEO. Every-time the poor guy opened his mouth in press briefings, the stock of GE went crashing down.

The company that had introduced the light bulb to the world, that had built the first electric power station in the US, the first nuclear power plant, and that was supplying the world with jet engines, was crashing down. "We bring good things to life" was the long-time GE slogan, but 128 years after it was born, this former giant was on the verge of dying.

The digital transformation of GE into a powerful platform player for the industrial world had failed miserably. After the implosion, more and more evidence surfaced that there had been a huge disconnect between the rosy rhetoric of Jeff Immelt, and the harsh reality of GE Digital. The initiative actually ended up like an internal development shop to supply IT to the various businesses of GE instead of soaring high like the radical business model transformation it had been intended to be. When Immelt claimed that Predix was already presenting $1 billion in revenue with only 1,500 employees, this was merely internal billing to GE's other business units. There were NO external customers.

GE fell into the trap that many companies encounter when they go through a digital transformation: they think that adding technology to the existing model will suffice. It never does. True digital transformation is about fundamentally rethinking your business model for the 21st century. Just don't make the same mistake as GE. You'll end up with an army of Red Shirts.

■ The (dumb) pipes, the pipes are calling

When you hear the horror story of GE's collapsed digital transformation, you might very well be thinking something along the lines of: "Let's stay clear away from these platforms. That's just risky business with a high chance of failure."

Perhaps. But consider the alternative: what if you don't.

Industries change all the time and business models evolve constantly, faster than ever before. We're living out the Schumpeterian prophecy of creative destruction[28] but in fast-forward and at 10X speed. If you stay in your comfort zone, you risk succumbing to the 'Dumb Pipe Syndrome'.

I have a personal history in the telecoms sector: as I wrote in chapter 2 on the Hourglass model, my very first (and only) employee experience was at telecoms giant Alcatel and a few years later, I sold my first startup to that very same company. When I was a young engineer, I liked to spend my lunch breaks wandering through its engineering halls where copies of the old 'telephone exchanges' were stored. These giant switching machines would connect the right 'wires' to allow telephone conversations to take place. They would diligently click and hum, and act as the network hubs of the telephone 'pipes'.

Companies like AT&T, T-Mobile and Vodafone have all driven countless technological innovations in the course of their history. AT&T, for example, is one of the world's largest telecom companies and its original corporate structure dates back to Alexander Graham Bell himself, who started the company when he invented the telephone. For no less than 120 years, AT&T had survived with its original business model essentially intact: 'connecting people'.

The business of AT&T resulted from extracting value from connectivity, but the technology to do so has radically been disrupted, time and time again. In the early days you had manual telephone operators setting up the right connections. Then came the massive disruption of 'automatic' telephone exchanges where people could 'dial' the number themselves. And another tidal wave arrived in the form of mobile connectivity. They were each and every one of them brutal transitions. But where the technological landscape for AT&T changed constantly, the fundamental value proposition remained pretty much unspoiled. AT&T was still 'connecting people'.

Then, all of a sudden, over the course of just a few years, the former telecom kings like AT&T found themselves completely dis-intermediated by a small number of radically new 'platform' players. The latter captured and controlled the value-add information flowing through the networks, and they basically reduced the telecom carriers to 'dumb pipes'.

The most beautiful illustration of that is when you land in a foreign country and switch off your phone's airplane-mode. You may receive a selection of a few mobile carriers to choose from. But what is the difference between them? Do you have any idea which of these carriers will offer you a better service? You don't. As a matter of fact, most people have programmed their phones to select these carriers automatically. They're all the same anyway, why waste our time selecting one? All these carriers have been reduced to the status of 'dumb pipes' and they are locked in a death spiral of diminishing costs. Why? Because when your telecom subscription provides you with 'unlimited' bandwidth, they will never be able to trump 'unlimited'. The only way to outsmart the other dumb-pipe competitors is by offering the service at a lower and lower price.

■ Essential? Or relevant?

At the same time, we see how platforms like Facebook and WeChat have positioned themselves 'on top' of the dumb pipes (the OTT, or 'Over The Top' players). They are the ones capturing a significant part of the value of mobile customers. They act as a 'platform' that captures user information to understand customers, turns that into practical services (like maps, taxis, content, or advertising) and then goes on to monetize that offering. These OTT players don't have to build expensive mobile networks, put pylons all over the place, and run huge operating centers to keep the mobile phones humming. They

merrily let the 'dumb pipes' spend all that money so that they can make billions by providing 'value added' services and content to the users.

All of this boils down to a very basic discussion: who is 'essential' and who is 'relevant'?

I would argue that when I started using mobile phones about 25 years ago, my telecom carrier was both essential AND relevant.

They were certainly essential. You couldn't operate your cell phone without a working SIM-card, supplied by the telecom carriers. If you didn't pay your bill, they could simply shut you off and disconnect you from the network. And they were relevant. They provided me with the capabilities to connect to and call colleagues, friends and family whenever and wherever I wanted. They supplied me with effective communication and basic services like text-messaging. They offered elementary directory services that allowed me to call a number to find an address, or somebody's phone number. They were essential, AND relevant. Back then, I mean.

Fast forward 25 years. Telecom carriers are STILL essential. I still need that SIM card for my phone, tablet or watch. Of course I can connect to a Wi-Fi signal, but these are not yet ubiquitous enough. We're still waiting for Elon Musk to launch enough satellites to allow me to connect everywhere in the world without my telecom carrier.

But essential though they (still) are, telecom carriers have almost completely lost their relevance. They have become dumb pipes: a non-differentiated commodity, providing virtually no real added value. When I want to look something up, I'll use Google. When I have to see where I am I'll use Google Maps or another app. When I want to connect to my family, I'll probably use WhatsApp. I use the services of platforms which are VERY relevant to me.

We see this phenomenon over and over again. It follows a pattern of disruption and commoditization.

A value-added provider – like telecoms operators used to be – are both essential AND relevant. Because of (technological) disruption, the added value erodes, and the provider becomes a Dumb Pipe. Then there are two strategic options to consider. You can innovate, leverage the power of 'platform' innovation and try to move 'up' towards offering new added value for your customers. Or you can stay in your swimming lane, and try to become an even Bigger Dumb Pipe to compensate for your dwindling margins.

Don't get me wrong, the latter is not necessarily a WRONG strategy. It is absolutely possible to grow, and very profitably, this way. Some company could very well become the biggest, and possibly the most profitable, dumb pipe. That is, until some technological disruption will change the equation once again, and they could lose it all.

In a way it is ironic to recognize that a player like AT&T helped make the 'digital revolution' possible, by the very nature of their 'dumb pipes'. But the revolution that they underpinned is now radically changing the rules of the game, and they are losing out. Somewhere up there Schumpeter must be smiling.

Largest Global Companies in 2018 vs 2008

2018

RANK	COMPANY	FOUNDED	USD
1.	APPLE*	1976	890
2.	GOOGLE*	1998	768
3.	MICROSOFT*	1975	680
4.	AMAZON.COM*	1994	592
5.	FACEBOOK*	2004	545
6.	TENCENT*	1998	526
7.	BERKSHIRE HATHAWAY	1955	496
8.	ALIBABA*	1999	488
9.	JOHNSON & JOHNSON	1886	380
10.	J. P. MORGAN	1871	375

2008

RANK	COMPANY	FOUNDED	USD
1.	PETROCHINA	1999	728
2.	EXXON	1870	492
3.	GE	1892	358
4.	CHINA MOBILE	1997	344
5.	ICBC	1984	336
6.	GAZPROM	1989	332
7.	MICROSOFT	1975	313
8.	SHELL	1907	266
9.	SINOPEC	2000	257
10.	AT&T	1885	238

* companies based on the platform model

SOURCE: BLOOMBERG, GOOGLE

■ Rage against the platforms

Someone in the 21st century will undoubtedly win a Nobel Prize for their explanation of the workings of platform-economics.

One of the strangest phenomena to flow from the rise of platform players is the birth of 'Category Kings': the absolute winner-take-all survivors in the age of disruption. In Europe, the market share of Google in search amounts to over 95%. Category King, clearly. Who is number 2? Well, nobody cares, right?

It has now become fashionable to frown upon the rise of these platforms and question their dominance in an industry. One of the most visible anti-platform evangelists is Scott Galloway, an early e-commerce pioneer, and occasional professor at New York University. In his book 'The Four: The Hidden DNA of Amazon, Apple, Facebook and Google' he criticizes the out-sized influence of the GAFA, and feels that they have so much power, influence and market-share that they should be broken up.

Galloway claims these four have grown to become almost like 'gods' of the 21st century, in that they are able to satisfy very basic human needs in an incredibly efficient and addictive way. "Die Religion ist das Opium des Volkes," wrote Karl Marx, loosely translated as 'Religion is the opium of the people'. Galloway claims that the GAFA are becoming the digital opiates of our era. The four major platform players have a combined value greater than the GDP of all but four countries on Earth. According to Galloway, together they are more politically powerful than any country in the world other than the US or China.

These platforms have also completely reshaped the laws of finance. Galloway argues that Amazon, through the excellent narrative of Jeff Bezos, has reshaped investor expectations, providing it with an abundance of long-term capital, at the expense of everyone else in the industry. The futurist Simon Wardley notes that Amazon inherently uses its ecosystem as a "future sensing engine" continuously eating a larger part of an even larger cake and that it is fated to conquer an even larger part of the market. In his words: "Amazon doesn't think like a retailer, it thinks as the retail industry."

■ Fair? Or clever?

Today it is not just high-profile professors taking aim at the platforms but it has clearly become a political theme. In the run up to the American presidential race in 2020, one of the democratic candidates, Elizabeth Warren, put up a big billboard in San Francisco, in the eye line of many tech-industry commuters that read: "Break Up Big Tech." Alexandria Ocasio-Cortez, one of the most vocal left-wing American politicians, called the dominance and monopoly of the new platform players "societally and economically unsustainable."

These sentiments articulate the political belief that these platform players should be 'broken' up, just like President Roosevelt broke up the holdings of the railroad barons. Or just like the breaking up of Rockefeller's Standard Oil Company. More recently in the eighties, the monopoly in the world of telephony was shattered when the Department of Justice broke up 'Ma Bell'.

The fundamental debate here is if these platform phenomena are 'Fair' or if the companies that operate them were merely being 'Clever'. I'm sure that if you work at Facebook, or Google, you don't think that what you do is 'unfair'. It's a different thing altogether when you corner a market, or squeeze out the competition, or even collude with competitors to rig up prices and manipulate the market. But these platforms evolved because WE as consumers WANTED to use them.

For instance, I'm a big fan of Waze. It's the dominant platform for those who want to find their way through traffic, but no one is FORCING us to use it. As a matter of fact, I love to use it, and I love to give it access to my information. The reason is that, as a consumer, the more information I give to Waze, the more intelligent its recommendations will be, and the more value I will get back as a result. With each extra data entry, Waze becomes better at navigating me through traffic.

I don't think that these platforms 'attract users like magnets'. It's actually the other way around. We, as consumers, 'feed' the platforms with data. We're constantly 'feeding the beasts', just like in that movie Gremlins. And we love those furry and cute animals at first. But when we feed them a little bit too much data, they turn into nasty horrible beasts.

And then we have to fine them.

In 2018, the European Commission gave Alphabet a whopping $5 billion fine as the dominance of the Android mobile operating system was an 'unfair economic' advantage, and therefore led to unfair business practices. Margrethe Vestager, the European commissioner in charge of competition claimed that "They have denied European consumers the benefits of effective competition in the important mobile sphere."[29] The ruling is highly questionable, and Bloomberg in an editorial stated: "Because Google's apps benefit from network effects and the power of Big Data, they get better as they become more popular. The better they are, in turn, the more people want them."[30] In other words, maybe the reason why these platforms demonstrate 'Category King' behavior is intrinsic to the way that platforms work?

Why would I join another social network if all of my friends are on Facebook? What if digital, connectivity and network effects by their very nature steer economics towards the generation of Category Kings? Does it still make sense to break them up, then?

Maybe we have to embrace platform economics as the New Normal, and we need to ask ourselves one crucial question: "Can I become a platform, or will I be a supplier to a platform?" In other words: will you be Batman, or Robin? This question seems loaded with judgment. However, to me, it is not. There's no judgment here. Not everyone can (or even should) be a platform. But I want you to think long and hard about the role of your company, should platform economics indeed become the norm. Do you fight the other platforms by becoming one yourself (huge benefits, but also huge risks), or join it, and use it to grow and better service your customers (low risk, and lower benefits).

■ Digital Ecosystems in the "We Economy"

In 1923 the Brit Arthur George Tansley spent a full year in Vienna studying psychology under Sigmund Freud. But when he returned to England he devoted the rest of his life to botany. He was the one who introduced the term 'ecosystem' to the world, to describe a community of organisms interacting with each other and their environment. In order to thrive, these organisms must compete and collaborate with each other on available resources, they must co-evolve, and jointly adapt to external disruptions.

It was the American business strategist James Moore – specialized in co-evolution in social and economic systems – who applied Arthur Tansley's biological concept of ecosystems to the world of business. In 1993 he authored the Harvard Business Review article called 'Predators and Prey: A New Ecology of Competition'.

In his article, Moore suggested that a company should not be viewed as a single firm within an industry, but rather as a member of a business ecosystem with participants spanning across multiple industries.

In todays 'networked times', with technology and globalization simultaneously shrinking the business world while speeding it up, the idea of a business ecosystem is an excellent way to help companies understand how to thrive. A business ecosystem consists of a network of interconnected companies that dynamically interact with each other through competition and cooperation to grow and survive. When an ecosystem thrives, it means that its participants have developed patterns of behavior that streamline the flow of ideas, talent, and capital throughout the system.

Each entity of an ecosystem affects and is affected by the others. This generates a constantly evolving network of relationships in which each entity must be flexible and adaptable in order to survive, just like in a biological ecosystem.

Paul Daugherty is the Chief Technology Officer of Accenture, and I've had the pleasure to collaborate with him on many occasions. I love his concept of the 'We Economy'. In his words: "The rapid evolution of technology is rewriting the business playbooks. Digital ecosystems are re-shaping entire markets and changing the way we work and live."

Tapping into the power of digital ecosystems creates opportunities that have the potential to bring about change on a global scale, faster than ever before. It realizes ambitions that transcend any single business or industry.

One of the most interesting sectors where we see ecosystems evolve, and transform an industry is in the world of healthcare. I personally believe that this is the #1 sector where the rules will be fundamentally rewritten over the course of the 21st century. Today, we may call it 'healthcare', but what we actually have is a system of 'sickcare' that treats patients when they become ill. We are in fact the last generation of humans to know so little about our bodies. Breakthroughs in sensors, measurement systems and algorithms to make sense of all this data, could fundamentally transform our ideas of treating disease, and truly reverse 'sickcare' into 'healthcare'.

■ An Apple a day...

The Apple Healthkit is an excellent example of such an ecosystem and platform evolution. Apple already launched this tool in 2014, at the same time they introduced their Health app. The app is for users and patients, but underneath it sits a set of APIs that allow fitness apps, activity trackers, sleep monitors, blood-pressure or glucose monitors, mindfulness apps or nutritional apps to streamline all the relevant health-related information into the Apple platform. These allow it to function as an open digital ecosystem platform which brings together all sorts of participants from across the world of medicine: from physicians, researchers, hospitals, and patients to developers of healthcare and fitness applications. The Mayo clinic,[31] for instance, was an early and very significant supporter.

The number of apps using the platform has been steadily growing since then and there are now millions of users that connect through the Apple Healthkit to track and stream their health-related information. All this data will allow the Apple platform to play a significant role in the development of new medicines, but it could also play a role in treatments, or in insurance. It forms a digital ecosystem, with Apple as the orchestrator of the many flows of health data, and the numerous connected parties involved.

Apple's move into health makes absolutely solid business sense: by integrating itself into the management of potentially life-long medical conditions, the company is creating a powerful reason to 'stick' to its products and services. It's one thing to switch to another phone, or watch, but when it concerns some of your most sensitive, even vital information, you might feel even less compelled to do so. Apple is increasingly positioning itself as the guardian of our privacy, and health could turn out to be one of the most important features in its portfolio.

■ JumPING to ANother market

But maybe we should look to the East for the most remarkable example of ecosystem and platform thinking, with the transformation of one of the largest insurance companies in the world: Ping An.

We tend to associate insurance companies with these old, stuffy and static institutions residing in stately buildings filled with grey-haired, grey-dressed and grey-minded clerks. Ping An – which means "peace and safety" in Mandarin – is different. Very different.

It was founded in Shenzhen in 1988. Only eight years earlier – in 1980 – Shenzhen had been launched as China's first special economic zone, and it was destined to become the East's very own version of 'Silicon Valley'. But it evolved far beyond that, into a unique Chinese blend of capital, innovation, technology and entrepreneurship.

Ping An is a beautiful consequence of that fertile cocktail. It started off with a fledgling staff of 13 and in just 30 years has evolved into a global financial powerhouse with more than 1,600,000 employees, and with three core businesses: insurance, banking and investments.

And then it decided to become the greatest healthcare platform in the world.

Peter Ma Mingzhe, the chairman and CEO of Ping An describes it like this: "Not only must we be the insurance expert for every one of our customers, we must

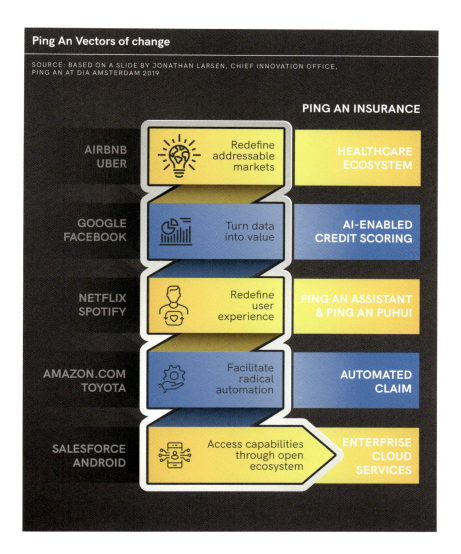

be their expert financial consultant and their assistant in every aspect of their lives." *Every* aspect of their lives. That means that Ping An not only wants to give you advice on your life insurance, it just as much wants to coach you on your health. So it controls both your death *and* your life. Clever.

At the end of 2018, more than 265 million customers had already registered to use Ping An Good Doctor, a platform that connects doctors and patients for bookings, online diagnoses, and suggested treatments. The platform had signed up over 3,000 hospitals and over 15,000 pharmacies in a record time. It now also operates a one-hour drug delivery service in almost 100 Chinese cities.

In 2019, Ping An went one step further and introduced its unmanned AI-driven "One-minute Clinic" booths, which allow patients to receive immediate medical services, including diagnosis and medicine prescriptions 24/7. These booths offer online consultations for more than 2,000 common conditions and tens of thousands of medical and health queries. Patients sit in the three-square meter clinic and chat with a doctor 'in the cloud' about their symptoms. Outside the clinic, there is a vending machine where you can directly procure the treatments and medication based on your consult.

All the data from the platform, the clinics and their users is constantly used to make the platform smarter. The beating heart of the ecosystem is the 'AI Doctor', developed by the Ping An R&D team with over 200 world-class AI experts. It has accumulated hundreds of millions of pieces of consultation data. The platform is being constantly nourished with healthcare data; the beast is always being fed.

In record time, Ping An Good Doctor has become China's one-stop healthcare ecosystem platform. In a country that is plagued by a monumental shortage of doctors, the company addressed an acute customer need in the smartest of manners. I love how they realized that if they kept focusing on their core business of finance and insurance, they would be in danger of becoming just another dumb pipe. Instead, they grabbed the potential of platform innovation with both hands and transformed from financial services provider into a 'health butler', allowing their customers to lead higher quality lives. They did not make GE's classic mistake of digitizing their existing business into a platform. Instead, they went for a new model, a new market and reinvented themselves like a Phoenix. They are also an excellent example of what Paul Dougherty calls the 'We Economy'.

Jonathan Larsen is the Chief Innovation Officer of Ping An. He was instrumental in turning the company into the major healthcare platform player in the region. We stand to learn a lot from the five key learnings of his company's transformation, or "the new vectors of the data economy" as he himself calls them.

The first of these is "redefining addressable markets". Think Uber. They were not replacing yellow cabs, they were addressing mobility for everybody, everywhere. In reference to the platform examples of Google and Facebook, he sees the second ingredient as "turning data into value." "The third ingredient is 'Redefining user experiences'": as the latter has been reshaped by the Netflixes and Spotifys of this world, patients want the same kind of top-notch seamless experience in healthcare. The fourth ingredient, according to Larsen, is 'facilitating radical automation'. As he states: "Our whole company was pivoted to becoming a technology-led company. The first thing was to go all-cloud, but it also meant replacing all legacy platforms across the company." Finally, if you want to succeed in this platform transformation, it means you have to learn how to leverage technology to access a wide range of new capabilities through the power of ecosystems. That meant a whole new mentality in the company, a fresh perspective on change, as Larsen concludes: "All these vectors of change came entirely from outside of the financial industry."

When asked why Ping An was so successful in reinventing itself, Jonathan remarks that: "We have, as a company, a fundamental innovation mindset. At the start of every year our CEO sends out a self-assessment. It's basically his scorecard. The first page is creating a permanent sense of crisis in the company. It's his assessment of how well we're doing and that includes challenging everything that we do, from the bottom up, all the time. So that's part of the culture." In other words, the company fosters this huge sense of urgency when it comes to innovation: they're basically in permanent crisis mode to make sure that everyone realized how crucial Phoenix-like self-reinvention is to their survival. There is no comfort-zone, only uncertainty and a great big hunger.

▪ Not just for the giants

Now, I'm sure that many of you think that only the truly giant corporates will be able to reinvent their atoms business into a platform model. I beg to differ. Above all, you need a powerful blend of pragmatic intelligence and chutzpah. Like in the case of my company nexxworks' customer: the 60-year-old family business Aertssen Group. This Belgian-based company has about

COPYRIGHT AERTSSEN

1,300 employees spread over 31 countries and operates in the construction and infrastructure industry. If we're being honest, it is not exactly an industry known for its digitization efforts.

The platform thinking at Aertssen started out very humble, but it has enormous potential. In fact, the company basically 'just' wanted to streamline a very tedious and stressful internal process in a more efficient manner. Every day, the Aertssen planners had to rent heavy machinery for their projects and – seeing that this could only be done 'efficiently' by phone – it was decided to completely digitize this repetitive and time-consuming task. It may not sound very 'sexy', but the planners ended up renting the materials 75% faster, and making 55% fewer mistakes.

And then the cunning Aertssen management realized that this internal efficiency-driven tool could have an enormous market potential. So they launched the platform Smartyard to the outside world, so that it would allow others – yes, a lot of competitors as well – to hire or rent out heavy construction machinery a lot faster, with less friction and ultimately, more efficiently. It's a pure platform approach, much like Uber or Airbnb. Smartyard does not own any machinery, it merely brings interested parties together and simplifies a process that used to be exceedingly friction-heavy. And the data underlying these interactions is used to continuously improve the experience. Just like with their core business of construction, Aertssen has big plans for launching Smartyard internationally, fully aware that the asset-sharing and the peer-to-peer economy still holds a lot of potential for growth.

Has it been a walk in the park? Of course not. Yves Aertssen, Co-CEO of the Aertssen Group is very open about the fact that the Smartyard startup and digital mentality sometimes clashes with the atom-based and more traditional way of thinking of the rest of the company. But the fact that adaptation to the market and innovation has always been a strong part of the company's DNA, is a big help. Aertssen has, in fact, always been a true Phoenix. And now that entire industries are evolving towards the platform economy, it's only logical that Aertssen is looking in that direction too. I can't help but be proud that our nexxworks Innovation Programs team has played a part in triggering the 'top of the Hourglass' Smartyard idea at one of our bootcamps. But that's a different story.

■ Operating in the age of platforms

Jennifer Schenker has been covering the tech industry in Europe since 1985. In 'The Innovator', the business executive's publication that she founded in

2016, she wrote: "At the beginning of 2019, seven of the 10 most valuable companies are now based on a platform business model: the creation of digital communities and marketplaces that allow different groups to interact and transact."

This is an age where physical borders no longer pose limitations for competition. Digital platforms and ecosystems have replaced and outmaneuvered traditional market operations, disrupting the old systems of intermediaries. The constant evolution of technology like Big Data, the cloud and artificial intelligence offers a quantum leap forward in capabilities, and all these changes are taking place faster than ever before, through flexible, scalable and open systems.

But as we discussed earlier: not every Phoenix will become a Platform. Some might be a Robin instead of a Batman: they will become the suppliers of a platform.

So how can you prepare? How can you learn to dance the platform dance? There are three things that you need to keep in mind.

1. Agility AND Scale
Muhammad Ali, nicknamed "The Greatest", is revered as one of the toughest and most expert boxers of all time. Most of us know him from his most famous quote "Float like a butterfly, sting like a bee", uttered just before his legendary match against Sonny Liston, who had been the world heavyweight champion until they fought. Ali was famous for being so quick on his feet that he practically danced around his opponents, but he also packed a hard and mean punch.

This perfectly describes the state of play that companies need to embody to be most effective in the age of networks. They have to focus on agility, being open-minded and having an extremely active long-range scan: in other words, they need a thoroughly developed 'top of the Hourglass'. At the same time, they have to 'sting like a bee': they need the power, efficiency and scale to 'knock out' the competition, and massively deploy solutions throughout the network. That's where their 'bottom of the Hourglass' needs to kick in. If you want to make it as a platform, you need Agility AND Scale.

2. Connected AND Controlled
In the age of networks, hierarchies are losing their relevance. Networks foster independence and thrive on creativity and risk-taking in all aspects of the organization. Decentralized creativity can unlock innovative entrepreneurship in all nodes of the network. But, as the great examples of the platform

approaches of Ping An and Apple Healthkit illustrate, you need a clear guiding direction, a north-star of strategy.

Ecosystems thrive because of the network effects. They are a true celebration of 'connected' actors and information. But successful platform orchestrators balance that with clear 'control', not by using the classic 'top-down' mechanisms of the past, but by clearly guiding the 'collective' towards new opportunities and direction.

3. Value for the beast AND the consumer

Concerns over 'privacy' and the 'control' and power that platforms have over their users are growing. A lot of us are scared that we have overfed the beasts. But let's be honest: platforms and ecosystems are *absolutely* economic phenomena. They exist to make money. And the more information and data they have, the more they can tailor offerings and services, the higher quality their value proposition, and the stickier these platforms become.

But. Customers will only stay if *they* sense this value creation and feel they are profiting from it as well. Just like in the case of Disney's MagicBands, where people don't complain about privacy because they receive value in return. True, Disney becomes smarter and richer, but the guests enjoy better services and experiences because of it. When you look at Ping An, the amount of information that flows through the Ping An Good Doctor network is incredible, and the more the beast is fed, the better it gets. But the added value for the patient is very tangible, transforming the traditional practice of medical consultation and enabling users to experience quality medical and healthcare solutions.

Value creation has to be bi-modal: feeding the beast will create enormous value for the platform and the ecosystem, as long as the customer feels that it's a fair exchange. They will keep feeding the beast if their personal perceived added value is real, effective and instrumental.

■ To the platforms, and beyond

The rise of ecosystems and platforms marks a fundamental shift in the business landscape: adventitious alliances are forged, the boundaries between markets and sectors are blurring. Clearly, long-standing power or influence counts for a lot less than it did in the past. This might be the most interesting economic systemic shift since the advent of the industrial revolution. And this is just the very beginning.

What can we take away from some of these narratives?

1. Platforms are more than a narrative

It's fashionable to talk about platforms and ecosystems. But rhetoric is not the same as fundamental business transformation. The GE example showed in painful detail what happens when you are brilliant at Talking The Talk, but horrible at Walking The Walk. There was a wide and growing disconnect between the promise of platforms in the industrial world, and the reality of the success of GE Digital. In the end two CEOs ended up going down in flames.

2. Challenge yourself on the Dumb Pipe roadmap

Are you at risk of becoming a Dumb Pipe in your market, industry or business? The telecom example is crystal clear, and it forces many companies to ask themselves if they are essential for their customers, and if they are truly relevant. Telco companies have been dealing with this existential crisis for quite some time, but now we are seeing the Dumb Pipe syndrome surfacing in many markets. It's appearing in finance, in banking and insurance...

As we discussed, becoming the most lucrative, biggest Dump Pipe is not necessarily a bad strategy in itself. But keep challenging yourself, and your organization, on the Dumb Pipe roadmap. Are you at risk of transforming into a Dumb Pipe? Would becoming an even bigger Dumb Pipe make any sense, if so? Think about what kind of player would be able to innovate at a 'platform' level in your industry, to provide value to customers on TOP of your market's Dumb Pipes?

3. Batman or Robin?

You can question whether platforms are 'fair', or just 'clever'. But the fundamental truth is that they become stronger the more they are used. They understand the power of 'feeding the beast'. And then you have to consider your options. Join them, or beat them. McDonalds decided to catch the opportunities of the home-delivery platform players by joining them. They teamed up with Uber Eats, instead of building their own platform. Decide what you want to do to leverage the possibilities of platforms: will you be a supplier, or do you want to be the platform? Do you want to be Batman or Robin?

4. Ride the Vectors of change

Ping An has leveraged the five 'vectors of change' to reinvent their insurance company into a healthcare platform. They redefined addressable markets. They turned data into value. They redefined user experiences. They facilitated radical automation. And they leveraged the power of open ecosystems. Above all, they proved that this can only happen if the entire organization is ready for disruption. Reinventing yourself necessitates a whole new mentality in the company and a fresh perspective on change.[32]

III CULTURAL DISRUPTION: THE CULTURE OF TRANSFORMATION

I have never tried that before, so I think I should definitely be able to do it. — PIPPI LONGSTOCKING [33]

Over the years, I've had the honor to encounter hundreds of companies, organizations and institutions all around the world and to observe their amazingly varied corporate cultures.

No two corporate cultures are exactly alike. They each have a unique fingerprint, allowing them to innovate and to grow, and yet it is virtually impossible to define what it specifically stands for. You can try to 'describe' a corporate culture, but it is inconceivable to fully 'identify' them, and just as hard to change them. Yet, as the famous line by Peter Drucker[34] goes: "Culture eats Strategy for breakfast."

You can try and understand a company before you join, read up on all the GlassDoor reviews to try to contemplate what it will be like, but it's only when you walk through the door and submerge yourself in the organization that you'll fully sense the 'smell of the place'.

■ The smell of Fontainebleau in the spring

That 'smell' refers to the late Sumantra Ghoshal, an incredibly gifted Professor of Strategic and International Management at the London Business School, who sadly passed away way too early, at the age of 55 in 2004. He was one of the top thinkers of his time, and he will always be remembered for his legendary speech at the World Economic Forum (WEF) in Davos. Ghoshal was born in Calcutta, the capital of India's West Bengal state, an incredibly vibrant and dense Indian megacity. He had also spent years teaching at INSEAD, the French business school that is situated in Fontainebleau, a splendid, densely forested area South of Paris.

In his famous WEF talk, Ghoshal compares the fatigue of downtown Calcutta in the summertime, with the freshness of the Fontainebleau forests in springtime. He brilliantly describes how each environment causes a very different energy and distinct type of behavior. If you've never seen his talk, just Google "The Smell of the Place", and watch the 8-minute video right now. Unfortunately, the quality of the video comes from a pre-Youtube era, but its content is still very valid today.

One small excerpt: "Go to the forest in Fontainebleau with the firm desire to have a leisurely walk, and you simply can't. The moment you enter the forest, there is something about the crispness of the air, about the smell of the trees in the spring, you want to jog or catch a branch or DO something… Most companies, particularly large companies, have created downtown Calcutta in summer inside themselves and then they complain."

Ghoshal claims that most workplaces today are unfortunately NOT like Fontainebleau in the spring, but much more like the very hot and humid Calcutta in the summer: the energy is low and people are tired and constrained. He argues that in these workplaces, the conditions that sap energy are driven by "Constraint, Compliance, Control and Contract." Workers feel Constrained by their organization and the processes that govern them. They sense they are primarily there to Comply with the rules, planning cycles and budgeting systems, that their 'boss', management and infrastructure are primarily there to Control them, and that their job is merely a Contractual obligation. Clearly, these values don't create the right context for people to proactively create change, take initiative, or cooperate towards the Day After Tomorrow.

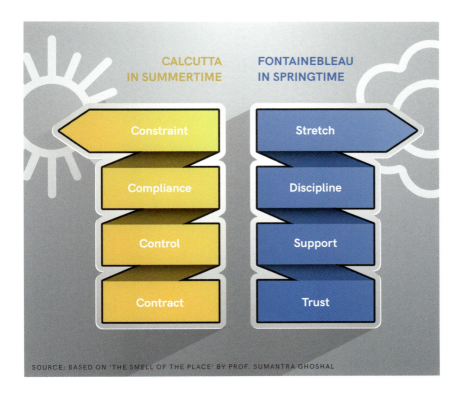

SOURCE: BASED ON 'THE SMELL OF THE PLACE' BY PROF. SUMANTRA GHOSHAL

At the opposite end of the spectrum, lies Fontainebleau in the spring. This is where leaders create conditions that trigger employees to reach for higher goals, where the energy is high and people are intrinsically motivated and excited. He argues that business leaders must create a context that values "Stretch, Discipline, Trust and Support."

This is an environment where workers are Stretched to do more rather than less, are Self-Disciplined in their engagements and commitments, see their leaders as mechanisms to Support them, and can operate creatively in a system of Trust.

I can absolutely vouch for Sumantra Ghoshal's observation. The moment I walk through the doors of a company, its vibrant 'Smell of the Place' rolls over me like an aromatic wave.

What is very clear is that culture is not a mono-dimensional concept. You can't put it on 'one' axis and then plot companies from left to right. There are many different facets that make up the complete 'culture portfolio' of an organization, and that define what 'smell' it gives. Just like you can't plot humans on a mono-dimensional axis to rank their abilities.

■ Culture is a web

One of the clearest mechanisms to understand this phenomenon is the template developed by Kevin Scholes and Gerry Johnson, who have co-authored some of the leading textbooks on corporate strategy in the last twenty years. Their model of the 'Cultural Web' and its 6 vectors still proves to be a very elegant way to explore the dimensions and complexity of corporate culture.

Stories and Myths: Organizations are characterized by stories. These are the narratives that cover pivotal moments and legendary people inside and outside of the organization. Who are the super-heroes and -heroines of the corporate narrative, and who are the villains? What are the plotlines and the cliffhangers? Leaders like Jeff Bezos, with his huge charisma and his "two pizza team" or "customer at the table" discourse, are experts at shaping and stimulating company culture through these recognizable and appealing stories.

Rituals and Routines: Companies are characterized by patterns of systematic behaviors that they perceive as completely 'normal'. These rituals and routines will determine what 'should' happen in particular situations. They can be positive (like the best practices of a customer service department), neutral (like who can fly business class) or negative (such as elements like sexism or

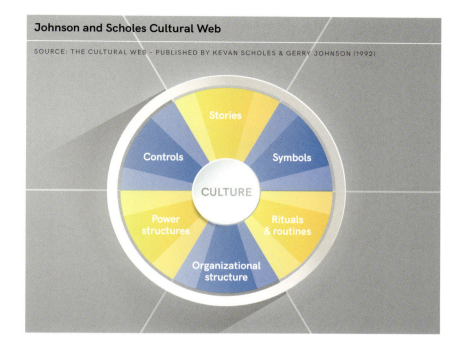

bullying). A positive example could be the empowerment of customer service employees at Zappos, who can control their own time and budget to better please customers. A negative could be that of the gender discrimination problems that surfaced at Uber in 2018.

Symbols: Remember the symbolism of a 'corner' office before we had open workspaces? Or the inflatable unicorns or ping-pong tables in a 'typical' start-up environment? Symbols can extend all the way to the branding of an organization, perfectly demonstrated by the 'uniform' that Steve Jobs wore during the later years of his life, the same outfit nearly every single day: a pair of blue Levi jeans, grey New Balance sneakers, and a black turtleneck designed by Issey Miyake. A repetitive approach that has since been copied by many well-known entrepreneurs, like Mark Zuckerberg and his grey t-shirt and ex-Theranos Elisabeth Holmes and her black turtleneck. These cultural symbols are not just about logos and fonts, even clothes – up till what the employees are allowed (or not) to wear – are never 'just' clothes inside companies.

Organizational structure: every organization has an 'official' hierarchy and structure that drives and influences its culture, but the 'unwritten' power of some particular people, teams or even entire departments is just as, if not even more, influential. Structures come in all shapes and colors, and it's safe to say that today, corporations are often more like networks than hierarchies. As I wrote in one of my other books, 'The Network Always Wins', the unofficial social power within a network can be even more instrumental than the 'org chart' to understand a corporate culture.

Control systems: This part is about the systems that control the organization: financial management, rewards and retribution or quality-control structures. Rewards, for instance, have a fundamental influence over a company's culture: if management rewards efficiency, compliance and perfection, this will suffocate the long-term experimental messiness that goes hand in hand with innovation. Some companies operate in heavily regulated environments, of course, and they will install more control systems than others. On the other hand, the many examples of the likes of Enron and Lehman Brothers clearly show that this is not an absolute guarantee.

Power structures: this is where the 'real' power lies inside the company and which people have the biggest influence on decisions, operations, and strategic direction. Who decides, who defines the strategy and what are the power mechanisms that drive evolution inside the organization? Formal power structures (supervisory boards, audit committees, the role of CEO and chairman) are often visible and clear, but, here too, many 'informal' power structures (from the control of a founder, or the implicit role of trade unions) can be just as important to describe the company's culture.

■ Uber-toxic

There might be many more dimensions to the cultural paradigms of organizations than these six, but Scholes and Johnson have provided a simple landscape that allows us to chart, navigate and evaluate corporate culture. It's also evidently clear that this well-orchestrated 6-pillar culture mix can completely lose its balance and change identities if only ONE of the elements of the cultural web shifts direction or otherwise changes radically. As touched upon above, Uber is perhaps one of the most visible and painful examples of a company that almost went belly up as a result of a colossal cultural meltdown.

I loved visiting Uber in their wonderfully swanky San Francisco headquarters over the last few years. The 'symbols' of their culture are of course highly visible. You cannot be a San Francisco startup-turned-Unicorn and not have the ping-pong tables, dogs, all-day gourmet-quality food or 'downtime' enablers for your employees (ranging from PlayStation-filled gaming-corners to sleep-pods for relaxation or top-notch gym exercise equipment). You'd be defying the laws of the universe if you did. So, there you have it: we can tick the 'Symbols' box right here.

But in 2017, it became increasingly clear that underneath all that polished Silicon Valley veneer flowed a bubbling undercurrent that was beyond toxic. In June of that year, Travis Kalanick – the high-profile Uber founder and chief executive – resigned after a series of costly missteps amidst growing criticism of his management style and behavior. He used to be a poster-boy for the next generation of Silicon Valley entrepreneurs, famous for his 'always be hustling' attitude, and the icon of the 'frat boy' style of entrepreneurial leadership. Unfortunately, he also embodied all of the venomous characteristics of that 'hustling frat-boy' image, too.

The press had a field day over the sexual harassment revelations at the Uber offices, various allegations of trade secrets theft, and even an investigation into efforts to mislead government regulators. An incriminating report into the company's 'toxic' workplace culture uncovered how the company condoned sexual harassment, bullying and retaliation against those who tried to report any problems.

The saddest piece of evidence was a video of the Uber founder himself who was caught on film yelling and bullying one of the company's drivers. But when Kalanick was ousted, the company's cultural problems were obviously not magically fixed.

When Uber filed for their IPO, the prospectus of the company preparing to list on the stock exchange gave a very sober narrative on the results of the cultural meltdown. In more than 300 pages, the document filed with the Securities and Exchange Commission (required to prepare Uber for becoming a $90 billion listed company) noted the dangers of cultural miscalculation. The prospectus stated: "Our workplace culture and forward-leaning approach created significant operational and cultural challenges that have in the past harmed, and may in the future continue to harm, our business results and financial condition."

The legal document is a goldmine for understanding the internal dynamics of the Unicorn that grew completely lopsided as a result of their destructive culture: "Our workplace culture created a lack of transparency internally, which has resulted in siloed teams that lack coordination and knowledge sharing, causing misalignment and inefficiencies in operational and strategic objectives."

All of this clearly had an immediate effect on the lifeline of an organization like Uber, which is the acquisition and retention of new talent. As the Uber IPO filing went on to state: "Challenges related to our culture and workplace practices have in the past led to significant attrition and made it more difficult to attract high-quality employees." It clearly concludes: "The loss of qualified executives and employees, or an inability to attract, retain, and motivate high-quality executives and employees required for the planned expansion of our business, may harm our operating results and impair our ability to grow. A failure to rehabilitate our brand and reputation will cause our business to suffer."

Safe to say that this high-profile startup did *not* hide a fresh and energizing Fontainebleau forest inside its walls. It smells a lot more like a really bad version of Calcutta during a summer heatwave.

■ Rules of the Garage

Notwithstanding some Uber-like horror stories, the Fontainebleau forest freshness is still deeply ingrained in the Silicon 'Magic' Valley discourse. It moves hand in hand with the obligatory myth of the fabled 'garage-startup' which is squeaky clean, vibrant and just as fresh. And it all dates back to the ultimate prototype of the Palo Alto seminal 'tech' garage, where Bill Hewlett and Dave Packard started a movement of their own.

In 1938, these two pretty square looking Stanford engineering students started working part-time in a rented garage with an initial capital investment of $538.

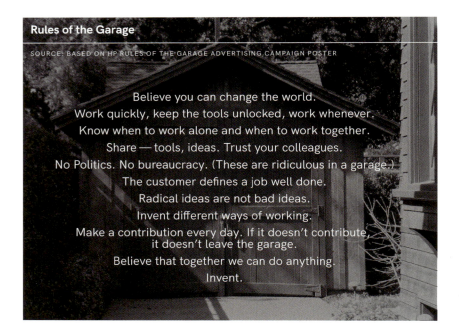

Rules of the Garage
SOURCE: BASED ON HP RULES OF THE GARAGE ADVERTISING CAMPAIGN POSTER

Believe you can change the world.
Work quickly, keep the tools unlocked, work whenever.
Know when to work alone and when to work together.
Share — tools, ideas. Trust your colleagues.
No Politics. No bureaucracy. (These are ridiculous in a garage.)
The customer defines a job well done.
Radical ideas are not bad ideas.
Invent different ways of working.
Make a contribution every day. If it doesn't contribute, it doesn't leave the garage.
Believe that together we can do anything.
Invent.

In 1939 they decided to formalize their partnership and comically tossed a coin to decide whether their company would be called Hewlett-Packard (HP) or Packard-Hewlett.[35] We all know who won. Their initial plan was to sell electronic testing equipment, but their business really took off after the Disney Company placed the first big order, asking them to build an audio frequency oscillator for the soundtrack of Fantasia.

Hewlett-Packard would evolve into one of the largest electronics companies in the world: a global producer of testing equipment, calculators, computers, and printers. They would reinvent themselves over and over again, as they grew into one of the giants in the world of IT.

But when they started out in those humble origins of the one-car Palo Alto garage, they crafted the 'HP way', clearly defining their culture and values, embodied in the famous '11 rules of the garage'.

It is just wonderful how this 'manifesto' – crafted way back in 1939 – is still so fresh and vibrant today that it could easily hang on the wall of any startup in Tel Aviv, Shenzhen or Berlin.

Let me analyze my own personal favorites of this wonderful list.

Believe you can change the world.
If there is one thing that defines the 'spirit of the garage', it is absolutely this one. It's just like the spring in Fontainebleau, where you just HAVE to do something, and believe it WILL have an impact. Unfortunately, in many companies the summer of Calcutta weighs heavily, and 'Constraint, Compliance, Control and Contract' keep the employees far from the notion that they can change the world.

When Steve Jobs wanted to hire seasoned marketing executive John Sculley away from Pepsi to appoint him as the CEO of Apple (a decision he would later greatly regret), he 'lured' him away from his comfortable position with these words: "Do you really want to sell sugared water for the rest of your life, or do you want to have a chance to put a dent in the universe?" He held that same Fontainebleau-fresh belief that he could change the world.

Share tools, ideas. Trust you colleagues.
The four C's of Sumantra Ghoshal's Calcutta limbo – constraint, compliance, control and contract – are all at root about mis- or dis-trust. That's because large systems tend to devour trust and replace it with artificial structures. So,

as companies grow, they almost inevitably gravitate towards layers of control to compensate for this growing dis-trust. Employees want the 'certainty' they are 'allowed' to do things without getting fired or compromised, and managers want to 'control' that their employees will perform as requested.

The only way to solve this almost paranoid type of context is through communication, sharing, and fostering proximity and understanding. Sharing tools in the HP garage may just have been a very physical way of collaborating, but sharing ideas is still very valid and essential today.

No politics. No bureaucracy. (These are ridiculous in a garage)
Bureaucracy has two linguistic roots. The French word 'Bureau' which means desk, or office. And the Greek word κράτος (kratos) which defines rule or political power. The German sociologist Max Weber was lyrical about the concept, believing that it was the best system to control large groups of unskilled workers during the industrial age.

The problem today is that many organizations still run on the bureaucratic system which was devised for the industrial age, even though the world has moved on. We expect our many highly skilled employees to be creative and come up with ideas and plans for the Day After Tomorrow, yet we restrict them with the rigid structures, rules and processes very reminiscent of the factory age. Time to start treating them as individuals rather than 'cohorts'.

Radical ideas are not bad ideas.
The freshness of the Fontainebleau forest makes people excited to explore new things and dream big. Today the word 'disruption' seems to have received a somewhat negative connotation, but if you're in that 'garage' type of spirit, you're very much drawn towards the Big Bold Day After Tomorrow Radical ideas.

How much 'radical' dreaming do you allow yourself in your job? I'm still amazed when I look at the faces of my audiences and see them suddenly realize that they virtually spend NO time thinking about radically new ideas, concepts or approaches. You *need* those pockets of radical experimentation in your company if you want to keep yourself relevant in the coming years.

Invent different ways of working.
It's not just the WHAT, it's the HOW. We've talked about the 'what' of innovation at length in this book, but, for me, the 'how' is the crucial one. And that means, above anything else, being permanently creative about new ways of

collaborating and co-creating: following the customer, creating ecosystems and even reaching out to the competition when you have to. No surprise actually that 'Invent' became HP's slogan around 1999.

Beautiful, right? The tricky part is this, though: you have to stay true to these rules, over and over again. It's great to draw up these radical rules, and let yourself be imbued by the Fontainebleau spirit, but eventually HP became one of the biggest, most boring companies in the world. At first, they were able to reinvent themselves, but in the early part of the 21st century, HP was struggling. Ironically, it had become a massive bureaucracy and it had lost its zeal in product innovation. The serious leadership troubles that ensued, would have made people think (or maybe sing) something along the lines of "Oh! Calcutta!"

So, even with the wonderful freshness of the garage spirit, is it inevitable that you will shed the Fontainebleau power one day, as your company keeps growing? Is this just an inseparable part of the senescence process that will eventually catch up with every company, and should we stop just kidding ourselves?

■ Day One, Part II

We talked about the Amazon 'Day One' philosophy earlier: how Jeff Bezos, almost religiously, wants Amazon to keep thinking like a startup, however big they become. Bezos constantly uses the rhetoric in his annual reports, and during his employee gatherings. The official Amazon Blog is called Day One, and the building in which Bezos works is called Day One.

But it's obviously more than just a mantra, or it wouldn't have brought Amazon to where it is today. Bezos is actually setting up a cultural insurance policy against the contentment that massive success can bring. In doing so, he creates a culture where everyone understands that past results do not automatically guarantee future success. He builds the cultural mechanisms that help every Amazon employee feel the importance of constantly innovating and being brutally open to change.

But that is an almost superhuman effort. It takes tremendous energy and charisma as a leader to pull off such a systemic tour de force and let it radiate through the entire organization. Day One is *not* a one-off, but an intense and continuous process. And the truth of the matter is that most companies don't have a Jeff Bezos or Tony Stark (if you prefer comics to rockets) running the company.

So let me bring you back to the Hourglass model.

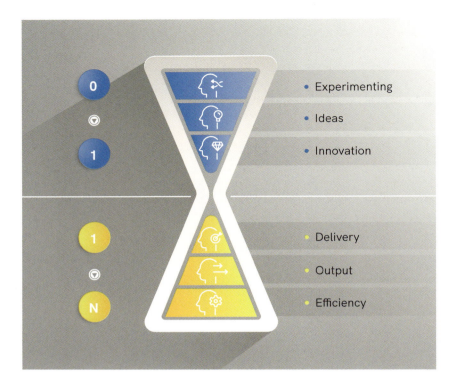

If you recall, the TOP part of the Hourglass model is the section of the organization that should activate the long term sensors. It should pick up on disruptive and radical ideas and technologies, experiment and try out new concepts and models, and ultimately focus on what the company's Day After Tomorrow strategy could be.

This is the part where you need the Fontainebleau freshness and the Day One spirit. This is where experimentation, risk taking and learning from failure is essential. This is where the Rules of the Garage should apply, over and over again. And this is also where we need brilliant charismatic leaders who can see things that others can't: the Steve Jobs, the Mary Barras, the Jack Mas and the Elon Musks. In fact, you should find these people not only at the very top of the organization, but throughout all its layers. They are the Garry Lyons (Mastercard), the Mickey McManuses (Autodesk), the Shannon Lucases (Ericsson) and the Ross Smiths (Microsoft).[36] of this world. Not always as visible as the Elon Musks, but just as vital, if not more so.

But back to Elon, disruptive innovation's poster boy. Just like any other company, Tesla knew humble beginnings, but when it scaled into a truly global automotive company, complexity grew and it had to leave the comfort of the garage (oh, the irony!) behind. Tesla once shone bright as the disruptive challenger, catching the automotive industry completely off-guard and shocking it into the age of electric mobility. It won over customers' hearts with its disruptive in-your-face attitude, and generated a loyal army of brand ambassadors, unheard of since the success of Harley-Davidson.

Then Tesla had to scale up production, with the introduction of its 'mainstream' Model 3. And the company struggled in a major way. It almost choked on the complexity of scale: from organizing its global customer service to shifting its production into a higher gear (yes, that *was* intended). At that time, Tesla might very well have thrived under a Jack Welch with his six sigma philosophy instead of the mercurial Musk.

That's because the BOTTOM part of the Hourglass is a completely different kettle of fish.

When you want to scale ideas and concepts – in volume or geographies – you need a culture and mindset that is focused on delivery and output. It's not about finding and trying out new things, it's about improvement and efficiency. Of course we can innovate too in that bottom part of the Hourglass, but here we're deeply focused on the existing business. Now, the cultural dimensions of the bottom part tend to be fundamentally different than those in the top part of the Hourglass. Not that we want to create downtown Calcutta in the summertime in the bottom part, but the 'smell of the place', and the skills needed to thrive there are radically different.

■ Do you know what you're doing?

After a long career in the startup scene and through my work with corporate customers, I've come to an extremely simple conclusion: there are only two fundamentally different types of people in business. There's the KWTD types and the DKWTD types.

The first category are the people who Know What They are Doing (KWTD). They are comfortable performing tasks for which they have been trained and which they have learned to master after years of practice. These people love the execution of concepts, relish in improving processes and focus on outcome.

The second category is a lot rougher, but oh so intriguing: they are the people who Don't Know What They are Doing (DKWTD). That does absolutely not mean that they are stupid, or ignorant. To the contrary, they are often incredibly clever. But primarily they are exceptionally brilliant in circumstances where they have to come up with answers without having all the experience, data and other ingredients needed to make a so called 'informed' decision. They shine when they have to do things that they have never done before. So, this group excels at working under uncertain and complex circumstances. They are comfortable with volatility and can function perfectly well with ambiguity. In short, they have a big-ass black-belt in the VUCA[37] arts.

So, what kind of a person are you?

During my presentations, I love to tease my audiences with the question "Would those of you who have absolutely no clue as to what they are doing in their professional lives, please stand up?" Of course, in all my years of giving keynotes, no one has ever stood up. There is this intense peer-pressure to keep sitting down, instead of showing to your colleagues that perhaps, maybe, you don't have all the answers.

But that may be the wrong attitude.

I believe that we will have to become much more comfortable with the VUCA landscape. Hard times are just around the corner, as we primarily have trained our people for the complete opposite in the 20th century. But we have to become much more apt at dealing with an increased number of Unknown Unknowns.

I'm absolutely not a fan of Donald Rumsfeld, but I do love this elegant statement of his:

> *"There are known knowns: these are the things that we know that we know. Then there are the known unknowns; that is to say, there are plenty of things that we know that we don't know. But then there are the unknown unknowns: the things that we don't know that we don't know."*

Rumsfeld used that wording when he was the United States Secretary of Defense, and when the US was under fierce international scrutiny about the lack of evidence linking the Iraq government with the supply of weapons of mass destruction. Rumsfeld paraphrased the concept based on the 'Johari' window, which had been developed by the psychologists Joseph Luft and Harrington Ingham in 1955. If you take the first two letters of Joseph and the first three (ish) of Harrington you may understand why it's called Johari. This Johari window has been used for a long time as an analytical technique by the national security and intelligence industry.

The concept is simple: imagine a two by two matrix such as this:

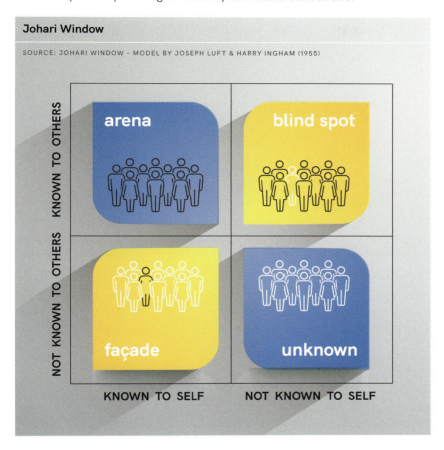

The first quadrant ('arena') is where you have a level playing field: what you know as an organization, and what the market knows is the same. These are the Known Knowns. The 'blind spot' and the 'façade' are variants of Known Unknowns, based on whether you or the 'others' are in the dark. But in our VUCA world it is the fourth quadrant that seems to be becoming increasingly relevant. These Unknown Unknowns will only increase in number and importance in a world that's continuously speeding up, increasingly connected and where every little change sets in motion a chain of other events and evolutions.

It is my opinion that in this VUCA world, you will need to hire more people that are comfortable dealing with these Unknown Unknowns, and you will need to staff the TOP part of the Hourglass with plenty of DKWTD people.

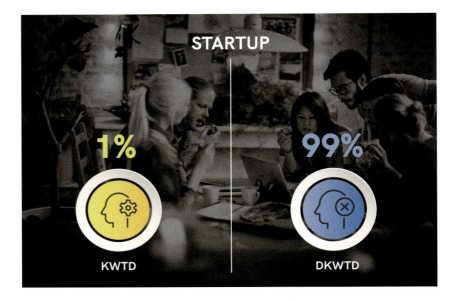

So, how many people in your organization Don't Know What They are Doing? Or let me phrase that even better: what is the ratio in your organization between those that KWTD and those that DKWTD?

Having had the privilege to observe the evolution of many tiny startups into larger scale-ups, and witnessing the behavior of the really massive corporations, I have developed a little theory on the evolution of this ratio.

▪ STARTUP = 1% KWTD + 99% DKWTD

In a startup, I would argue that the ratio is the most extreme. At the very onset there might be up to 99% people working there, who are comfortable doing things that have never been done before. That's where they get their kicks. In fact, these people only feel 'alive' if they can attempt to do something that has never been done before.

The 1% of people that (think) they know what they are doing, are definitely a minority here. It might be the obligatory seasoned and probably grey-haired 'serial entrepreneur' on the advisory board. That is probably all you need if you want to put a 'dent in the universe'.

▪ SCALEUP = 10% KWTD + 90% DKWTD

The bigger the startup gets, the more it scales and the more that ratio changes. You will need more structure, more control, more governance, and more 'overhead'. You will need to build mechanisms to guide your evolution, since you're outgrowing the 'garage'. A simple set of rules nailed to the wall won't cut it anymore.

■ GOOGLE = 80% KWTD + 20% DKWTD

Companies like Facebook and Tesla, as they reach hyper-growth, typically run into trouble if they can't grow their KWTD quota fast enough. As I stated above, Tesla faced production challenges at their Fremont factory, when they were unable to deliver enough Tesla model 3 cars. Clearly, they didn't employ enough 'German Precision' engineers who really knew what they were doing. The same went for Facebook spinning out of control after being hit by the Cambridge Analytica scandal and realizing that they just hadn't invested enough in people who KWTD when it comes to content quality control.

If you see a company like Google that is more than 20 years old, has more than 100,000 employees and more than $100 billion in annual revenue, I would argue they've passed the 80/20 ratio of KWTD/DKWTD. It's not downtown Calcutta in the summer. Not yet. But the company has had to invest in a LOT of 'traditional' people that just know what they were doing to be able to scale their business. Their 'bottom' part of the Hourglass has become really powerful and effective, running the $100 billion in revenue with Swiss Clock precision. And they definitely run the danger that their TOP part (like Google X) is no longer fully aligned to the BOTTOM part of the Hourglass.

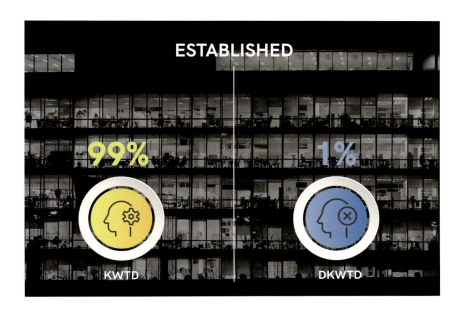

■ INCUMBENT = 99% KWTD + 1% DKWTD

And then I get invited to the traditional players, the incumbents. You enter a bank for example, where the ratio seems to be 99% versus 1%. These 99% of people, they all know EXACTLY what to do, how to do it, and they've done it that way for years and years on end.

I always sympathize with the 1% in those banks, insurance companies, retailers or other traditional players. These are the people that are trying to innovate and put disruptive ideas into the mainstream business. These are the tugboats trying to change the direction of the massive tanker made up of the 99%.

These 1%'ers are what I call the 'Positive Troublemakers' and the 'Frustrated Enthusiasts'. These are the people that are truly committed to making a difference, or a dent in the universe, if you will. But so often, they are frustrated, sometimes bitterly so, because they have to keep fighting against the status-quo mindset that makes up 99% of their company.

They are also the ones that Apple glorified in their fabled 'Think Different' campaign. I love to re-read the narrative of that advertisement from time to time, since it almost reads as the 'Manifesto of the 1%':

> "Here's to the crazy ones. The misfits. The rebels. The troublemakers. The round pegs in the square holes. The ones who see things differently. They're not fond of rules. And they have no respect for the status quo. You can quote them, disagree with them, glorify or vilify them. About the only thing you can't do is ignore them. Because they change things. They push the human race forward. And while some may see them as the crazy ones, we see genius. Because the people who are crazy enough to think they can change the world, are the ones who do."

If you work in the TOP part of the Hourglass, this manifesto will fit you like a glove. You can nail that on the wall next to the 'Rules of the Garage'.

My main message is that if you want to keep milking the cash-cows of old business models as long as you can, you don't need to invest in the TOP part of your Hourglass. Your 1% of people that DKWTD will be just fine. Probably heavily frustrated too, but fine. But, if you want to keep your company relevant in the Day After Tomorrow, that won't do. You have to massively invest in the TOP part of the Hourglass, staff it with people that are comfortable doing things they've never done before, and then – just as hard – align that with the bottom part of your Hourglass organization.

As this might take 'a while', I'd advise you to start right now.

■ What's next?

So, when culture does eat strategy for breakfast, what are the things that you need to think about right now?

1. What's the smell of your cultural web?

Sumantra Ghoshal took two extremes to describe corporate cultures: the Fontainebleau springtime and downtown Calcutta summertime. But what's the smell of your organization? What are the different dimensions of your 'cultural web'?

Imagine that you are a fresh young talent that enters your organization for the very first time: what would that smell reveal about you and your ambitions? And what would you need to do to adapt any of those dimensions, should they prove to turn out as stale as day-old bread?

2. How clear are the rules?

You're probably not really working in a garage. But what would your rules look like if you made them explicit? Talking TOP and the BOTTOM of the Hourglass, companies should probably become more comfortable with the different subcultures in their organization. Perhaps we need to abandon our heritage of one-size-fits-all systems and look in the direction of more ambidextrous structures, where different types of cultures peacefully (-ish) live and work together.

The rules of the 'garage' in the TOP Hourglass part of the organization might sound quite different from the 'processes' that live in the BOTTOM part of the Hourglass. Think about how you can make those explicit, and how you can make sure that they 'fit' together, and are aligned. Even when you have different subcultures, how do you insure that everyone feels a part of the same ambition and set of beliefs and values?

3. How to boost the output of the 1%'ers.

Depending on where you are in your journey as an organization, you will have various levels of people that are comfortable doing things that have never been done before. What is your ratio of people in terms of KWTD and DKWTD?

If you want to put more emphasis on transformation, on radical responses to fundamental disruption, you will have to focus on the TOP part of your Hourglass. And then you will have to increase the number of people that are comfortable and even thrive in a VUCA environment.

But the main question will be this: how you, as a leader can boost the output of the DKWTD crowd. How can you move the needle, and fundamentally use the energy of the 1%'ers to focus on innovation output, rather than fighting the 99% of the established oil-tanker.

I really hope you do find that Fontainebleau forest inside your organization.

IV ORGANIZATIONAL DISRUPTION: REMASTERING THE SYSTEM

In the past, we learned in order to work;
Now and into the future, we must work to learn.
— HEATHER E. MCGOWAN

■ Digitally Remastered

One of the most beautiful pieces of classical music is without a doubt the 'Goldberg Variations' by Johann Sebastian Bach, known in true German #gründlichkeit as number 988 in the Bach-Werke-Verzeichnis. 'Goldberg' refers to the German virtuoso harpsichordist Johann Gottlieb Goldberg, who is believed to have been the original performer of this heavenly piece. Goldberg often performed for Count Kaiserling, the Russian ambassador to the court of Saxony, who suffered from extreme insomnia. Bach's aria and its 30 variations helped the count through his many sleepless nights and he was so happy with what he called 'his' variations (Bach had already been working on the variations when the count suggested such a piece, though)[38] that he rewarded Bach handsomely with a golden goblet filled with 100 louis-d'or pieces of gold.

The most wonderful performance of this Bach masterpiece is just as much of an outlier. It's by the hands (and fingers) of the Canadian classical pianist wizard Glenn Gould who actually recorded the Bach masterpiece twice: once analog, and once digital.

The analog recording launched the enigmatic and eccentric Gould as an international musical wunderkind. He recorded the Goldberg Variations back in 1955, and this became the breakthrough work that introduced the world to one of the most stubborn, creative music geniuses known to mankind.

Gould was not just a mastermind performer; he was also a technology fanatic: an almost obsessive perfectionist who wanted to create the 'ultimate' recording of a piece of music. And at the end of his life he became fascinated by digital technology and its promise to make a 'perfect' bits and bytes recording that would never lose its quality.

That persuaded the celebrated artist to carry out one more recording of the Goldberg Variations, which would be immortalized – as of 1981 – as one of the very first digital compact discs ever. It has not been out of print since.

For me, the contrast between the two recordings helped me appreciate the almost magical art of Bach more than ever before. The 1955 'analog' version is fresh, vibrant, hungry, energetic and impatient. The 1981 'digital' version however, performed just a few months before Glenn Gould passed away, is more melancholic, contemplative, introspective and almost meditative. The violence of youth heavily contrasts with the philosophical counterpoint of wisdom.

At least we now have the 1981 version in full digital splendor, and indeed this will be preserved for all eternity.

But the older 'analog' recordings of masterpieces, be they music or film, were flawed since they were pressed on temporary carriers such as vinyl, or cellulose film. Or worse, those dreadful VHS tapes.

When digital technology became mainstream a whole lot of 'old' analog audio and vintage video material was remastered to fit the new digital era. I myself shelled out a small fortune in purchasing the 'digitally remastered' classics of my favorite artists, whose work I had already had on vinyl.

I actually love that term: 'digitally remastered'.

In a world where digital has become normal, have we all 'digitally remastered' our organizations?

I would argue that this transformation has progressed incredibly well on the customer side. Many companies have 'felt the heat' in this domain, where the advent of digital changed behavior faster than what had previously been imagined possible. Companies knew they needed more insight and therefore embarked on transforming their analytics capabilities. Ten years ago, not one marketing department would have heard of 'Big Data'. Today, marketing has been completely 'remastered' through analytics, algorithms and data science. The skills inside a marketing department, too, have been fundamentally 'remastered' to include data scientists, and people who understand the programmatic nature of dealing with customers.

So, the 'customer-facing' side of companies has effectively been 'digitally remastered'. But what about the rest? Have we digitally remastered our talent, organizations, learning and leadership?

If we're honest, the short answer is: not enough. And in a world where digital has become 'normal', perhaps we ought to move beyond merely remastering for 'digital'. Perhaps we need to remaster for a VUCA age, for disruption and for the Day After Tomorrow, too.

■ Remastering Talent

Any organization continuously needs infusions of fresh, raw, and unsoiled talent. It's as essential as oxygen. And, yet, this inflow seems to lack momentum in many traditional organizations and markets.

When I was a fresh university graduate, eager to make my mark on the world (and to earn some 'real' money, of course), I landed a job in the research department of Alcatel (as I mentioned earlier, it was at that point a major French telecoms infrastructure player… but no more). I was ecstatic. But right from my very first day on the job, I felt there was something wrong. Perhaps naïvely, I had been expecting to be submerged in an energizing and inspirational intellectual maelstrom of brilliant ideas and novel concepts. I thought I would become part of a privileged elite group of engineering masterminds setting out to change the world with technology.

But the harsh reality sunk in when I was escorted to my barren desk, in a stale cubicle occupied by four engineers. Right in the middle of this depressing sight, shone a Sun Microsystems workstation that we would have to share amongst the four of us. The person residing next to me had pinned Dilbert cartoons all over his flimsy walls. I had never seen a Dilbert cartoon up till then, but he told me: "You'll soon understand. I think Dilbert actually works here."

He was right. Bureaucracy, politics, pettiness, and incompetence revealed themselves in every aspect of our everyday office life. And I was getting mightily depressed. I thought I had just chosen the wrong company at first, but when I reached out to my study-friends – who had moved on to jobs in banks, insurance companies, manufacturing or oil companies – they all told the same kind of stories about the same Dilbert-esque experiences. I was trapped in Downtown Calcutta in a perpetual summertime heatwave, with a big clock on the wall, ever so slowly ticking down towards my retirement.

Surely there *had* to be more to life than those ghastly boring memos, mind-numbing meetings, and dreadful PowerPoint presentations delivered by unbearably un-inspiring bosses? Right?

So, after a mere 18 months – that felt more like two very long lifetimes – I quit my job, realizing that I would slowly die on the inside if this is how I had to spend the next 40 years of my life. I wanted to do something that made me feel alive. I wanted to invest my heaps of energy into something that would have an impact, something that I would actually enjoy and – above all – something that would give ME a boost back. I wanted to feel passion and vigor.

The life I chose was the life of startups, which was still an uncharted path back in 1995. Much has changed since. But I felt reborn. I loved building something from scratch. I was thrilled to do something 'that had never been done before'. I got energy from finding the DKWTD people and unleashing their potential. More than anything, I enjoyed finding new customers to buy into something that they had never seen before.

▪ We, or Me?

Only later in life did I discover the 'We-Me' model that helped me understand why I had made those decisions.

I love this art installation by the artist Dewey Ambrosino,[39] where you see a big WE on the wall which is reflected as a ME on the floor. It was inspired by the "shortest poem in the world" which was created on the spot by Muhammad Ali in 1975, at the end of his Harvard University Commencement Speech. The enthusiastic graduates had suddenly called for a poem, to which he replied "Me," pointing to himself, and "We," pointing to himself and the entire assembly. The shortest poem indeed, but perhaps also one of the most fundamental ones.

PROJECTED WE/REFLECTED ME (MUHAMMAD ALI, 1975 HARVARD UNIVERSITY COMMENCEMENT SPEECH), 2005, PROJECTION, MIRROR, 48" X 52" X 48". SOURCE: WWW.DEWEYA.COM

It's an age-old conundrum, which has kept us occupied ever since we became conscious of ourselves and our surroundings. "What is the WE and what is the ME?" Now, if you apply this to an employee's relationship with their organization, it's about this: which part of our commitment to a company is based on our self-interest and personal development, and which part is focused on the collective? What is the 'WE' part of our engagement, allowing us to contribute to a bigger collective purpose? And what can that collective knowledge, wisdom, or network generate for 'ME' as an individual?

In short: how will the 'ME' feed the 'WE', and equally how will the 'WE' feed the 'ME'?

That fundamental balance between 'We' and 'Me' may well change over time, be culturally defined, and even greatly contribute to the 'cultural web' of how an organization behaves and prepares for the Day After Tomorrow.

If we want to keep attracting the best and the brightest talent needed to shape our future, perhaps we should more actively manage that balance between this 'me' and 'we'. When I joined Alcatel, I have to admit that I was first and foremost concerned about 'me'. But now that I use the lens of my children and observe the ambitions of the young talent flowing into the companies that I'm close to, I realize that this generation is a lot more focused on the 'we' element. They seem to think a lot more about how they can contribute to a collective purpose, which will then also offer them more value in return.

One of my favorite thinkers in 'remastering' organizations is probably John Hagel III, the founder of Deloitte's Center for the Edge, based in San Francisco. With his 35 years of Silicon Valley experience as a management consultant, entrepreneur, speaker and author, John knows *a lot* about the digital transformation journey of companies. But I've seen his thinking evolve from the 'technology' side of the Day After Tomorrow and disruption equation towards the human component.

One of the interesting elements of John Hagel's narrative is the difference between mindset and what he calls 'heartset'. He argues that many companies focus too much on the 'mindset' component, assuming that our beliefs shape what we feel and what we do. In this limited 'mindset' view of the world, emotions are merely a distraction, or at best a second order effect. But John Hagel thinks otherwise: "We need to move beyond mindset and expand our horizons to address our heartset: what are the emotions that filter how we perceive the world, shape what we believe and influence how we act?"

That's why, if we want to start 'remastering' our organizations, we need to respect and nurture the following three dimensions: Skillset, Mindset and Heartset.

▊ Skillset

This is one of the most essential questions of today: what kind of skills do we need inside our companies to be prepared for the Day After Tomorrow?

It is already painfully obvious that there will be a real shortage of people who are proficient in the STEM domains of Science, Technology, Engineering and Mathematics. STEM is in fact the most natural 'second language' to help us understand the implications of the world of tomorrow. But the type of 'jobs' unfolding out of that domain are constantly evolving.

Surely the world will need people that can build Blockchain based applications, have mastered Machine Learning, and know how to develop Artificial Intelligence based algorithms. We will definitely need 'Digital Twin Engineers' and may have to cope with a shortage of Quantum Computing experts. The problem is that many of these 'jobs' didn't even exist a few years ago. Which means they did not appear on the strategic horizon of most education systems, let alone become integrated into the actual curriculum of universities.

There is a fundamental need to speed up the 'remastering' of our education frameworks in order to keep up with the exponentially changing technology landscape and prepare the workforce for the future.

But what will we do with the employees that no longer 'function' in this 21st century economy? How can we 'reskill' them to be ready for the Day After Tomorrow? We MUST think about this, if we do not want to end up with the very depressing vision of what futurist Yuval Noah Harari calls the "useless class." He believes that just as mass industrialization created the working class, the AI revolution may create a new 'unworking' class. Yuval believes that we cannot compare the threat of automation and job loss in the 21st century to what happened in the 20th century:

> *"In the 20th century you saw automation in agriculture, so lots of unemployed farmworkers moved to working in industry, and then when automation reached the industries they moved to working as cashiers at Walmart. But in those cases what happened was that people lost low-skill jobs and transferred to other low-skill jobs. Moving from being an agricultural worker to working in some car factory in Detroit you moved from one low-skill job to another low-skill job. When you lost your job at the Detroit car factory and got a new job as a cashier at Walmart, again you moved from a low-skill job to a low-skill job."*

His concern is that with the advent of smart automation, the 'low skill' worker will have no more places to move. "But if the next stage means I am losing my job at 45 as a cashier at Walmart and now there is an opening as a software engineer at Google designing virtual worlds, this is going to be much more difficult than moving from the car factory to Walmart." He adds that it is nearly impossible for us to predict what the job market will look like in 20 years, or which types of skills will be needed. Completing this rather bleak picture, he concludes that we really don't even know how we will need to adapt our education systems to cope.

Safe to say that Yuval is not an upbeat kind of guy. He fears that we may end up with, on the one hand, a new elite of 'superhumans', enhanced by bioengineering and brain-computer interfaces. And on the other, a new, massive and 'useless' class with no military or economic usefulness and, therefore, no political power. Luckily, we're not there yet and AI is still too flawed to replace most of us. For now. But we HAVE to think about how we can prepare our workforce for all of these changes.

I've had the absolute pleasure of working with the future of work strategist, keynote speaker and author Heather McGowan on many occasions. She has a very clear vision of the future of skills and employment and is convinced that "The Future of Work is Learning". She knows that in such a fast-evolving world, and with human lives lasting much longer than they used to, remastering education and corporate training is absolutely critical.

She brilliantly visualized the impact of longevity and increased change rates in the eye-opening chart on the right.

In the 'old paradigm' of work, where human life expectancy was about 75 years, we used to gather and 'store' plenty of knowledge until we were about 22 years old. Then we would hope to maximally leverage that knowledge in our professional careers. Eventually, we would retire, around the age of 65. During the final years of our life, we kicked back and relaxed, and let society take care of us so we could enjoy our final moments. It was much like deeply inhaling air, swimming under water all the way across towards the far end of the pool and hoping that you had enough oxygen to make the full distance.

Kids today have the almost mathematical guarantee that they will reach 100 years old. That's the good news. But in a Never Normal world, a completely different pattern of gathering skills and sharpening our knowledge will need to emerge. We will need to work longer. A lot longer. Perhaps we might 'never' retire, merely migrating towards a pattern of 'less intensive' engagement as the end of our life nears. But the most vital part is that we have to be prepared for a professional experience of life-long learning. We will need a continuous and persistent mechanism for keeping ourselves 'up-to-date', employable, and relevant.

How are we preparing our next generation for 'lifelong learning'? How many 22-year-olds do you know that shout "Wow! That was awesome! I want to go again!" when they graduate?

And how to keep the current workforce – that grew up and were motivated under the 'old paradigm' of learning – engaged? How do we 'sell' to them that they should 'remaster' their skillset to stay relevant through the 21st century, and – even more difficult – that they might never retire? This will *not* go down easily.

This challenge will eventually become the top priority of virtually every nation on every continent in the world. And yet, our current politicians hardly even address the issue. Worse, the education systems in almost every country have become the slowest moving part of society.

Why does it matter: longevity + change rates

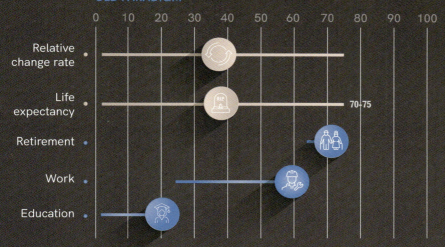

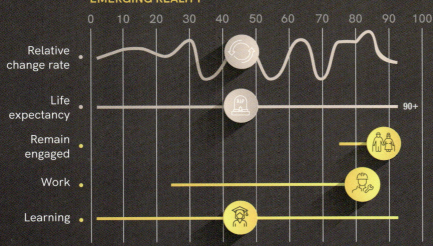

CONCEPT BY HEATHER E MCGOWAN

■ Make America Skilled Again

In the US an employer led platform called 'UpSkill America' is actively trying to remaster the skillset of American employees. They promote training and re-skilling practices to help workers progress in their careers and move into better-paying jobs, ultimately allowing the economy to thrive.

A company like AT&T for example, is investing no less than $1 billion in reskilling its employees. It realized that almost all the technical talent they had hired in the 20th century was no longer adequate for the 'digital' world of telecommunications. Just as landline phones are disappearing, the skills of the AT&T workers were no longer up to par. And as 'fresh' tech talent is almost impossible to acquire at scale, the corporate giant decided to massively reskill its employees, embarking more than 100,000 of them on its 'Future Ready' program.

The ambitious multiyear program retrains employees through web based approaches via new educational players like Coursera and Udacity. Udacity, for instance, is a great example of a new education platform that has offered training in some of the most sought after skills and technologies of the 21st century, long before any classical university.

The platform was famously founded by Sebastian Thrun, the rock star developer of the first prototype of the Google driverless car. He was teaching Artificial Intelligence at Stanford, when he launched the first Massive Open Online Course (MOOC) in 2011. This pioneering online 'Introduction to Artificial Intelligence' course attracted more than 160,000 students. When Udacity was first launched, they tried to focus on this 'MOOC business', of single course. However, they soon pivoted towards providing 'nanodegrees'. These are very specific trainings for a focused set of skills; a perfect example is Udacity's nanodegree in the field of 'Self-Driving Car Engineering', which virtually no 'traditional' university would think to offer.

But although STEM will clearly play a vital role in the Day After Tomorrow society, perhaps we should look at reskilling through a completely different lens? Perhaps rather, we need to prepare our next generation by stimulating their creativity, imagination, and curiosity? It all starts with examining the very nature of work, in order to understand its future.

Since the industrial age, 'work' has been centered on the 'transactional and predictable', and the flawless execution of routine and tightly defined tasks. We installed bureaucracies and organizational structures in order to allow large groups of unskilled workers to collaborate: each of their tasks highly specialized, standardized and specified yet highly limited in scope.

The problem, as John Hagel points out, is that this highly orchestrated system is increasingly being disrupted by technology. As he brutally points out: "Machines are more accurate, they don't get tired or bored, they don't break for sleep or weekends. If it's a choice between human or machines to do the kind of work that requires compliance and consistency, machines should win every time."

But instead of lamenting the fact that technology could destroy the 'old' jobs, would this not be the opportunity to 'redefine' work altogether? Isn't it actually a shame that we put so many brilliant minds and creative individuals into a straitjacket that forces them to work solely within the confines of their specialty and set of tasks? Wouldn't it provide a lot more value to their organization if their full creative potential were deployed?

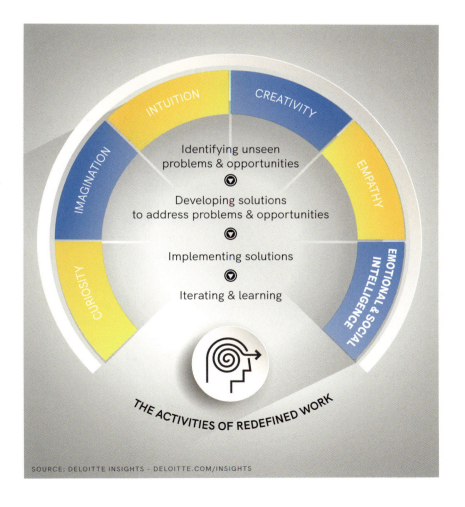

SOURCE: DELOITTE INSIGHTS - DELOITTE.COM/INSIGHTS

One thing is certain, in a VUCA world, with an increased number of unknown unknowns, we will need more DKWTD type of people to staff the 'top' part of our Hourglasses. Work will continuously evolve, and probably faster and faster. Shouldn't we prepare the next generation to be comfortable with VUCA? Shouldn't we think about what kind of human capabilities will become key in the Day After Tomorrow?

John Hagel's 'Center for the Edge' frames this redefinition of 'work' in the context of the 'human' capabilities we need in order to thrive in an increasing technological world. In a VUCA world where our employees will need to identify unseen problems and new opportunities and to develop solutions to challenges that they have never encountered before, the heart of the matter is that they will need a completely different set of capabilities. Instead of focusing on "information storage" in our brains – replicating facts and memorizing content – we have to focus on brain plasticity by sparking curiosity, unlocking the imagination, developing intuition, energizing creativity, empowering empathy and advancing social and emotional intelligence.

▪ Mindset

That brings us to the next essential element in our 'remastering' process: how can we foster a mindset that can keep us relevant in the Day After Tomorrow?

In the aftermath of the industrial revolution, we experienced intense global developments of scale, which necessitated the creation of 'management science'. We built processes, systems of governance, scorecards, reporting mechanisms, as well as a myriad of financial and operational constructs, which allowed huge scaling, profit maximization and unrivalled efficiency and quality.

But the world has changed.

Don't get me wrong: we still do need the 'Scale and Run' capabilities of the bottom part of the Hourglass. But if we want to stay ahead of the curve and avoid devaluating ourselves into 'dumb pipes', we should not only develop new skills, but also foster a different culture to populate the 'top' part. We need a culture where innovation runs deep, where an 'entrepreneurial' attitude is more prevalent than a 'managerial' approach, and where FAILURE is accepted as part of the game.

So there you have it. The F- word finally reared its ugly head.

Samuel Beckett, one of the greatest artists of the last century is now often quoted by starry-eyed entrepreneurs: "Ever tried. Ever failed. No matter. Try again. Fail again. Fail better." I'm quite sure, though, that Beckett didn't really have Silicon Valley in mind when he wrote Worstward Ho, back in 1983.

Ah, the magic of the startup garage, where failure is accepted and sometimes even idolized. 'Failure' definitely did not feature in the original 'Rules of the Garage' of Hewlett-Packard, but today it is deeply ingrained into the mantras of many Silicon Valley companies (and their copycats) all over the world. Fail Fast, Fail Often and Fail Forward! It has evolved into some borderline communist-style propaganda to promote the sensationally badass concept of Failure.

Laugh with it all you want, but it's incredibly important to create that precise 'fail and learn' mindset because it helps accelerate the rate of innovation and learning.

■ Psychological Safety

Today, that fashionable concept has become widely known as 'Psychological Safety'.

A company like Google – with more than $100 billion in revenue, and more than 100,000 employees – talks *a lot* about 'psychological safety'. It's one of the major results of its extensive research into what makes teams work effectively inside large global and rapidly expanding companies. It was easy in the beginning, of course, when they were all still toiling in the garage. In the early years, 'all' they needed to do was allow everyone to experiment and try new stuff with 20% of their time. But what do you do when your company has become massive, and traditional thinking is slowly creeping in? How can you keep stimulating a culture and mindset that allows people to stay creative? One that allows them to try new things and experiment, without the fear of punishment whenever they make a mistake?

The Google People Ops team (basically, just a cooler version of the traditional Human Resources department) set out on a two-year study to find out how they could empower teams to move beyond the 'normal', and be as effective as possible. They learned that these five key dynamics could make all the difference:

1. Psychological safety: Can we take risks in this team without feeling insecure or embarrassed?
2. Dependability: Can we count on each other to do high quality work on time?
3. Structure & clarity: Are goals, roles, and execution plans in our team clear?

4. Meaning of work: Are we working on something that is personally important for each of us?
5. Impact of work: Do we fundamentally believe that the work we're doing matters?

As it turns out, their study proved that 'psychological safety' was far and away the most important of the five dynamics, and absolutely key for understanding team effectiveness. We've known for some time that positive emotions like trust, curiosity, confidence, or inspiration can help broaden our mind. The Google study showed clearly that we become more open-minded, resilient, motivated, and persistent when we feel safe. And that this helps us become more 'ready' for the future.[40]

In Google's fast-paced, rapidly changing and highly demanding business environment, their success greatly depends on their capability to build teams who dare to experiment and take risks. And these types of high-performing teams only really work in a context of psychological safety.

But how do you build such a context? How do you generate 'psychological safety'?

■ Cognitive diversity

My colleagues at the London Business School, David Lewis and his partner Alison Reynolds, uncovered an interesting correlation between psychological safety and cognitive diversity. In a 2017 Harvard Business Review article,[41] they concluded that teams solve problems faster when they're more 'cognitively diverse'. When we think of diversity inside companies, we tend to think in terms of gender, ethnicity, or age. But cognitive diversity is not just limited to these characteristics: it's about how individuals think about and engage with new, uncertain, and complex situations.

When these types of challenges and opportunities surface, people will have various ideas and reactions. Unfortunately, all too often, the ideas that eventually make it tend to come from a minority: the most confident, most senior or most vocal people in a group. And from this already restricted set of ideas, often the 'safest' option is chosen because of a typical corporate aversion to risk and fear of failure. The result is suboptimal, at best, and, at times, disastrous in terms of strategic decision making.

David and Alison conducted research into this, and they came up with 4 distinct 'mindsets' and cultures, depending on the degree of psychological safety, combined with the extent of cognitive diversity in teams.

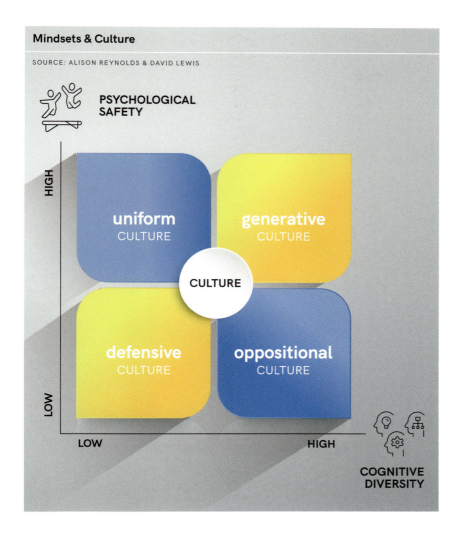

What they describe as the 'Generative' mindset culture, is a combination of maximum cognitive diversity and maximum Psychological Safety to generate the very best results. This 'Generative' mindset is characterized by behaviors such as "curiosity, experimentation, nurturing, enquiring, being forceful and encouraging."

If we want to build organizations which are prepared for a VUCA world and if we want to populate the top of our Hourglass with open-minded, curious and creative individuals who have an 'entrepreneurial' mindset, we will have to look into those two vital ingredients for success: how can we optimize psychological safety and how can we maximize our cognitive diversity?

I wrote earlier about the wonderful transformation that took place at Microsoft, with the advent of Satya Nadella as the new CEO, and how the concept of 'mindset' played a crucial role in this transformation.

In his book 'Hit Refresh', Satya Nadella writes that his wife Anu gave him a copy of a book written by Dr. Carol Dweck: 'Mindset: The New Psychology of Success'. Carol is Professor of Psychology at Stanford University, and has done extensive research on overcoming failures by believing that you can. Dr. Dweck divides the world between 'learners' and 'non-learners', demonstrating that a 'fixed mindset' will limit you, while a 'growth mindset' will enable you to move forward. People with a 'fixed mindset' are more likely to stick to activities that utilize the skills that they've already mastered, rather than to risk embarrassment by failing at something new. People with a 'growth mindset' make it their mission to learn new things, understanding full well that they might not succeed (at all of them) at first.

Satya Nadella used the concept of the 'growth mindset' intensely while transforming Microsoft from a culture of 'Know-it-Alls' into a company of 'Learn-It-Alls', stimulating a mindset of curiosity and learning in employees throughout the organization.

■ Heartset

The 'heartset' is the final element of 'remastering' talent inside our organizations. Mastering new skills and life-long learning will be essential to remain relevant in the Day After Tomorrow. On top of that, the VUCA mindset and acceptance of failure will become vital. But if we really want to make a difference, we will also have to take the heartset into account: what are the emotions and passions that filter our perception of the world, that help us shape what we believe in, and that influence how we act?

Believe that you can change the world. That's the very first rule of the garage, about wanting to make a 'dent in the universe'. It's about believing that what you do every single day matters, that it makes a damn difference. That there is a reason why you drag yourself to work, why you fight the 99%, and why you overcome your fear of failure to create an impact. Because you believe that it is the right thing. Because your heart tells you so.

John Hagel believes that we have been too obsessed with 'mindsets' in the past. According to him, this is a direct result of the engineering and managerial beliefs that shaped the 'scale and efficiency' cultures that dominate most of our current institutions. The Enlightenment, 'the age of reason', gave us absolute faith in the power of the mind. The industrial revolution gave us the 'engineering method' and the belief that if you have the right data and execute the right analytics you can accomplish absolutely anything. You just need to break down any complex problem into tiny little parts, standardize components, and execute the monolithic tasks in order to increase efficiency and predictability.

Hagel thinks we now have to move beyond that. That humans feel absolutely miserable when they are treated as 'cogs in the machine'. In his words: "Numbers and charts alone are not going to drive the change required. Seek to understand the heartset – the fears and hopes that are motivating the actions of those in the organization." This means rekindling our professional 'passion'. Most of us often feel passion in our personal lives, but the hard truth is that unfortunately this is felt a lot less often in our professional activity. The numbers don't lie: research from the Center of the Edge indicates that only 13% of workers in the US workforce would describe that there is any element of 'passion' in their work.

How can we motivate ourselves to give our very best if we can't believe in what we do, and if we don't think we can make an impact? Just look at the negative impact that cultural meltdowns can have when the 'purpose' of an organization falls apart. We've seen the enormous (financial) impact when Uber went through its cultural collapse, and then had a really hard time hiring the best and brightest.

Heartset and passion might even be more relevant for the generation born in the 21st century, which tends to cherish a different set of beliefs and values, as well as a different 'We-Me' balance, than those who have come before. Heather McGowan says this is the generation that "believes in Purpose more than just a Paycheck." Trying to stay realistic, I'm sure this won't apply to all the jobs out there. There might still be plenty of manufacturing jobs – working the night shift in a cookie-factory for example – where workers are understandably not too preoccupied with their 'ability to change the world'. But if you want to lead an organization into the Day After Tomorrow, and you DO need to fundamentally change and adapt, then this could be to your advantage. Perhaps you need to HIRE people who believe in that purpose. Perhaps you need to HIRE for heartset.

Gary V (V stands for Vaynerchuk) is one of the most popular – and visible – entrepreneurs of our time. I have loved working with him on a number of occasions. He really does understand the art of polarizing an audience: you either instantly love him or you hate him with a vengeance. But one thing is certain:

you will always know exactly what his opinion is. In 2006, Gary launched Wine Library TV, a daily webcast about wine, to boost his family's wine business. Since then he started his own very successful digital marketing and communications agency VaynerMedia. In this highly competitive and fast changing market, attracting the best people is core, but attracting the right people is perhaps even more crucial.

Gary V fundamentally believes in the importance of 'heartset'. He always encourages people to hire for culture first. In his words "I don't care how smart someone is – if they are a jerk or have some kind of caustic attitude they will become a liability in your team building process. When hiring people you want to look for what Eric Schmidt in Trillion Dollar Coach refers to as 'smarts and hearts.' Seek competency and compassion that are a cultural fit for the 'why' and the 'how' of the organization you are building. You want diversity of thought but not diversity of heart. Make cultural fit a top priority when selecting people to join you on your entrepreneurial journey."

In a rapidly changing 'Never Normal' world, we will have to fundamentally look at other mechanisms, skills and cultural dimensions to stand out. John Hagel sums it up perfectly: "Until we recognize and address the heartset that shapes our actions, and its complex interactions with our mindset, we'll find that fear and stress will increase resistance to change. On the other hand, if we can draw out hope and excitement, we'll find that we'll be able to learn and change at an accelerating rate. Our heartset can be both the barrier and the enabler of change – it's up to us which one will prevail."

■ Leadershift

My absolute favorite Steve Jobs quote is "If you want to make everyone happy, don't be a leader. Sell ice cream." It touches on one of the most delicate challenges in organizations: what makes a great leader? And how can they help their company keep reinventing itself like a Phoenix in these VUCA times? As Heather McGowan likes to point out: innovation begins with learning.

Sumantra Ghoshal is not only known for his wonderful description of the freshness of Fontainebleau in springtime and the 'smell' of downtown Calcutta in summertime. He was also one of the most vocal critics about how we train managers. Ironically, although he taught at INSEAD (next to the forest), and later at London Business School, he was also one of the harshest critics of these institutions. While he picked up on the faults of leadership in creating a 'smell' of constraint, compliance and control, he also blamed the business schools for attempting to teach management as a science to these very same future business leaders.

This criticism was already there in the 20th century. Imagine the situation today. Although I really enjoy working with schools such as London Business School, I also have to admit that the 'traditional' managerial training seems to grow increasingly out of sync with the current VUCA reality. In the 20th century the 'art of business management' was perfected with the creation of the MBA – the Master in Business Administration – with the very first program run at Harvard in 1908.

Mary Parker Follett was an American social worker, born in 1868, and one of the pioneers of the study of organizational behavior. She is known as the "Mother of Modern Management" and believed to have once said that Management is the "art of getting things done through other people."

MBAs primarily focus on four domains. First is the analytical side of management – finance, economics and accounting – and then the operational elements: operational management, marketing management, human resources management etc. On top of that we teach the governance elements including control, audit and the operating role of boards and committees. Finally, time is spent on the elements of strategic management.

Great. For a 20th century company, that is. But if you want to lead both the BOTTOM part and the TOP part of the Hourglass in these VUCA times, I would argue that a lot of crucial elements are fundamentally missing here. And yet, we still send so many unsuspecting managers to the MBA-template-machinery that will mold them into the 'perfect' leader.

Buckminster Fuller, one of the most intriguing American designers, inventors and futurists believed that "You never change things by fighting the existing reality. To change something profoundly, you must build a new model that makes the existing model obsolete." Perhaps a true 'LeaderSHIFT' is long overdue, introducing a completely different model and approach to creating leaders for this century.

By the end of the 20th century, some American corporations were realizing that the 'American way' of management was beginning to fail. In his famous book called 'The Art of Japanese Management: Applications for American Business', the author Richard Pascale coined the 7-S Framework: Strategy, Structure, Systems, Skills, Staff, Style, and Shared goals. The first three of these 7 S's were called 'hard' factors, and this is where American companies excelled. But most were failing miserably at the remaining four – soft – factors.

Since then, I believe our training of managers has caught up to include those other last 4 elements, with an increased emphasis on the aspects of Skills (competencies), Staff (people), Style (culture) and Shared Goals (purpose). But the disconnect between 'entrepreneurial' and the 'managerial' styles of leadership is still immense.

In this early stage of a new century, we might have to make a new leap, though. Leaders should not only be trained in the Bottom part of the Hourglass (Scale and Run), but just as much in the leadership skills necessary to excel in the Top part of the Hourglass (Sense and Try).

If we want to educate leaders to operate in VUCA times, if we want them to excel in leading organizations through radical change, then we will have to help them be more comfortable with uncertainty, deal with ambiguity and make decisions without knowing all the facts. We will have to teach them to deal with experimentation and create a culture of psychological safety. They'll need to learn to make decisions with increasing complexity, to abandon linear thinking and embrace network dynamics. And let's not forget about the deep cultural aspects of creating purpose, of building environments where people want to engage and give their very best, and attracting the very best and brightest in terms of skill, mind and heart.

■ Opportunity as well as danger

I believe we might need to design the leadership development of the 21st century from scratch. We'll need to build an entirely new model, as Buckminster Fuller would say.

Charles Handy is one of the great management thinkers of our time. He's a wonderful professor as well as a contemporary philosopher, and one of the people who believe it is time for a systemic change in how we teach future leaders. He says: "Uncertainty brings opportunity, as well as danger, and we need to prepare for it. And educating for it requires a radical departure from the mindset that has traditionally characterised our educational institutions, including business schools."[42] As he points out, the current approach to business education is very much the idea that the past is the most appropriate model to understand the future.

That might be so for the BOTTOM part of the Hourglass, but it is certainly not the case for the TOP part.

If we want to rethink the concept of education for uncertainty, the biggest obstacles will be the professors and teachers. In Charles words: "They will have to radically change, from being the 'expert' laying down the law to obedient listeners; they will have to evolve and be more like the master in an art class, mentoring and encouraging." Charles believes that we have to completely rethink our leadership development: "Curiosity and imagination could be spotted and encouraged in classes, but resilience in the face of adversity, the courage to stand up for what you believe in, and the necessity for compromise in order to move forward, and the wisdom to know when, will be essential to develop."

This does not only apply to business education, of course.

Yuval Noah Harari, the Israeli historian and best-selling author of 'Homo Deus' (who we met a couple of pages ago), has an extremely interesting view on the future of education. He asks: "Humankind is facing unprecedented revolutions… How can we prepare ourselves and our children for a world of such unprecedented transformations and radical uncertainties?"[43] Much of what kids learn today in school will likely be completely irrelevant by 2050. He claims that in a world where information is at our fingertips, where Youtube and Wikipedia are prevalent, that last thing a teacher needs to give their pupils is MORE information; they already have far too much of it. Harari believes that even computer programming might become obsolete as perhaps an artificial intelligence algorithm would be able to code much better and faster than humans. I don't necessarily agree with this, as I fundamentally believe we humans should still be able to remain in the driving seat of the technological revolution.

But where I do agree wholeheartedly with Harari is when he says: "Most important of all will be the ability to deal with change, to learn new things and to preserve your mental balance in unfamiliar situations. Many pedagogical experts argue that schools should switch to teaching 'the four Cs' – critical thinking, communication, collaboration and creativity." In our current 'production line' approach of education, we will have to bundle all our efforts to rethink our concepts of learning.

Alvin Toffler, the author of 'Future Shock', phrased it beautifully when he explained how the 'illiterate' of the 21st century are NOT the ones who cannot read or write, but "those who cannot learn, unlearn, and relearn."

And that will be the only way to truly remaster our organizations for the Day After Tomorrow.

V STRUCTURAL DISRUPTION:
A Never Normal Design

BY LAURENCE VAN ELEGEM — Content & Communications Director at nexxworks

Laurence Van Elegem has been my loyal communications companion for the last decade, carefully orchestrating all of my social and other media activities and acting as the extremely talented (but ruthless) editor of my latest books, including this one.

Over the years, she has also crafted a unique and intriguing voice of her own on one of the most pivotal aspects of transformation: the radical shift in organizational systems thinking, vital to becoming a true Phoenix.

That's why I've asked her for a signature contribution of her own on this pivotal aspect.

Take it away, Laurence!

"It is not love or money that makes the world go round but flow and design."
— ADRIAN BEJAN

I've always been fascinated by the tension between opposites, both real and imagined. One of the first 'big' texts I ever wrote – my Germanic Languages master's thesis – dealt with the clash between the Ojibwe (native American) and western, catholic culture in the work of the novelist Louise Erdrich. And since then, this fascination with duality has never left me. It's the reason why I'm so obsessed by the antithesis and synthesis of technological and human systems. And why – lately – I've been so drawn to how organizations structure their existing business on the one hand, and their emerging business on the other.

Over the course of my career, I have come into contact with many organizations that have struggled with innovation. One of the things that keeps puzzling me, though, is how the human structures that support the existing business are designed the exact same way as the parts that are responsible for reinventing the business, in a Phoenix-like fashion. People at the top of the Hourglass require a very different approach and management system than the bottom of the Hourglass crew. And yet we tend to put them in neatly fixed silos, with fixed roles and fixed colleagues. Giving them hip names like 'Lab' or 'Idea Factory' does not change the fact that their structures don't match their purpose.

■ Complexity requires experimentation

I first learned about the Cynefin Framework in a podcast interview with its creator Dave Snowden, an ex-IBM Director and knowledge management expert, who went on to found Cognitive Edge, a Singapore-based management-consulting firm specialized in complexity and sensemaking. Cynefin – pronounced kuh-nev-in – is a Welsh word that means "the multiple factors in our environment and our experience that influence us in ways we can never understand."[44] The framework was designed to help leaders assess which contexts require which type of response and leadership style.

The most powerful frameworks tend to be the simplest, and Cynefin is no exception here. When I read an article about it that described how "different situations require different responses to successfully navigate them,"[45] my brain simultaneously responded with "Well, duh" and "That's exactly what's wrong with how most organizations organize and structure their innovation."

When you compare the visualization of the Cynefin framework to others of its kind, it's delightfully messy, very much on par with the reality of decision making, and organizational design. The edges are curvy rather than straight, and instead of using 4 neat quadrants, there's an almost imperceptible core in the middle.

The heart of the framework – disorder – is the most challenging. It's when you don't know which situation you're in, and how you need to respond to it. The trick is to gather as much information as you can to get out of there and then take the appropriate action, according to the 4 types of context that the framework addresses.

The 'obvious' or simple context is not surprisingly the easiest one. It's the predictable area of the 'known knowns': your options are clear and cause and effect relationships are apparent to all involved. There is often only one solution and, even better, everyone knows what it is. But when you find yourself in the quadrant of the 'complicated' context – the area of the 'known unknowns' – it gets a bit trickier. There may be a clear relationship between cause and effect, but it may not be visible to everyone. That's because the problem is too complicated for 'regular' people to solve. You need experts. An example could be a car that breaks down: most drivers don't know what the problem is and how they can fix it, but they will always know someone who can.

The most relevant quadrant of the framework, however, is the one describing the 'complex' context, which is the domain of unknown unknowns and of emergence. Many business situations fall into this category, and I think that we all agree that it fits innovation to a tee: what happens here is 'subject to flux and unpredictability'. "There are no right answers, only many competing ideas." Often, we don't even know the right questions to ask.

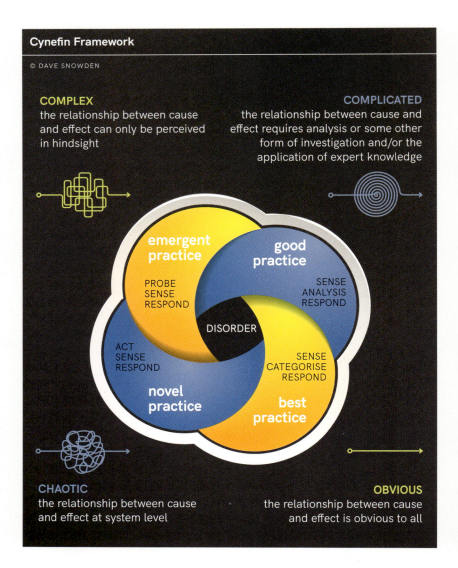

According to Dave Snowden, trying to control the situation or insisting on a plan of action is the worst possible response in the face of complexity. What you need to do here is to increase the level of interaction and communication, seek diversity, be accepting of failure and, above all, to experiment as much as you can. He calls the latter "Probe" (which I'm sorry to say always brings to mind weird UFO stories), which allows patterns and possible courses of action to emerge.

Finally, there's also the high turbulence 'chaotic' context. This is the realm of 'unknowables'. Searching for 'right' answers would be pointless here. The relationships between cause and effect are impossible to determine because they constantly shift, and no manageable patterns exist – only turbulence. The events of 9/11, for instance, fell into this category. In the chaotic domain, a leader's immediate job is not to discover patterns but to staunch the bleeding and then respond by working to transform the situation from chaos to complexity.[46]

The hard part of Cynefin is to realize with which situation you are dealing, and that's no different from when it comes to designing innovation. However, many organizations fundamentally commit a category error and fail to recognize that this falls into the complex context. Instead, they tend to approach it as if it were a complicated or even obvious type of situation. Often, they even use a mix of both. Those that treat it as 'obvious', are the ones who think that one 'Big' answer is enough. They have a yearly hackathon, a three day management symposium, a co-creation session or even one fixed innovation team (the same four people that stay in the same room coming up with the same type of answers) and think that it will be enough. And then these organizations are disappointed when very little is accomplished.

Those who regard innovation as merely complicated are very common too. They believe that calling in the expert consultants will fix any kind of innovation ailment. And sometimes they can, but if you want to embed innovation deep into the fabric and design of your organization, a 200-page consultancy report won't be much of a help.

Though some pockets of innovation can indeed be 'merely' complicated, the bulk belongs to the realm of the complex context. And so, what innovation 'wants' is experimentation. And interaction. And diversity. Because as circumstances become more complex, simplifications, control and order will fail to deliver.

True, a lot of companies *do* experiment, but they experiment with ideas, products and services, and very little with organizational design. So if we apply this experimentative approach to our companies, it means we must let go of order, command and control. We need to experiment a lot more with our structures, team formations, functions and roles.

It means we need an experimenting Never Normal Design: with fluid departments and roles that continuously morph and shift. It means we need to create as many connections as possible to strengthen the fabric of the organization. It does *not* mean suffocating the stream of innovation with fixed departments, with fixed team members who constantly sit in fixed roles.

■ **Designing for innovation flow**

"Design is not just what it looks like and feels like. Design is how it works." — STEVE JOBS

If you think that this type of fluid design is merely a side issue, a speck of dust in the multiverse that innovation is, think again. In fact, design and flow lie at the very basis of pretty much everything, if we believe Adrian Bejan. Bejan is a Romanian-American professor and bestselling author who has made many contributions to modern thermodynamics and developed what he calls the constructal law. He believes that "everything that flows and moves generates designs that evolve to survive (to live)." According to him, all designs evolve according to this same constructal law of physics which he thinks governs "any system, any time, anywhere": from rivers and lightning bolts to trees, animals and technology and even knowledge, language, or culture."[47]

Any system. That means your company too.

According to this constructal law, flow systems have two basic properties. There is the current that is flowing: for instance heat, mass, information or, in our situation, innovation. And then there is the design through which it flows: in this case, the company. Now, the design of the flow system will always have to deal with various forms of friction. But it will also always seek to facilitate the flow, by bypassing this friction. Because this flow is what keeps it evolving. It's what keeps it alive.

And yet, ironically, we tend to design our organizations with so much friction – be it static, or closed-off parts – that it completely destroys the natural flow of information, ideas and experiments. Successful systems will evolve in such a way that provides easier access to the currents that flow through it. Microsoft and Ashoka, for instance, are excellent examples of that, as I explain below. Finite-sized systems that are not designed to 'flow', on the other hand, will not persist in time as they will no longer evolve fast enough, according to Bejan.

If you want to keep innovation flowing through your organizational system, you need to create a fluid undercurrent of teams and individuals that continuously navigate the rest of the organization, and who switch roles, positions and tasks. Your innovation design cannot be static but must offer freedom and facilitate faster and easier movement. If it is immobile, the current will stop, and the system will dry up and die. Never make the mistake of underestimating this.

How you structure your organization is essential.

Inside flow: role experiments

Of course, the first thing that comes to mind when talking about a Never Normal Structure is the concept of fluid architectures, with team members who frequently switch roles. Now, I *do* realize that this approach is not new. There's a lot of literature to be found on it. But the thing is, it's mostly theory. You can find a lot of opinion leaders who explain the benefits and how you *could* organize it. Most of these articles offer very few concrete examples.

Yet out there, there are companies that do apply this type of fluid flow-enabling structure. Microsoft is one. I had the pleasure to talk to its HR Director BELUX, Elke Willaert, about how the company encourages individual employees to switch roles every 3 or 4 years. This unofficial policy is designed to enhance learning and encourage a growth mindset, agility, and familiarity with change. Social entrepreneurship company Ashoka, too, is a fantastic example of such a mobile architecture. The composition of its teams keeps shifting over time, as their needs evolve. They are not organized around fixed roles and responsibilities, but are oriented around common problems whose nature obviously keeps on dynamically morphing.

So yes, organizations experimenting with a Never Normal organizational design do exist. But they are still few and far between. And an important reason for this is the flexibility of the individual. We humans like our comfort zones, and we like sharpening our existing expertise. Switching roles and functions induces stress. For some types of personality, it's a healthy kind of stress, but others tend to suffer greatly from it. They have trouble adapting to their new environment, new colleagues, new roles and new skills requirements. Now, if this flowing design and role-switching is accepted as the standard, many will learn to perceive it as part of the process, rather than something to be feared.

But however revolutionary this may all sound, it is just not enough. There are some ways of looking at these problems which offer some paths for the future. Frederik Anseel told me about one such simple but brilliant 'mind trick' that's perfectly in line with the Cynefin advice of tackling complex situations with experimentation.

Frederik used to be a Head of Department at Ghent University but then moved on to King's College London, where he became Vice Dean of Research at the Business School. He's not 'just' an academic, but an entrepreneur too, and has founded two HR-tech oriented consulting firms. I've had the pleasure of interviewing him twice for our nexxworks blog and have come to know and appreciate him as one of the most original thinkers in organizational behavior today. Perhaps one of the things I like most about him is his low tolerance for unresearched and unfounded 'vision' by 'thought leaders' with no industry experience. In this, he's a bit of a rebel, sometimes even daring thought-leaders to put money on their predictions. But above all he's this devilishly smart and funny guy. He's also the one who taught me that you can soften transitions for change-shy individuals by simply encouraging them to begin new roles 'as an experiment'. It creates a really ingenious safety net.

When employees transition to a new function, it is always presented as an official and often long-term move. And then, if the new role does not pan out, employees tend to treat this as a (personal) failure. Now, if this perception is turned upside down and the transition is presented as an experiment, with employees told that they "do not need to transition to this role permanently, just try it on for size", a great deal of stress and fear of failure is taken away.

This type of experimental HR migration is the most non-threatening way to allow employees – even the most change-averse and insecure ones – to find new potential within themselves. It releases the pressure of changing into a new role and alleviates the uncertainty that comes along with that. Going back or moving on to something else will never be perceived as shameful if it's presented as an experiment. It's a much more natural process.

In fact, you could say that – even if the new role turns out to be a bad match – the person in question will have grown and learned a lot. We tend to believe that only positive data – about our successes – is useful, but 'negative' data about failure – how NOT to do something or learning what you're NOT good at – can be just as useful. Silicon Valley's "fail fast and learn" adage is absolutely applicable to this facet of the business world as well.

When you think about it, it's quite strange that this flow-inducing experimental approach to role switching does not happen more often. There is so much talk out there about how companies have to experiment with products, services and business models. And yet we almost never apply this experimentation, this "fail fast and learn" approach, to roles and careers. If you don't make it frictionless and safe for employees to 'reinvent' themselves – by allowing them to experiment with their own careers – how can you expect them to keep reinventing your processes, or products, or business models? It simply doesn't add up. It's the responsibility of HR to allow for the Never Normal structures inside a company to compensate for that. And too often, there's a discrepancy there.

▪ Outside flow: talent consortia

But it won't suffice to just stimulate the flow *inside* the design of your organization. Innovation works best at the crossroads between companies, industries and markets. And complex contexts require communication, interaction and collaboration with as diverse a set of profiles as possible. That's why the most successful companies build bridges to others, sometimes even competitors. Like BMW and Daimler joining forces to enter the ride sharing business.

Now, to induce the flow between your organizational system and others, and reduce the friction between them, attending congresses, network events or trainings won't suffice. As long as these connections are not structural, the ideas and actions flowing from this will remain non-committal.

It's a happy accident that the solution for this can be found in the response to another very relevant problem, which is just as challenging: finding and keeping top talent. These top profiles are an especially restless breed that are exceedingly sensible to 'payment' in growth and learning.

Sometimes, the learning cycle that a company can 'repay' them with, halts. It's a very uncomfortable truth that companies can sometimes no longer help develop a certain person's talents within the confines of their own organization. A lot of companies choose to ignore this, for obvious reasons.

Frederik Anseel told me about his rather radical solution for this conundrum. One which a lot of organizations will be afraid of: he believes that in these unfortunate cases, companies must set these talented employees free to another company, and then try to bring them back again after 5 to 10 years. It's a scary but irrefutable logic: if you can't help your top talent grow and learn, they will leave you regardless. But letting them go, retaining a dialogue and mutual understanding, will allow you to keep communication channels open.

And that's the absolute crucial part. For two reasons.

First, when top employees leave and maintain a good relationship with their former employer, they function as connectors and boundary spanners. This has the same effect as when companies introduce fluid teams inside their organizational structure, as employees travelling between the teams also function as connectors. Innovation thrives at the edges of systems and if these former employees will connect their former employers with new systems – new organizations, new industries, new methodologies – their added value will keep resonating well beyond the end of their formal employee-ship.

And second, when the ties are maintained when talent leaves, they might one day decide to return. And just imagine how much value will flow from that: not only will they still have a firm understanding of the company, but they will be able to look at its processes, methods, team structure, customer centricity (and all other facets of your company) with a wholly new and critical perspective. On top of that, they bring an entire set of new experiences, insights and knowledge to the table that they would never have acquired had they stayed within the safe confinements of the 'mother ship'.

Now imagine the richness and the agility that would result from embedding this approach in a structural manner in your organizational flow design. What if non-competing companies could set up some sort of consortium for sharing their top talent? What if they would share certain very hard to find and keep profiles – like machine learning and blockchain experts, or very creative T-shaped individuals – allowing them to move from role to role, between said companies? That way, the individual could keep developing their skills and talents within the different functions and sectors of the consortium. And at the same time the companies can still keep them quite close, and broaden their own Hourglass-outlook through their network of consortia-partners from very different sectors.

These types of highly fluid intra-company structures, with employees moving between the peripheries of different systems, would greatly stimulate agility and innovation flow, both on an individual level and an organizational level. Employees that kept switching between networks and industries might become very talented at the top part of the Hourglass: sensing new tendencies and customer behaviors and experimenting with them, and interconnecting the different organizations in the talent-sharing platform.

▪ Don't fuck up the structure

Company structure has always been greatly underestimated. Next to its big, hip and happening, Instagram influencer worthy brother, "Culture", Structure was the nerdy knocked-kneed, spectacle-wearing junior of the family who kept posting anonymous – but possibly useful messages – on Quora.

Culture received all the attention and Structure had to cope with the fact that all the cool quotes were directed at his popular sibling: from Peter Thiel's "Don't fuck up the culture" to Peter Drucker's "Culture eats strategy for breakfast."

Well, I'm here to tell you – badly quoting Patrick Swayze – "Nobody puts Structure in a corner." It's a crucial part of the flow of innovation inside your company, and you have to keep your Never Normal design morphing, switching and experimenting to keep your system alive. You cannot expect people to change, adapt and grow – themselves or your company – if you fix them in static structures.

But a fluid structure – creating flow inside and outside – goes so much beyond that and is the basis of many other organizational benefits.

It's about stimuli: about employees moving between departments and even companies (in the case of the consortium or when you keep communications open with former employees) and becoming inspired by new ideas, new approaches, insights, skills or even cultures.

It's about connections: the more people are strongly linked within a company – by creating these types of mobile employee nodes that connect to many others – the stronger the fabric of your organization becomes.

It's about putting people where they belong. Sometimes, we expect too much flexibility from employees: just think about someone working in marketing today compared to 15 years ago. People don't always have the elasticity to evolve along with their functional role. But what if, instead of keeping them unhappily (knowing that they just don't fit anymore) where they are or firing them, we could put them in another place of the organization where their skills and talents *do* match at that certain point in time?

It's – and this is a very big one – about integration: so many fantastic innovation ideas and experiments fail to emerge from the innovation part of an organization and don't become integrated into the existing business because of a lack of interconnection. The innovation team flies solo, and their ideas never fulfil their potential. In a fluid organization, with teams and people switching places and broadening their network, the integration becomes easier because the entire organization is – in itself – a lot more connected.

And last but not least, it's about lifelong learning. Learning is no longer something you do once in your life. It's not even about following a training every four months. Remember the 1%, the people who 'Don't Know What They Are Doing'? If you're doing something for the first time, something that has never been done before, there won't be any training program available. Online or offline. In this case, you learn by doing. And what better way to 'train' your brain for this type of agility by moving from role to role every so often and familiarizing yourself with 'doing something new' over and over again?

Structure *does* matter. It's the undercurrent of everything that happens in your organization.

So, whatever you do, don't fuck up the structure.

YOUR TURN

So that's essentially how successful companies are able to reinvent themselves. Innovation takes a village. Don't let yourself be discouraged by how much is involved. Just work in baby steps. And right now, I want you to do some soul searching. Ask yourself some questions that might be long overdue, because you have been focusing so much on Today, or even cleaning up Yesterday's shit.

Do you have "an offer you can't refuse"?
Are you keeping your offer relevant for your customers? Are you connecting data in a smart way so you can deliver them what they want, when they want it? Or are you perhaps focussing too much on yourself, your own products and services? And what exactly are you doing to create "an offer you can't refuse" for your customers? As Steven Van Belleghem would ask: how are you helping them save time, accomplish their dreams and even help with BIG world problems?

Could you be, or could you join, a platform?
If you want to become a platform, go big or go home. Don't make the mistake of just 'digitizing' your current business model into a platform, but completely reinvent yourself, like Ping An and Apple Healthkit did. Otherwise, your well-intentioned but misplaced transformation will still end up with you becoming a dumb pipe. And there's always the option of joining forces with a platform, like McDonalds did with Uber Eats. Think about what you want to be: a Batman platform or a Robin supplier?

Are you fresh like Fontainebleau in the Spring?
What does your company culture 'smell' like? Are your people scared to fail? Are they stressed out? Or are they thriving, experimenting and really passionate about what they are doing? I want you to take some time to write down the rules of your company. Do not copy its official rules. We all know how big the divide can be between a company's mission and vision and what's really going on. Just think about what needs to be done inside your company to be regarded as a success, and you'll have the real rules. If they 'smell' like Calcutta in the summer, tear them up, and rewrite them. And then work backwards to what needs to happen to make them real. You may need to hire more people "who don't know what they are doing". Just be brave. Wanting to rewrite your culture is the first step, like Satya Nadella did when he first entered Microsoft.

Are you VUCA-proof?
Are lifelong learning and a growth mindset firmly incorporated in your company? Are you hiring for diversity, for culture fit and passion? And is there a balance between the value for the company and the value for the individual employee? And above all, are your leaders comfortable with complexity and ambiguity?

I know, it's a lot to think about. But just start with the part that makes you most excited, even if you are scared. Trust me, things will get a lot scarier the longer you wait.

5

The Proof of the Pudding

> To succeed in this world,
> you have to change all the time.
>
> — SAM WALTON, FOUNDER OF WALMART

SO, TELL ME. CAN IT BE DONE?

During all my years as a keynote speaker on disruption, radical change and the Day After Tomorrow, I've received primarily two questions after a presentation. First, is what people's children should study in order to prepare for the future. That's a big one. But just as often, people inquire after examples of companies in their industry that succeeded in transforming themselves to thrive in the Day After Tomorrow.

My answer to that second question is always that they should not wait. They should definitely not delay reinventing themselves until one of their competitors has led the way, so that all they have to do is copy that pattern. But it's obviously a little bit more complicated than that.

My brother in arms at London Business School is Professor Costas Markides. He is a brilliant teacher of corporate strategy, who co-developed the London Business School course 'Exploiting Disruption in a Digital World' with me. Costas is the author of many books, one of which is 'Fast Second: How Smart Companies Bypass Radical Innovation to Enter and Dominate New Markets'.

In this book, Costas argues that in many cases it pays off to NOT to be the first mover in a market. He contends that – if you take a classic S-curve – 'startup' companies operating at the 'bottom' of the S-curve are much better at the zero-to-one game, and will excel at innovation, while the established firms are just better equipped at the scale-game – going from one-to-N. Sometimes you just have to wait for markets to become 'ripe' for scaling.

One of his favorite stories is that of disposable diapers. In the 19th century, diapers were essentially cotton towels, held together with a safety pin. But in 1947, the Scottish housewife Valerie Hunter Gordon started developing and making a product called 'Paddi', a 2-part diaper system consisting of a disposable pad worn inside an adjustable plastic garment. She got a patent for her invention in the UK in October 1949, and it was successfully sold through the Boots stores for many years.

But in those days, it was still seen as a luxury item. The Paddi diapers were only purchased by affluent mothers who wanted to travel in comfort with their babies when they would go on a long train-journey. But at home, they would not use the 'expensive' Paddi diapers, and would revert back to the traditional cotton ones.

And then, in 1956, Procter & Gamble began researching disposable diapers. They figured out how to design the product and scale production in such a way that the Pampers product (launched in 1961) could completely capture the market, and in so doing, fundamentally change behavior. Today, the Pampers business generates more than $10 billion in annual revenue for P&G. The brand grew so big it has become synonymous with diaper.

Costas fundamentally believes that it is the unique capability of the P&G's of this world to scoop up embryonic innovations like the Paddi, and then use the efficiency, power and scale of their massive 'machines' to execute to success.

As you can see, it's absolutely true that it does not always pay off to be the first.

Google was not the first search engine. Some of us are old enough to remember our first Internet queries on 'vintage' web service providers like Yahoo or AltaVista. Google was a 'Fast Second' company that understood the dynamics of an emerging market, realized how to improve the customer experience and increase relevance, and then developed the underlying business mechanics to grow into a $100 billion business. And now they have to reinvent themselves, all over again.

Amazon, too, has kept gloriously transforming itself in the last 10 years: from becoming the dominant online retailer in the West, to positioning itself explicitly as a technology company by emerging as the largest Cloud Computing player on the planet. We could hardly call them a Fast Second, though, since they almost single-handedly invented the entire new category of 'Computing as a Service'. So, perhaps not a 'Fast Second', but it was definitely a brilliantly executed Phoenix move.

As a matter of fact, I would assert that EVERY last one of the top four US Digital Giants – the fab four of the stock market or the 'GAFA' (Google, Amazon, Facebook and Apple) – have gone through, or are currently executing, a Phoenix transformation.

Google has to pull off a Phoenix move in order to transform itself beyond the world of advertising. Amazon has masterly executed the ingenious Phoenix move towards the Cloud. Microsoft, too, is reinventing itself at this very moment under Satya Nadella, through the power of Cloud computing. Since then, they have been rewarded as one of the most valuable companies on the stock market. Safe to say that their Phoenix maneuver is paying off.

But Apple might very well be the most badass Phoenix of them all, with the battle scars to prove it. In fact, it should have died a long time ago. If business life were a zombie movie, Apple would be the one that suddenly surfaces out of the barren ground and grabs us by the throat, because we all thought it had kicked the proverbial bucket.

If William Shakespeare would be alive today, he would not write about Kings or Princes, he would write about Steve Jobs.

I've called Apple the 'Ultimate Phoenix' before in this book. Unfortunately, I'm not sure Apple as a company offers much of a 'handbook' in terms of innovation guidance. Many of its breakthrough moments, and pivotal radical strategic shifts, are ultimately traced to the erratic genius and undoubtedly controversial leadership style of Mr. Jobs himself.

Jobs was at his brilliant best when he single-handedly embarked upon the creation of the Apple Macintosh, a breakthrough in the field of computing, and still very much alive almost 40 years later. If you enter a Palo Alto coffee shop, all you see is young entrepreneurs carrying around the direct space-grey descendants of that original Macintosh, launched way back in 1984.

But the truth is: Jobs' leadership couldn't (and probably shouldn't) be copied. Andy Hertzfeld was the chief software designer of the original Macintosh team, and he used to describe Jobs' unique style with a term from Star Trek: 'The Reality Distortion Field'. In his words: "Jobs possessed an eerie quality to convince anyone of practically anything. His reality distortion field was a confounding mélange of a charismatic rhetorical style, an indomitable will, and an eagerness to bend any fact to fit the purpose at hand. If one line of argument failed to persuade, he would deftly switch to another. Sometimes, he would throw you off balance by suddenly adopting your position as his own, without acknowledging that he ever thought differently."

He must have been an incredibly difficult person to work with, but he also pushed people beyond their limits. He unlocked their creativity in ways many of them had no idea that they could. People like Andy would describe their astoundingly intense collaboration as both the worst and the best experience he and the rest of the team ever had in their professional careers. But Jobs unlocked a culture of striving for perfection, and putting a 'dent in the universe'. He would inspire others to turn up their nose at good ideas: "You must work on great ideas, not good ones."

Ultimately, he fundamentally believed that brilliant people can only do brilliant work if they are truly empowered to unlock their creativity. That's why he isolated the Macintosh team in a separate building – with a Pirate flag waving at the top – and told them, "It's better to be a pirate than to join the navy." I just love how he wanted all the creators who built that breakthrough icon of innovation to sign their names on the inside of the plastic case of the machine. As Jobs put it: "Since the Macintosh team were true artists, it was only appropriate that they sign their work."

As Andy Hertzfeld phrased it: "We were excited because we thought we had a chance to create something extraordinary. Most technology innovation is incremental, but every once in a while there's an opportunity to make a quantum leap to a whole new level."

That's the moment you have to grasp. You will probably encounter those opportunities to radically change something in your organization just a few times over your entire professional career. Maybe two or three times you will truly be able to make a difference. I am talking about that moment where you can join a movement that will truly make a 'dent in the universe'.

Will you be able to recognize that moment?
And would you know what to do when it happens?
Are you truly, really ready?

THE PHOENIX FROM BENTONVILLE

Having a Reality Distortion Field will probably not help you reinvent yourself as a Phoenix. It might have worked for Jobs, but it's certainly not a recipe for absolute success.

So what *is* a methodology that could assist you in your Phoenix journey? My good friend Costas helped me discover an incredibly simple put powerful framework to address these challenges. I'll illustrate that framework with one of the most wonderful Phoenixes that I've ever had the chance to study: the radical and inspiring transformation story of the largest 'traditional' retailer in the world. That of Walmart.

A few years ago, I was invited to talk at the birthplace and headquarters of Walmart, located in Bentonville, in the North-West of Arkansas. I have spent quite a lot of time in the US – giving lectures in glorious places like New York, Miami, Dallas or San Francisco – but take it from me: if you want to experience the 'real' United States, then Bentonville is the perfect place. It will also help you understand the true values and beliefs that lie at the heart of Walmart.

In downtown Bentonville, you can even visit the original "Five and Dime" store that Sam Walton started in 1950. Back then, he was a bright young man, who had learned all about the art of 'retailing' while he worked at J.C. Penney. And then, on a stroke of genius, he decided to start on his own in the retail business.

The growth of the company was beyond spectacular.

His first 'real' Walmart was opened in Rogers, Arkansas in 1962. A chain of other discount department stores followed in rapid tempo. By 1967, the company had grown to 24 stores across the state of Arkansas, and it had reached $12.6 million in sales. By 1975, when Walmart had moved on to Texas as well as six other states, there were 125 stores with 7,500 associates, and total sales of $340.3 million.

By the company's 25th anniversary, the community of Walmart employees had grown to over 100,000 people. Sam Walton was not a technologist, but he was an insatiably curious man, who was always on the lookout to improve efficiency. Walmart had grown to such a size that they were instrumental in pushing the 'radically' new concept of barcodes into the retail ecosystem. By 1988 Walmart had equipped 90% of their stores with barcode readers.

By 1995, Walmart had become the largest retailer on the planet, with almost $100 billion in sales, and more than 675,000 associates. From that moment on, Walmart started to quickly expand internationally, moving into regions like Mexico, Canada, Brazil, the UK and China.

Walmart was not the first supermarket. They were not the first discount retailer. They were probably what Costas Markides would label a top-achiever in the 'Fast Second' category. Their recipe for success: a laser-like precision focus on strategy, flawless execution, faith in technological innovation and a fundamental belief in their core values to engage their associates. And last but not least, the absolute conviction that there is only ONE boss: The Customer. That is the combination that made Walmart the largest retailer, and the largest private employer in the world. In the US, Walmart accounts for 2% of the entire economy.

In 2018, Walmart managed more than 11,000 stores worldwide in more than 27 countries, and did more than $500 billion in revenue. And yet, despite all this scale, they needed to reinvent themselves all over again.

Walmart was King. Walmart had been the retail 'disruptor' of the 20th century. They had followed the 'Fast Second' playbook religiously and had created an economy of scale like no other had done before.

Until that pesky technology startup from Seattle with a name like a rainforest had started selling books online, and gently but firmly rain had started falling on Walmart's parade.

I would argue that it took a relatively long time for Walmart to realize that the world of retail was fundamentally changing. They 'ignored' the e-commerce revolution for quite some time, thinking it was merely a small ripple in a big pond. But when companies like Amazon grew increasingly aggressive and moved into the core space that Walmart occupied, they decided to engage. Big Time.

That is why, for me personally, Walmart is one of the most visible and inspirational Phoenix stories out there. And let me illustrate that with the innovation model that Costas Markides has taught me.

1 Sense of Urgency

You cannot embark on a 'Phoenix' transformation, without an utterly clear and absolutely vigorous Sense of Urgency.

That might seem obvious, but realize that there is such a thing as a 'Fake' Sense of Urgency. Companies can suffer from *Eisenbahnscheinbewegung*:[48] they might 'think' they have a sense of urgency, but in reality, often most people in the organization don't feel it. In fact, they secretly think that 'it will all blow over'.

It's a bit like fire alarms. When they go off, we all tend to think that it's just a harmless (and annoying) fire drill. It's the story of the Boy who Cries Wolf,[49] who is eventually eaten by the beasts. In exactly the same way, many people in the organization think "Whatever" when their CEO delivers a (pseudo-)passionate speech about 'disruption' at the annual company event.

In my opinion, Walmart's absolute sense of urgency surfaced in 2017, when Amazon decided to purchase the American organic supermarket chain Whole Foods Market for $13.7 billion. The whole world had been watching in awe, and Walmart received a wake-up call. Don't get me wrong. It's not that e-commerce had NOT been on Walmart's radar before that moment. Of course it was. Walmart had built e-commerce infrastructure and had even made a few pricey acquisitions like jet.com, back in 2016, for more than $3 billion.

But what truly created Walmart's sense of urgency was the stock-market's reaction the very moment that Amazon had acquired Whole Foods Market. It had paid $13.7 billion for the supermarket chain, and intriguingly, its market cap jumped $15 billion as soon as the deal was announced.

Amazon had substantially grown its grocery delivery business for the previous few years. It had invested in building out Amazon Fresh and had systematically evolved from selling books towards a whole spectrum of goods. Goods that people *used* to buy at Walmart. There was even a book written about Amazon called 'The Everything Store'.[50]

But when Amazon plunked down $13.7 billion for the up-market inner-city organic food chain with its digitally savvy mobile New Normal user base, Bentonville was put on Red Alert.

The CEO of Walmart, Doug McMillon, put it like this: "At some point, Walmart became big and expectations changed. And we missed the memo." Missing 'the memo' can be fatal in a world that is moving so fast. But if you wake up just in time, you might be able to correct your course. The sense of urgency came at exactly the right moment for Walmart, when it was vital for them to redesign themselves as a Phoenix.

And if we turn that around, we just end up with 'All Talk, but No Action': these are the companies that don't have such a CLEAR sense of urgency, even though they have all the other necessities in place for transformation. Don't be that company. Be more like Walmart.

2 Clear Vision

Having established the sense of urgency, the next question becomes: what's your vision for the road ahead?

The CEO Doug McMillon started talking about Walmart as a 'technology company' in speeches, magazines and newspaper articles. That may be a fantastic aspirational goal, but it does not entirely measure up to reality. Yet. You could claim that from the very start, Amazon was a technology company which happened to build a platform that disrupted the retail sector. But at heart, Walmart is a retailer that needed to dramatically beef up its technological powers.

Which they did.

Its Pickup Towers are one of my favorite examples of this. These are gigantic, ultraconvenient and superfast in-store vending machines – almost the size of an upright school bus – where you can pick up the goods that you ordered on walmart.com.

When the company started to successfully expand its online offering via walmart.com, some customers liked the idea of picking up their order in a nearby Walmart store on their way from or to work or their children's schools. But when it takes only 10 seconds to order something on your phone, but then you

© WALMART

have to wait for 10 or more minutes in line for the Walmart associate to find your package, that really takes all the fun (and point) out of online ordering.

Enter the Pickup Towers. These automats were actually conceived by ex-Estonian postal employees, and Walmart believed they could brilliantly solve their conundrum: they allow customers to order online, walk up to a Pickup Tower in a nearby store, scan the code on their app and pronto, receive their parcel in less than 10 seconds. Customers loved it, and now Walmart is rolling them out everywhere in their physical network.

That is exactly what Walmart's vision of the future is all about.

They leverage their amazing existing retail infrastructure and combine it with ultraconvenient and seamless online experiences. When we talked about Omnichannel as one of the New Normals, these Pickup Towers are just the perfect embodiment of Walmart's Online-Meets-Offline vision.

It is not only customers that love that clear combination, but analysts do as well. "The Walmart brand is at the center of a new ecosystem that integrates shopping, services, and marketplace e-commerce," one financial analyst wrote. "Walmart is seizing the moment to transform through innovation and utilization of unique store, product and people assets."

They excel at marketing, too. Remember that viral US commercial with the famous movie cars from the last century – The Delorean from Back To The Future, KITT from Knight Rider, or the Scooby-Doo van – that brilliantly illustrated the convenience of ordering online, and picking up your groceries with your car just outside your local Walmart?

Walmart's vision of the Online-Meets-Offline approach is crystal clear: leverage the enormous footprint of the current Walmart stores, and develop that network as the enabler of e-commerce for the Walmart customer of the future. It's simple, really: if you don't know where you're going, you're just playing around and will **Hit the Wall**. And Walmart is dead serious about reinventing itself.

3 Right Mindset

Establishing a sense of urgency about adaptation and transformation as well as developing a clear vision is essential for budding Phoenix companies. But it's just as important that the entire company fully understands the mindset of change: that each and every employee has a clear vision about the urgency of innovation and a thorough understanding of how to get there. If only the top of the company is on board, it simply won't work.

Walmart still feels like a family business.

Sam Walton became one of the richest men in America when his company floated on the stock exchange on the 1st of October 1970. But Sam Walton was also known for his frugality. Inside the original Bentonville store – which has been turned into a museum – stands the beloved old rusty pickup truck that he drove for most of his life.

Today the Walton family still owns about half of the Walmart shares. And although Walmart is publicly traded, you still clearly feel some of the typical 'family owned' business atmosphere. An example of that family perspective is the strong focus on long term thinking, instead of merely looking at the next quarter.

That is now clearly voiced as well by the CEO, when Doug McMillon addressed that very specific issue of the 'Time Horizon' in his 2019 shareholder letter: "We're playing the long game. Our priority is to position the company for long-term success. History has shown us that companies that focused too much on the short term were doomed to fail. Managing our business on a daily basis is important, but most of our strategic decisions are made in light of what we want our company to become for the next generation."

That typical Day After Tomorrow belief in preparing for the next generation is very difficult to find in many corporations. Most tend to run primarily for short-term returns, and aim at maximizing short-term gains. But a company like Amazon is notorious for playing the long game. In fact, it refuses to even think about short term profits or dividends, because that would jeopardize its 'Day One' spirit. If you're competing with Amazon, then you have to play along and harbor a long-term perspective too. No other way around it. To do this, your shareholders have to support you wholeheartedly.

It also means that you need the right mindset to enable a long-term engagement towards and from your employees. Sam Walton was famous for walking around his stores and talking to his 'associates' in order to understand what he could do for them. Today Walmart is the largest private employer in the world. In this day and age of rapid technological change, how does a company of that size ensure that this enormous community of associates can make the transition? How does such an organization re-skill for the Day After Tomorrow?

Well, through massive and frankly impressive investments in the training and re-skilling of the Walmart associates. As Doug McMillon puts it: "The ways we can use technology today and in the future are exciting, but our business is still a people business. We are people-led and tech-empowered, and that makes investing in our associates a strategic priority."

Creating the right mindset to prepare for the Day After Tomorrow is crucial: you need everyone on board, or none of your beautiful transformation plans will stick. And everyone needs to face the same direction. Otherwise, Panic ensues.

4 Shared Direction

So the fourth 'ingredient' for a successful transformation, and a Phoenix imperative, is an explicit Shared Direction.

When you enter the massive Walmart 'Home Office' – as their headquarters are characteristically called – the first thing you'll notice is a massive sign on the wall that reads: "There is only one boss. The Customer."

That customer has always been the guiding 'North-Star' of the company, from the very beginning. And, yes, long before expensive words like 'Extreme Customer Centricity' became popular.

That statement comes from the man himself, of course: Sam Walton. Actually, his version was just a bit longer, and a tad bit more brutal: "There is only one boss. The customer. And he can fire everybody in the company from the chairman on down, simply by spending his money somewhere else." I suppose that was just too long to put on the wall.

For a long time, Walmart's focus on the customer was related to the quality of the products, to the variety of selection, but primarily to price. Walmart even codified that in its 'Every Day Low Price Guarantee'. The latter even grew to become a fixed acronym inside the company, part of its standard jargon and a cornerstone of the Walmart strategy: EDLP, the Every Day Low Price.

With Walmart's sheer volume of sales, the bargaining power this gives them with suppliers, and the knack that the company has always displayed for keeping operational costs as low as possible, it had built a powerhouse that can deliver on that lowest price guarantee.

But what Walmart started to understand, as Amazon.com kept growing, is that the behavior of their customers was changing. Of course it remained important for customers to find the products they wanted, at the lowest price. But platforms like Amazon had similar economies of scale which also allowed them enormous bargaining power. Walmart was no longer part of the happy few on the market to be so price conscious. And for the average customer, saving time was becoming just as important as saving money.

If you are a working mom, combining two jobs to pay the bills, you'll try to spend as little time as you can wandering around in a supermarket. It doesn't matter how friendly the associates are nor how cheap the products, quality time with your loved ones during your precious non-working hours will always be more important. In the 21st century, where we are all busier than ever, convenience has become the new 'loyalty', as my friend Steven Van Belleghem would say.

And Amazon truly excelled at that part. You would just be able to order your goods by talking to Alexa, and when you come home at night, your groceries and other goods would be nicely delivered on your doorstep. Amazon helped customers save money AND save time.

That shared direction, The Customer, has not changed for Walmart. The customer is still the boss. But they have started to behave very differently.

Today Walmart is massively investing in this area. If you don't want to swing by the local store to pick up your goods, that is perfectly fine. It is experimenting with driverless vans, and delivery robots to drop off the goods right at your doorstep.

And for those who really don't like robots, Walmart has launched a brilliant 'In Home Delivery' service. A Walmart associate enters the customer's house via a 'Smart' lock, and they will stock the refrigerator with the groceries that were ordered online, so that they can remain fresh. For those with trust issues about a complete stranger entering their house: you can follow the entire process on the Walmart app on your phone.

The North-Star is still the customer. But today, Walmart associates help the customer save money and time. Fresh, or worse, frozen groceries can't be left on the doorsteps for hours, and now Walmart found a way to deliver an ultra convenient experience right into our home, with smart entry technology combined with proprietary cameras worn by the associates. This experiment is a great example of that 'Shared Direction'. Companies who lack this are merely ruled by **Anarchy**.

5 Execution Support

The last vital element in a successful 'Phoenix' metamorphosis might be the most important one of all: absolute, consistent, and genuine Execution Support.

You can have brilliant ideas, amazing talent, smashing technology, and even a fantastic award-winning vision. But if it fails in execution, it's all worthless.

How does a company's management enable everyone to actually move when the Red Alert is blinking? That is the essence of Execution Support.

It starts at the top. I have seen too many executives talk a lot about change but never really commit to it. But at the end of the day, the CEO should lead the pack. The fascinating thing about Walmart is that the current CEO Doug McMillon has had tremendous international experience, and that he saw firsthand what was happening in other parts of the world. Digital disruption originated in the US, but it certainly is a global virus. Evolutions in China were advancing even faster than back home, and Doug could feel the need for fundamental change.

Execution support means building amazing teams that understand how to operate in the two halves of the Hourglass. Teams that Run and Scale the traditional business and maximize efficiency and productivity, but at the same time know how to play the second game of 'Sense and Try'. The one where you pick up concepts, ideas and technologies, experiment and explore, and then bring it to the 'machine' for flawless execution.

But above all it's about empowering people. I have met some truly brilliant people at Walmart, who could have easily worked at Google, Facebook or Amazon. Instead, they were having an amazing time running the 'Machine' of Walmart. The company decided not to isolate innovation too much from the 'main ship'. They believe that, when you compartmentalize or isolate novel ideas and concepts, it becomes incredibly hard to influence the mothership.

But when you put innovation at the very heart of an organization and truly empower those brilliant maverick minds that thrive on experimentation and change, then you can generate phenomenal results. But if you don't, and isolate the DKWTD 1%'ers too much, and they end up spending all their beautiful energy in fighting the 99% who KWTD, you will only **frustrate and demotivate** them.

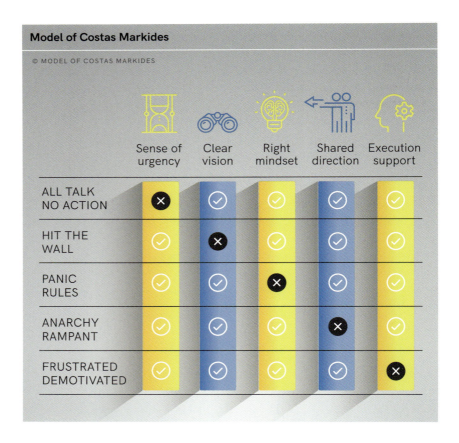

The film director James Cameron (known from hit movies like Titanic and Avatar) once told us that "Luck is not a factor. Hope is not a strategy. Fear is not an option."

If you are up against a technology colossus like Amazon, whose strategy it is to become "the world's biggest laboratory", you *will* need more than hope and luck. And fear is probably the worst counsellor for the Day After Tomorrow.

Phoenixes do exist. They are not mythical creatures. They are out there, and they are just as (if not more so) fascinating as Unicorns. They are the Microsofts, the Assa Abloys, the Volvos, the General Motors, the McDonalds and the Disneys of this world. Heck, I even found a Phoenix in Bentonville, Arkansas, of all places.

If you too have ambitions to rise like the Phoenix, you'll need the golden combination of a fearless sense of urgency, a clear vision forward which respects your history, the right mindset that encompasses both customers and employees, a shared direction for your entire team, and – above all – the enabling and support of those brave souls willing to tackle the Day After Tomorrow.

In the end, it all boils down to leadership. James Freeman Clarke once said: "A politician… is a man who thinks of the next election; while the statesman thinks of the next generation."

That's exactly the state (pun intended) of mind you need to lead a Phoenix.

BEFORE WE PART

10 questions to spark your inner Phoenix

Before we part, I want to leave you with a few questions that will hopefully help you decide upon the first steps towards your new beginning as a Phoenix. I hope that it will allow the insights of this book to resonate a little bit longer and perhaps even create some sparks.

1 Do you know what your New Normals are?

Think about all the newborn startups in your environment, and others in adjacent markets. Which technologies make up their foundation? What type of skeleton supports their muscles and flesh, and allows them to move so much faster than you? And are you making use of that same foundation? Is the answer "No"? You know what to do. Is it "Yes"? Great! But it may also be time to revisit them. Because New Normals keep changing. All the time.

2 Is your bottom heavier than it should be?

Let's go back to the Hourglass model, and then try to figure out what the exact ratio inside your company is. How much resources are you investing in the top 'Sense and Try' part, and how much are you focusing on the bottom part, where you 'Scale and Run'? Don't be discouraged if the bottom part overshadows the top. You'll definitely not be the only company in that position. But do think about how you can reallocate your resources from now on, to give you this much needed telescope view on the future.

3 How are you reinventing yourself?

I want you to think about the types of innovation going on in your company: are you reinventing your products, your market, your services or your business model? If it's only one of those, it might not be a bad idea to investigate the others as well, to avoid putting all your eggs in one basket. The more you experiment, the bigger the chance that something will stick.

4. What's your "offer you can't refuse"?

Customers are changing all the time. Are you *really* listening to them? Is your offer relevant and are you delivering it to them in the smartest, most timely and best connected manner? Or are you offering them what works best for *you*? And how are you making your products and services indispensable, as Steven Van Belleghem explained with his "offer you can't refuse"? Are you 'buying' time for your customers? Are you trying to speak to their dreams? And are you helping solve some of the world's biggest problems with and for them? The times when you 'just' offered something convenient and useful are over. Only the brands that go *far* beyond that will survive.

5. Are you Batman or Robin?

This is the age of platforms. You have two options: fight them by becoming one yourself – the most exciting but also most challenging option – or choose to become their Robin-like sidekick, joining forces and become a supplier. However, just ignoring the platforms is a really bad idea. Acknowledge the ones that are really useful for your customers and then decide which relationship you want to have with them.

6. What do you smell like?

Does your culture smell like a fresh Fontainebleau forest in the spring or a stale Calcutta in the summer? If it's the latter, figure out why. Is there a culture of toxic masculinity? Are people scared? Is the level of competition so high that people stop sharing information? Is there a lack of openness and trust? It's important that you're really honest: is this the type of company where you would like your children to work? Where they would be happy and passionate and able to grow? No? Then what can you do about that? Think of what bothers you the most, and then start talking to your colleagues about what could be done about it. If you won't tackle these problems, the best talent *will* leave you and you'll only end up with the mediocre and 'grey' employees, lacking in passion and commitment.

7. Do you know what you're doing?

Does everybody in your company know what they are doing? If the answer is yes, go back to square one. Not one single person that innovates knows what they are doing, as they are doing something that has never been done before. You can't be 'experienced' at innovating. So it's a good thing to have people in your company who feel comfortable not knowing what they are doing, are great at improvising along the way and at adapting to unexpected situations. Find, hire and empower those mavericks. If everyone inside your company knows what they are doing, you're simply not experimenting and innovating enough.

8 But are you experienced (at learning)?

How are you helping your employees to keep redefining their knowledge, experiences and skills? Today, individual employees, too, should be like Phoenixes: able to reinvent themselves along with the customers, the market and society. How are you supporting them in that: both emotionally (the pressure that comes with agility can be overwhelming at times), structurally and with training, coaching and position switches? And are you doing enough?

9 Safety first, or last?

Do your people feel safe enough to experiment? Just to give one example: according to innovation guru Clayton Christensen, 95 percent of all new products fail. In other words: failure is the mother of innovation, and you simply can't have one without the other. If you punish your team when a project goes sideways, they'll simply stop offering new ideas and experimenting. And you really don't want your top of the Hourglass activity to come to an end or even slow down. Find a way to incorporate acceptance of failure. And use the learnings from those mistakes to make your organization smarter.

10 Where's the love?

These are trying times for your employees. Very exciting times… but challenging too. Because we expect a lot of flexibility and adaptability from them, and for them to continuously recalibrate their function and skills. So, more than ever before, we need to take their fears, hopes and stress into account. And above all, we need to rekindle their passion, their purpose and their motivation so that, together, we can make a dent in the universe… So, where's that 'love' in your company? And what are you doing to keep it alive? Or do you need a new spark to light that fire again?

That's it for Today. May these questions set fire to your glorious Day After Tomorrow. And I mean that quite literally. Don't panic. There's no creation without a little bit (or sometimes even a lot) of destruction first.

So, dear faithful reader, our book journey stops here. This is where it ends.

And where it begins.

Are you ready?

ENDNOTES

1. The Pursuit of Power: Europe 1815–1914, By Richard J. Evans
2. Organizational Behavior: Foundations, Theories, and Analyses, John B. Miner
3. https://en.wikipedia.org/wiki/Social_Credit_System
4. https://en.wikipedia.org/wiki/Standing_on_the_shoulders_of_giants
5. Why Software Is Eating The World, By Marc Andreessen, The Wall Street Journal, August 20, 2011
6. Desert Island Discs, Sue Lawley in conversation with William Gibson.
7. Playboy Interview, February 1985, http://reprints.longform.org/playboy-interview-steve-jobs
8. https://en.wikipedia.org/wiki/Gloster_Meteor
9. https://en.wikipedia.org/wiki/Hans_von_Ohain
10. https://edition.cnn.com/travel/article/nasa-supersonic-flights-testing/index.html
11. https://globetrender.com/2019/03/03/boom-supersonic-overture/
12. Concorde research shows way to the next generation, FLIGHT International, 3 February 1972
13. https://en.wikipedia.org/wiki/Tupolev_Tu-144
14. https://archive.org/stream/roleofconcordeth00horw/roleofconcordeth00horw_djvu.txt
15. https://www.assaabloy.be/en/local/be/news-lp/news-articles-2014/news-category-2014/news-forbes-again-innovation/
16. https://www.cnet.com/news/meet-the-company-reinventing-the-way-we-unlock-doors-everywhere/
17. https://en.wikipedia.org/wiki/Design_thinking
18. https://nl.wikipedia.org/wiki/Blue_Ocean_Strategy
19. https://en.wikipedia.org/wiki/Skunk_Works
20. https://en.wikipedia.org/wiki/Kitty_Hawk,_North_Carolina
21. Ant Financial raises $14 billion in world's largest-ever single fundraising, Adam Jourdan, Cate Cadell – via Reuters
22. TransferWise valued at $3.5 billion after $292 million secondary funding, Paul Sawers, Venturebeat
23. https://en.wikipedia.org/wiki/Animal_Farm
24. These 10 job profiles will lead auto industry into the future, says Mary Barra of GM; auto.economictimes.indiatimes.com
25. https://en.wikipedia.org/wiki/AlphaGo
26. https://en.wikipedia.org/wiki/CRISPR
27. Control Your Destiny or Someone Else Will (Collins Business Essentials), by Noel M. Tichy & Stratford Sherman.

28 https://en.wikipedia.org/wiki/Creative_destruction
29 European Commission – Press release: Antitrust: Commission fines Google €4.34 billion for illegal practices regarding Android mobile devices to strengthen dominance of Google's search engine
30 Bloomberg – Europe Misfires on Europe, 19 July 2018
31 https://en.wikipedia.org/wiki/Mayo_Clinic
32 https://www.digitalinsuranceagenda.com/thought-leadership/the-vision-behind-ping-ans-success-story/
33 Some sources claim that Astrid Lindgren never wrote this, even if you find the quote all over the Internet, but I thought this was too fitting not to share here.
34 https://en.wikipedia.org/wiki/Peter_Drucker
35 https://en.wikipedia.org/wiki/Hewlett-Packard
36 London Business School's Julian Birkinshaw wrote a brilliant case study about Ross Smith.
37 https://en.wikipedia.org/wiki/Volatility,_uncertainty,_complexity_and_ambiguity
38 https://en.wikipedia.org/wiki/Goldberg_Variations
39 http://deweya.com/ME-WE
40 "The five keys to a successful Google team", Julia Rozovsky, via https://rework.withgoogle.com/
41 "Teams Solve Problems Faster When They're More Cognitively Diverse", Alison Reynolds and David Lewis, via https://hbr.org/2017/03/teams-solve-problems-faster-when-theyre-more-cognitively-diverse
42 "Educating for uncertainty" – Charles Handy – via https://www.london.edu/lbsr/educating-for-uncertainty
43 "21 Lessons for the 21st Century" – Yuval Noah Harari
44 https://cognitive-edge.com/
45 "Understanding the Cynefin framework – a basic intro", by Julia Wester in https://www.everydaykanban.com
46 A Leader's Framework for Decision Making, by David J. Snowden & Mary E. Boone, Harvard Business Review
47 "The evolution of design to amplify flow", by John Hagel on https://edgeperspectives.typepad.com
48 The sensation when sitting in a stationary train that you are moving, as you can see another train out of the window which is moving.
49 https://en.wikipedia.org/wiki/The_Boy_Who_Cried_Wolf
50 Written by Brad Stone, and published in 2013.

ABOUT PETER HINSSEN

Peter Hinssen is a serial entrepreneur, adviser, author and keynote speaker on the topics of radical innovation, leadership and the impact of all things digital on society and business.

SOUGHT-AFTER KEYNOTE SPEAKER, BUSINESS SCHOOL LECTURER & BOARD MEMBER

Peter is a world-renowned thought leader on radical innovation who has given numerous keynote presentations around the world, for companies such as Google, Apple, Facebook, Amazon, Accenture, Microsoft, … and has been the keynote headliner for many internal conferences for Fortune1000 companies. He lectures at renowned business schools like the London Business School, the MIT Sloan School of Management and the Paul Merage School of Business at UC Irvine. He is also a multiple board advisor on subjects related to innovation and technology.

SERIAL ENTREPRENEUR

For more than fifteen years, Peter led a life of technology startups. His first company e-COM was acquired by Alcatel-Lucent, his second, Streamcase, by Belgacom, and Across Technology by Delaware Consulting. His third venture (Porthus) was quoted on the stock exchange in 2006 and acquired by Descartes. Between startups, he has been an Entrepreneur in Residence with McKinsey & Company, with a focus on digital and technology strategy. Peter's current company **nexxworks** helps organizations become fluid, innovate and thrive in The Day After Tomorrow.

OTHER BOOKS BY PETER HINSSEN

THE DAY AFTER TOMORROW (2017)

In 'The Day After Tomorrow', Peter writes about an exponentially changing world and its consequences for organizations of Today. He introduces those pioneers who managed to move (way) beyond Tomorrow-thinking in innovation and were able to change the course of entire industries. Above all, he writes about the business models, the organizational structures, the talent, the mindset, the technologies and the cultures needed to maximize our chances for survival in the Day After Tomorrow.

THE NETWORK ALWAYS WINS (2014)

This powerful guide shows you how to keep your company up to speed with your market, engage with customers at a time when loyalty keeps fading into the background, and transform your organization into a network in order to thrive in this era of digital disruption.

THE NEW NORMAL (2010)

In The New Normal, Peter Hinssen looks at the way companies have to adapt their information strategy, their technology strategy, their innovation strategy and the way they are organized internally. This book is an interesting read for any manager who is concerned with the future of his company as it is hit by the digital revolution.

BUSINESS/IT FUSION (2008)

Organisations have to go beyond 'aligning business and IT'. They have to 'fuse' business and IT. Fusion will allow companies to focus on technology-enabled innovation, instead of just on the commodity-saving potential of technology. Fusion will allow a new type of IT organization, that will evolve from an 'executional technology function' towards a 'proactive strategic innovation function'. Fusion will allow companies to focus on maximizing value from technology innovation.

The Phoenix and the Unicorn
© Peter Hinssen and Newton Engineering BVBA, 2020

In collaboration with: nexxworks NV
Ottergemsesteenweg Zuid 808 bus 331
9000 Ghent, Belgium
books@nexxworks.com

ISBN 9789463963671 (ENG) NUR 800

Author Peter Hinssen
Layout Armée de Verre Bookdesign
Infographics and cover Vera Ponnet
Project Managers Cathy Boesmans, Kim Indeherberg and Laurence Van Elegem

Printed in Belgium by Graphius
Published in Ghent, January 2020.

Copyright images:
Istock: p44, 45, 46, 47, 58, 83, 109, 111, 115, 144, 174, 175, 217
Shutterstock: p111, 112 (Ivan Marc / Shutterstock.com), 117 (Sushiman / Shutterstock.com)
Dreamstime: p111, 116 – D 160621373 © Joni Hanebutt | Dreamstime.com
Rob Clayton: p236

All rights reserved.
No part of this publication may be reproduced, stored in a retrieval system,
or transmitted, in any form or by any means, without the prior written consent
of the publisher. An exception is made for short excerpts, which may be cited
for the sole purpose of reviews.